The Development
of Commonsense Psychology

The Developing Mind Series

Series Editor
Philip David Zelazo
University of Toronto

Co-Editors
Dare Baldwin, *University of Oregon*
David F. Bjorklund, *Florida Atlantic University*
Judy DeLoache, *University of Virginia*
Lynn Liben, *Pennsylvania State University*
Yuko Munakata, *University of Colorado, Boulder*

The Developing Mind Series brings you readable, integrative essays on fundamental topics in cognitive development–topics with broad implications for psychology and beyond. Written by leading researchers, these essays are intended to be both indispensable to experts and relevant to a wide range of students and scholars.

The Development
of Commonsense Psychology

Chris Moore
Dalhousie University
and
University of Toronto

2006

LAWRENCE ERLBAUM ASSOCIATES, PUBLISHERS
Mahwah, New Jersey   London

Copyright © 2006 by Lawrence Erlbaum Associates, Inc.
All rights reserved. No part of this book may be reproduced in any form, by photostat, microform, retrieval system, or any other means, without prior written permission of the publisher.

Lawrence Erlbaum Associates, Inc., Publishers
10 Industrial Avenue
Mahwah, New Jersey 07430
www.erlbaum.com

Cover design by Tomai Maridou

CIP information for this volume may be obtained by contacting the Library of Congress

ISBN 0-8058-4174-1 (cloth : alk. paper)
ISBN 0-8058-5810-5 (pbk. : alk. paper)

Printed in the United States of America
10 9 8 7 6 5 4 3 2 1

Contents

Preface

The study of the early development of social cognition has enjoyed a renaissance over the last 25 years, and there have been many good authored books on the topic during that time. Leading the way was Judy Dunn's (1988) *The Beginnings of Social Understanding*, which showed how the early development of children's thinking about the social world was highly dependent on the interactions children experienced. As research on social understanding became dominated by the theory of mind approach from the late 1980s through the 1990s, a number of classic volumes appeared. I was most impressed by Henry Wellman's (1990) *The Child's Theory of Mind*, Josef Perner's (1991b) *Understanding the Representational Mind*, and Janet Astington's (1993) *The Child's Discovery of the Mind*.

Through the early to mid-1990s, like some others, I became dissatisfied with the almost hegemonic theory of mind approach and I was pleased to see other approaches start to gain ground. During this period, I was most influenced by Peter Hobson's (1993) *Autism and the Development of Mind*, James Russell's (1996) *Agency*, and a bit later Michael Tomasello's (1999a) *The Cultural Origins of Human Cognition*. These volumes all articulately presented conceptually sophisticated alternatives that profoundly influenced my thinking. However, none quite provided the right balance between self and other development that I thought was vital.

My ideas on the development of social understanding started to really take shape during the mid-1990s as a result of working with two people at Dalhousie University. Valerie Corkum was my graduate student and the person with whom I started the program of infancy work that expanded my research range beyond the overpopulated preschool period. Valerie set up our infancy laboratory and with her doctoral work she forced me to think deeply about what social understanding in infancy means. John Barresi was and still is a faculty colleague in the Psychology Department at Dalhousie. We came from different corners of our discipline-his interests were in personality theories, social psychology, and the history of both-but I could not have asked for a better intellectual sparring partner. Out of the many rounds of jabs and blocks came a novel theoretical approach that provided the guiding principles for virtually all of the research I have conducted in the last 10 years. John is the most intellectually generous colleague I have ever known. He is also a close friend. He deserves significant credit for helping develop the themes of this book.

By 2001 I could feel the book taking shape. Fortunately, at that time, Philip Zelazo had negotiated with Lawrence Erlbaum Associates (LEA) to edit a series of monographs in developmental psychology. Phil invited me to submit a proposal and I was happy to agree. I was particularly pleased to get a contract with LEA. They have provided important support to developmental psychology through some difficult recent times as scientific societies and their society journals have reorganized. They deserve the support of developmental psychologists in return.

I started planning the book out and even wrote a couple of chapter drafts in 2001. There then occurred a 2-year hiatus during which I served as Acting Dean of the Faculty of Science at Dalhousie. I found myself devoid of inspiration as I tried to manage the demands of that administrative post. Nevertheless, I think I grew hugely during those years and I thank Sam Scully, Vice President Academic at Dalhousie, for his support and confidence in me. I also thank Phil Zelazo and Bill Weber, then editor at LEA, for indulging me during that period and not pushing me to meet my contract deadlines.

When trying to decide what to call social understanding, a number of choices were available. Within developmental psychology, *theory of mind* is still the most popular term. There is an argument for cleaving to the consensus term in that everyone in the field immediately knows essentially what the topic is. However, there are also costs. *Theory of mind* has particular connotations—that the understanding is theorylike and that it involves primarily mental entities—that I do not support. I strongly believe that a mature account of the development of social understanding will to need to move beyond these notions. In philosophy the kinds of issues that are considered in this book are more commonly placed under the rubric of *folk psychology*. *Folk psychology* has fewer theoretical connotations than *theory of mind* but it has been the phrase used most often in philosophy of mind, a field that has been rather preoccupied with the special status of beliefs and desires as the explanations for action. As we will see, the concepts comprising social understanding range far beyond beliefs and desires. Furthermore, for the first period of development-infancy-there is a form of social understanding that does not involve beliefs or desires at all. In the end, I chose to employ the phrase *commonsense psychology* because I wanted to recognize the fact that we are studying a conceptual system that is part of everyday thinking and that it is essentially psychological without being necessarily mental.

It was because of a visiting fellowship at New York University in late 2001 arranged by Bruce Homer that I realized that if I was ever going to get back to research and actually write the book, I would have to leave Dalhousie. I needed a research environment where there would be few administrative demands, like-minded colleagues, and a fresh perspective. I discussed my feelings with Janet Astington, a longtime colleague and friend, and it was she who initiated the process that ultimately led to the offer of a Canada Research Chair at the University of Toronto. I arrived in the Department of Human Development and Applied Psychology in the summer of 2003. Protected from administrative work and with supportive colleagues, notably Jenny Jenkins, Marc Lewis, and Keith Oatley, I was finally able to make good progress on the book and finished the first draft over the next year. I am extremely grateful to Janet for her support over the last 2 years. It is a source of some regret to me that as I left behind university administration, she took it up so that we never really managed to forge a collaborative research relationship.

One of the real joys of academic life is the opportunity to interact with stimulating colleagues around the world. It is extremely difficult to reconstruct the process through which one's ideas develop through the joint attentional interactions that occur at scientific meetings and university visits. Over the years, however, the following have certainly influenced my thinking considerably: Dare Baldwin, Doug Frye, Peter Hobson, Josef Perner, Danny Povinelli, Jim Russell, Mike Tomasello, Amanda Woodward.

Other members of my department in Toronto provided help during the writing of the book. Jenny Jenkins discussed quite a few of the ideas with me and had great suggestions on how to make the story more accessible. Lisa Ain, Ivy Chiu Loke, and Rebecca Todd read drafts and gave me immensely valuable feedback. Other students at Dalhousie and Toronto with whom I discussed the ideas in the book are Sandra Bosacki, Nancy Garon, Keelan Kane, Karen Lemmon, Amy MacPherson, Carly McCreath, Shana Nichols, and Carol Thompson. I would particularly like to thank Kaja Montgomery and Carly McCreath, who assisted with such care in the preparation of the references and figures for the manuscript.

As the book reached its final stages, Phil Zelazo provided absolutely invaluable help. Phil is a superb editor. He went through the first draft in fine detail and offered suggestions of all kinds ranging from what content to include to stylistic devices to typographical errors. Readers should be thankful to Phil for his care.

Finally, I want to thank my two girls who have followed the ups and downs of the last few years. Although thankfully my madcap idea to carry out a joint attention diary study with her failed very early (it is hard to be both an observer and an interacter, and the latter was far more important), Mackenzie has always been a source of inspiration. Shannon took the return trip between Halifax and Toronto with me, indulging my need to find an academic context that was conducive to intellectual progress even if it meant a cost to the stability of our home life. For that I will always be grateful.

1

Introduction

As human beings, we all spend a considerable amount of time and effort trying to understand ourselves and those around us. Think for a moment about the significant events that have happened to you in the last week. By significant, I mean those events that have taken up a noticeable amount of your conscious energy. Probably these events involved actions on the part of yourself or someone you know, and those actions impacted in some way on someone other than the actor. When you reflect on such events, it is likely that a central part of your thinking involves trying to understand and explain the protagonists' thoughts and opinions, feelings and emotions, desires and intentions. Such thinking may be referred to as *commonsense psychology* because it is our everyday attempt to explain, as academic psychology does, the workings of the human mind and its relation to behavior. What is clear is that as adults we all do it much of the time, either alone or in conversation with others.

Commonsense psychology is not just about understanding why people did what they did in the past; it is also about trying to determine what those people will do in the future. Again, just as academic psychology is aimed at formulating theories of how past behavior may allow us to make predictions about future behavior, commonsense psychology is important in allowing us to predict how people will act in the future. Accurate prediction is important because it may enable us to anticipate how others will act in relation to us and in relation to each other. In turn, prediction and anticipation of others' action will also allow us to formulate a plan to achieve our own goals. Achieving our goals often depends on others, either through cooperation or competition. Forming friendships requires an alignment of opinions, desires, and emotions. Achieving competitive goals may require action to stymie others' intentions.

Commonsense psychology ranges from the very simple and automatic to the very complex and effortful. Figure 1.1 depicts an example of

1

FIG. 1.1.   Pointing illustrates a simple act of commonsense psychology.

a relatively simple and automatic act of commonsense psychology—one person directing the attention of two others using a pointing gesture. Note that three characters are engaging in commonsense psychology. The man tries to manipulate the attention of the two women. He wants them to attend to something located some distance away. The women shift their attention from the man to the distant object or event. They understand that the man wants them to attend over there and therefore that there must be something of relevance there. This example illustrates that our shared commonsense psychology allows us to communicate effectively with, to manipulate, and to be manipulated by those around us. It also illustrates a basic fact of commonsense psychology: that the psychological states we all experience are referential in that they occur in reference to something else. The man's pointing gesture and the attention shifts it produces in his listeners are directed toward something, presumably some object or event in the world.

Figure 1.2 presents an example of commonsense psychology expressed through language that is rather more complex. This example shows again the role that commonsense psychology plays in predicting the future and regulating interactions. Charlie Brown is using his reasoning about Lucy's mental states to try to predict what she is going to do and that prediction guides his own choice of action. In addition, it illustrates two more points nicely. First, the thing to which any particular psychological state refers can be another psychological state. Thus, Charlie Brown's representation of

FIG. 1.2.   *Peanuts*, Copyright © United Features Syndicate, Inc.

Lucy's thought is that Lucy's thought is about his own thought. In this way, commonsense psychology allows for psychological states to be embedded within other psychological states. Second, commonsense psychology can occur in reference both to the psychological states of self and to the psychological states of other people. I return to these points in chapter 2. Indeed they will be a central part of this story.

So commonsense psychology describes our natural tendency to try to understand and predict the activities of people (and sometimes other agents such as animals). It is clearly a very salient component of mental life. Because we regularly participate in social interactions and we are embedded in overlapping sets of social networks, much of our activity impinges in some way on those around us and their activity impinges on us. Commonsense psychology is the conceptual system that we use to make sense of the social interactions and relationships that we observe and in which we participate. Just as we generally interpret the nonsocial world in terms of mechanical causes and effects, we generally interpret the social world in terms of psychological causes and effects. The causes are emotions, intentions, meanings, and other psychological categories; the effects are actions. Commonsense psychology is also a tool we use to negotiate our interactions and regulate our relationships by making predictions about future action and guiding our choice of action. In a very general way, commonsense psychology is the glue that binds us to our social worlds, allowing us to interact with others, to participate in meaningful relationships, and to function as members of a social network.

THE STUDY OF COMMONSENSE PSYCHOLOGY

The fact that this conceptual system is part of common sense does not mean it is unworthy of scientific scrutiny. It is well established that human beings throughout the world are endowed with natural forms of psychology that equip them for navigating their social worlds (Callaghan et al., 2005; Lillard, 1998). The recognition of the ubiquity of commonsense psychology in people has led in the last 20 years to the emergence of a vigorous program of scientific research in the cognitive sciences. There are various goals for this scientific enterprise. Researchers want to understand how commonsense psychology is normally involved in the organization of social action. At the same time, it is productive to consider the departures from typical social interaction seen in different forms of psychopathology as disruptions in commonsense psychology. The classic example here is autistic spectrum disorders, which have been fruitfully viewed as involving disturbances in the development of commonsense psychology (Baron-Cohen, Tager-Flusberg, & Cohen, 2000; Hobson, 1993). Recently there has even been interest in how understanding the nature of commonsense psychology may be useful in the construction of intelligently social robots (e.g., Scassellati, 2002).

Because the first step in any scientific enterprise is to describe accurately the phenomena to be explained, we start in the next chapter with a general description outlining the major features of commonsense psychology and laying the groundwork for the rest of the book. Some of these features may seem quite obvious and perhaps unworthy of comment (they are, after all, common sense). However, there is good reason to consider them closely because they provide clues to the construction of a case for how commonsense psychology is made possible. In science, it is true that insights are sometimes gained from the observation of the novel and exotic-for example, Charles Darwin's (1839/1989) observations of creatures unique to the Galapagos Islands provided an important clue to the process of evolution by natural selection. However, insights may also be gained from taking a fresh look at phenomena that are so familiar that we barely notice them in everyday life—witness the impetus to Isaac Newton's development of the laws of motion from the observation of an apple falling to earth. A careful consideration of certain obvious features of commonsense psychology will guide us in our explanation of its place in human psychology.

If we are to understand the place of commonsense psychology within human psychology, then we have to be able to recognize and describe it when we see it. However, here the commonsenseness of commonsense psychology may actually be an impediment because it may subtly influence our identification skills. Commonsense psychology is just as much a part of the psychological makeup of scientific psychologists as it is of everyone else. When describing the behavior of both people and many social animals, such as chimpanzees, dogs, and so forth, it is difficult not to see the expression of commonsense psychology everywhere. But, in order to describe accurately when commonsense psychology is present, we need a way of assessing commonsense psychology independently of our intuition. So how can we ensure that our scientific descriptions are not simply a reflection of our common sense? As we shall see at many points in this book, when it comes to describing the commonsense psychology of young children the situation is particularly worrisome. Adults can tell you how they understand themselves and others and to some extent we can study their commonsense psychology directly through their verbal reports. But young children, and in particular infants, are not so capable. Too often we have to infer how they think of things from observations of their actions. So, for example, when a 12-month-old infant points or follows her mother's point, can we be sure that she understands that her mother can see something? Whether an infant is using commonsense psychology is not directly evident from the outside because we cannot observe directly the conceptual system of that infant.

So, how do we determine if and when infants and young children are using commonsense psychology? A simple answer to this question might be: "You just watch what they do and if they show behaviors that depend on commonsense psychology in an adult, then you can be fairly sure that commonsense psychology is indeed involved." Sometimes called the *argument by analogy*, this strategy has a venerable history (e.g., Hume, 1739–1740/1911; Povinelli, Bering, & Giambrone, 2000; Romanes, 1883/1977; Russell, 1948;). But notice that there is a problem here. Because as adults we are inveterate commonsense psychologists, we tend to see the workings of commonsense psychology everywhere. So our tendency to ascribe commonsense psychology is not a good basis for determining whether infants actually do use commonsense psychology. It may well reflect our own natural application of commonsense psychology rather than the real properties of the infants themselves.

In the history of psychology, this problem provided an early challenge to the development of the scientific study of nonverbal creatures. When the scientific study of behavioral psychology was in its infancy in the late 19th century, the argument by analogy was explicitly used to interpret animal behavior. A beautiful example comes from Georges Romanes, an early follower of Charles Darwin, and one of the first writers to explore possible continuities in behavior between animals and human beings. Indeed he was the originator of the term *comparative psychology* to denote the systematic study and comparison of the behaviors of different species. In one passage, he described the behavior of a dog:

> The terrier used to be very fond of catching flies upon the windowpanes, and if ridiculed when unsuccessful was evidently much annoyed. On one occasion, in order to see what he would do, I purposely laughed immoderately every time he failed. It so happened that he did so several times in succession—partly, I believe, in consequence of my laughing—and eventually he became so distressed that he positively pretended to catch the fly, going through all the appropriate actions with his lips and tongue, and afterwards rubbing the ground with his neck as if to kill the victim: he then looked up at me with a triumphant air of success. So well was the whole process simulated that I should have been quite deceived, had I not seen that the fly was still upon the window. Accordingly I drew his attention to this fact, as well as to the absence of anything upon the floor; and when he saw that his hypocrisy had been detected he slunk away under some furniture, evidently very much ashamed of himself. (Romanes, 1883/1977, cited in Mitchell, 1986, p. 444)

In this example, Romanes (1883/1977) attributed a variety of acts of commonsense psychology to the dog, of which the most complex is that implicated by the final attribution of shame. According to Romanes, the dog was ashamed because he knew that Romanes knew that he had tried to make Romanes think that he had caught the fly. This is certainly a complicated bit of psychological reasoning for a dog. Now, maybe the dog did indeed understand the complexity of the interaction between himself and his master and, as a result, experienced shame. The problem is, we cannot know for sure just from observing the dog's behavior. It is entirely possible that rather simpler explanations are possible—perhaps the dog detected a dominance display from Romanes in the final denouement and responded as a subordinate animal in a species-typical way.

It is interesting to note that this approach to the interpretation of animal minds concerned many of Romanes' contemporaries (e.g., Morgan, 1894; Thorndike, 1898/1965) and it was an important part of the reason that scientific psychology over the next 50 years moved in rather a wholesale manner away from attributing complex mental states (and then indeed any mental states) in the explanation of behavior of animals and humans. Whereas we have few qualms about attributing mental representations as scientific explanations of behavior these days, we would nevertheless do well to keep in mind the dangers of using our natural tendency to use commonsense psychology. Attributions of commonsense psychology to the subjects of our study may reflect our own psychology rather than that of our subjects.

In the domain of human psychology, verbal reference to concepts of commonsense psychology constitutes evidence that the speaker is using commonsense psychology. But, if we are not to rely on the argument by analogy, how do we explore the commonsense psychology of infants and very young children, who cannot show us through their language that they conceive of people's action in psychological terms? Developmental psychology provides a more objective approach than simply relying on our own commonsense psychology. Within developmental psychology, researchers have developed a variety of scientific techniques to study what children of different ages know about people and their behavior. I examine many of these techniques in the rest of the book.

THE PLAN OF THE BOOK

We begin in chapter 2 with an outline of some of the key characteristics of commonsense psychology. This chapter also points to certain aspects of commonsense psychology that, although core features of this conceptual system, are shown to present considerable challenges to any nonverbal organism attempting to acquire and use it. These aspects of commonsense psychology are challenges in the sense that they appear not to be evident to naive learners from observing either themselves or any other organism. The challenges provide organizing themes for the explanatory account of commonsense psychology offered through the remainder of the book. In particular, I pose four challenges. The first, which I call the challenge of *self-other equivalence*, starts from the straightforward fact that we think of ourselves as being similar to others in the sense that we are all individuals with conscious minds. But how are we initially able to recognize this similarity between self and others when we have no direct access to others' conscious minds and only limited experience of ourselves as objective entities? The second challenge begins with the recognition that we assume people's psychological experiences are meaningful in the sense that they are about things in the world. We assume people see and hear things, feel emotions about things, believe things, and so on. Yet, all we ever know at the outset of other people's psychological states is their behavior—facial expressions and actions—and we can never observe directly what other people are seeing, feeling happy or sad about, or thinking about. I call this the challenge of the *object directedness* of psychological states. The third and fourth challenges take off from the fact that we do acquire a commonsense psychology that recognizes self-other equivalence and object directedness. The third challenge is that of *psychological diversity*. If we do grasp the notion that people have similar psychological orientations to the things in the world, how do we come to the realization that different people may have different orientations to the same things, or that the same person may have different orientations to the same things at different times? Finally, how do we come to understand that despite this psychological diversity, people retain an individual identity through time? In particular, why is it that I assume that the self I know myself to be now is continuous with my self from the past and with my self in the future? This fourth challenge is that of *personal identity*. These questions may seem trivial at the outset (after all, they reflect basic assumptions on which commonsense psychology is founded), but we will see that they are not. It is particularly toward the provision of solutions to these challenges that the rest of the book is directed.

Once we have considered an account of what commonsense psychology is, we turn to the task of this book: elaborating an explanation of the nature of commonsense psychology and how it arises through development. In the science of psychology, there are various approaches to the understanding of its phenomena—behavior and the mental and neural bases of behavior. Experimental psychologists study how behavior varies under different conditions and thereby seek to understand how perception and cognition organize action. Neuroscientists explore the brain bases of the organization of action. Developmental psychologists use both of these approaches and others, but critically they attempt to understand psychological phenomena by examining how they change with age. The study of development is a fundamental way of understanding the nature of psychological characteristics by examining how they were built from less mature forms. The idea is that the complexity of psychological phenomena is in part explained by its transition from earlier developmental forms. Just as if we wanted to understand why Europe is partitioned into its current intricate structure of national borders, we would examine the historical record of the interactions of the peoples of that continent, so if we want to understand the form of the mind at any stage of maturity, we must study the earlier influences that led to that organization.

Throughout its more than 100-year history, developmental psychology has periodically addressed the deep issues of commonsense psychology. James Mark Baldwin, often credited with being the first experimental developmental psychologist for his systematic studies on perception and reaching conducted on his own two daughters, was particularly concerned with exactly the issues we examine in chapter 2. Baldwin (e.g., 1894, 1906) argued that infants begin life with no knowledge of themselves or others but that they acquire an understanding of both self and other through observation and, particularly, imitation of the actions of self and others. For Baldwin, imitation provides the means for children to project their own subjectivity onto others and at the same time use their knowledge of others to learn about themselves. Although he lacked the scientific methods to provide evidence for his proposals, his theories are not radically different from contemporary proposals founded on a considerably larger body of evidence (e.g., Barresi & Moore, 1996; Meltzoff & Gopnik, 1993).

No one had a greater influence on shaping modern developmental psychology than Jean Piaget, the Swiss psychologist. Like Baldwin, Piaget (e.g., Piaget & Inhelder, 1969) argued that infants start life with no understanding of either themselves or others. For Piaget, psychological development is in large part a gradual overcoming of *egocentrism*, the failure to make a distinction between self and other. Egocentrism initially exists in the sense that infants make no distinction between the self and the rest of the world and believe implicitly that the world is an extension of their own actions. Even once children have gained a sense of the self's place in the world, egocentrism at the level of perspectives remains in that young children do not recognize that others may see the world differently from the way it appears to them.

Contemporary developmental psychology tends to explain development in terms of information-processing mechanisms that build knowledge from exposure to information available in the child's world. In chapter 3, we consider some general aspects of the information-processing systems of young children. A guiding assumption is that developments in commonsense psychology depend to some extent on the same information-processing mechanisms as any other aspects of the human conceptual system. The most important of these processes that I identify in chapter 3 are the capacity for forming mental representations of objects and events and the capacity to detect patterns in stimulation. The capacity to form mental representations is important because it allows children to imagine things independently of, or at the same time as, whatever is available to perception. Because others' mental states are intrinsically not directly perceptible, they have to be represented or imagined. Pattern detection is important because it allows children to make sense of the objects and events to which they are exposed. Pattern detection capacities continually operate on information available through perception and through mental representation. In this way, development is progressive because at any particular point in development, further development proceeds through an interaction between the existing state of children's knowledge and the information to which they are exposed. This fundamental principle is applied in the rest of the book to the case of developing commonsense psychology.

The bulk of the book traces the development of commonsense psychology from birth to the later preschool period. We begin in chapter 4 with the starting state of life outside the womb. In examining the very earliest stage of postnatal development infants begin life with certain predispositions that lead them to tune in immediately to their social worlds. Newborns are sensitive to both the sights and sounds provided by other people in their immediate environments. They are also able to monitor their own activity so that they can recognize how external stimulation is tied to their action. In addition to their perceptual capabilities, young infants are endowed with a small but important variety of signals that are best elicited by people. These signals serve to keep those people close and to regulate the complexity of the stimulation they provide.

Although there is nothing yet in the repertoires of infants that could be thought of as commonsense psychology, their early social adaptation allows infants to quickly become participants in social interactions and social relationships. In chapter 5, we look at how interactions with people arise and how interactions with certain other partners—in particular the primary caregiver—become emotionally tuned to the extent that, by the second half of the first year, infants can be said to have formed relationships with those special partners.

Human infants are social from birth. It takes them a little longer to develop an active interest in the wider world of objects. As infants gain control of their postural and manual coordination through the middle of the first year, they start to want to reach for and manipulate objects. This newfound interest in objects is soon transported into the preexisting social interactions so that during the second half of the first year, social interactions start to be focused on objects. In chapter 6 I describe this development and consider its importance for the origins of commonsense psychology. Perhaps most importantly, for the first time infants can use other people's actions to make discoveries about the world. This not only teaches infants about objects but also teaches them about people's psychology. We locate the earliest forms of commonsense psychology at this stage of development.

The second year of life witnesses profound changes in social functioning and commonsense psychology. In chapter 7 we consider some of these changes. Toddlers start to show a new appreciation of the subjectivity of other people and a corresponding awareness of themselves as objective entities. For the first time, they appreciate both themselves and others as independent psychological agents. At the same time they become able to engage in symbolic functioning whereby they can communicate with others using a conventional symbol system—language. Language is of unique importance in subsequent development because it allows a new level of representational capacity and at the same time allows children to become exposed to a whole new world of information. As such it deserves special treatment in this book and I provide that treatment in chapter 8.

Chapters 9 and 10 review the changes in commonsense psychology that occur during the early preschool years. Through these years, children acquire an explicit commonsense psychology in the sense that they become able to communicate with others about their own and others' psychological states. They also start to recognize the perspectival nature of mind—that the way that people see or think about the world may differ—and that these different perspectives may lead people to act differently even if the objective circumstances are the same. Understanding the perspectival nature of mind also plays an important part in developing a temporally continuous sense of self. Children start to piece together their memories of the past into an autobiography that includes their present. They also become able to appreciate that their interests may change over time and that it is important at times to act in the interests of their future selves.

With chapter 10 we come to the end of the developmental story. In chapter 11 I provide a summary of the developments in commonsense psychology reviewed through the book. I show how commonsense psychology is the product of general purpose pattern detection mechanisms operating on perceptual and then representational information provided from children's experience of their own psychological activity in relation to objects, the observation of others' activity in relation to objects, and the combination of both that occurs in the interactive structures within which children are embedded from birth.

2

Commonsense Psychology and the Organization of Social Behavior

As seen in the last chapter, commonsense psychology is used by all typically developing children and adults as a way of understanding and predicting behavior. It invokes a variety of psychological concepts that are assumed to underlie action and in some sense to cause that action. Thus, for example, we may say that President George W. Bush ordered the invasion of Iraq because he believed that Saddam Hussein had weapons of mass destruction and he wanted revenge for the September 11 attacks on the World Trade Center. In this way, we attribute to actors beliefs, desires, and other psychological states that explain their action. As we have also seen, we use such concepts to predict what actors will do in the future. In this chapter, I provide a description of the nature of commonsense psychology. It is important to point out at the outset that the conceptual domain of commonsense psychology is a rich and complex one. Commonsense psychology plays a central role in the way we think about our social worlds and there are literally thousands of words and phrases in English that refer to broadly psychological characteristics. Trying to fit this complex domain into a handy set of descriptive principles inevitably means that some of the richness will be lost. However, the payoff is that if we can achieve some guidelines for what counts as commonsense psychology, we will have gained some traction on the next stage—attempting to explain its development.

PSYCHOLOGICAL RELATIONS

I begin by providing more of an analysis of commonsense psychology. In doing so, it is important that we deal with certain aspects that are shared by all forms of commonsense psychology. In general, although we often speak of psychological states, such as feelings, thoughts, or desires, this is in fact misleading because psychological states never exist in isolation. Rather, commonsense psychology is relational in structure in that it invokes psychological acts performed by agents in relation to objects or events. In each and every case there is some agent who is performing the psychological act, there is the act itself, and there is the object toward which the act is directed. In this way, the agent is linked to the object through the psychological act. We can consider these components in a little more detail.

Agent

Commonsense psychology applies first and foremost to animate entities, most importantly people. Now, we certainly have no trouble applying commonsense psychology to other animals and even some apparently purposeful inanimate objects, however as we move away from people, the range of psychological activities that we might attribute to these nonhuman agents becomes more restricted and it is more likely commonsense psychology is being applied metaphorically. For example, we may be perfectly comfortable saying that the family dog saw the ball and wanted to play, or that he heard the can opener and thought he was going to get something to eat. With organisms very different from us in both structural and phylogenetic senses, such as a fly buzzing around the jam pot, we may be willing to attribute certain simpler psychological relations such as the fly wanted the jam. But we would probably not go so far as to say that it had any thoughts about the matter. Clearly the difference between flies and dogs is that the latter display more complex behavior that makes considerably more sense to us in the context of our interactions with them. It is this behavior that leads us to apply our commonsense psychology. Along the same lines, although they may not display *behavior* in the usual sense of the word, the fact that we can have quite complex interactions with certain artifacts, such as computers, leads quite naturally to a willingness to interpret the activity of these artifacts with reference to psychological categories. However, it is to people that we most easily apply commonsense psychology.

It is important to note that the category of agents to whom we apply commonsense psychology includes ourselves. This is an obvious but nevertheless remarkable fact about the application of commonsense psychology. Self and other are effectively treated as equivalent when it comes to commonsense psychology. Thus I can talk about my own feelings and thoughts in the same way as I can talk about yours. This fact is so self-evident that it may seem unworthy of further comment. However we will see shortly that it is a source of considerable intellectual concern.

Object

There are many different kinds of psychological activity in commonsense psychology, but the vast majority involve some kind of psychological relation to an object. By *object* here, I do not mean necessarily a real, concrete object, although such objects can be involved. I use the term *object* in a generic sense to mean anything toward which a psychological relation is directed. Some psychological relations are indeed directed at real objects, for example, the perceptual relation expressed in (1), the intention action expressed in (2), or the desire expressed in (3). Others are directed at real events expressed in propositional form (4). Given that the objects of psychological relations can be propositions, it is easy to see that recursion of psychological relations is possible. That is, the object of one psychological relation can be another psychological relation (5) and so on.

(1) Columbus sees land.
(2) Mackenzie reached for the marker.
(3) Salome wants the head of John the Baptist.
(4) I saw Amy kiss Brian while Candace was in the kitchen.
(5) I saw you look at me.

However, the object of psychological relations can also be imaginary and nonexistent. In (6), although exposure to mall Santas may in part have led to the existence of this psychological relation, it is the mythical Santa at the North Pole not the actor in red garb that is the true object of the love. By active exertion of my imagination I can create other imaginary objects at will (7).

(6) My nephew loves Santa Claus.
(7) I'm thinking of a purple cow.

The fact that psychological relations can be directed at nonexistent objects reveals that the validity or coherence of any particular psychological relation does not depend on the existence or truth of that to which the relation is directed. Psychological relations can be directed at mental objects, which may or may not correspond to real-world objects. That psychological relations may be directed at nonexistent objects is also evident when we consider objects of psychological relations that are statements or propositions (8). Imagination makes possible elaborate fantasies, which are, of course, the regular products of the creative minds of artists, writers, and small children.

(8) John thinks of his team winning the World Cup.

Now, in some situations the agent may be particularly concerned about the correspondence between the object of the psychological relation and the real-world state of affairs. Such correspondence can work in two main ways. In some cases the object of the psychological relation is taken to be a reflection of, or a perspective on, the way the world actually is (9). This has been termed a *mind-to-world direction of fit* (Searle, 1983) because the aim is to make the mental perspective match the way the world is. In such cases, we can speak of the object proposition having truth value because it is either a true or a false representation of reality. In other cases (10), the object proposition is a perspective that the agent would like the world to match (whether or not it actually is). Here we can speak of *world-to-mind direction of fit* (Searle) in that the aim, if possible, is to make the world fit the mental perspective.

(9) John thinks that his team won the World Cup.
(10) John wants his team to win the World Cup.

The difference between (8) and (9) is a very subtle one, but it is important. In (8) there is no concern that the object bear any form of correspondence with some actual state of affairs, whereas in (9) that correspondence is implied. Linguistically, this difference hinges on some relatively simple syntactic changes: the substitution of the word *that* for *of* (Perner, 1991a) and a change from the present progressive to the future tense. To introduce a piece of terminology, we can say that those objects of psychological activity that have some correspondence to the actual state of the world are *perspectival* objects because they entail a particular perspective or way of relating to the world. Beliefs about the world, such as (9), are directed at perspectival objects that have truth value, in other words, those objects can be true perspectives on the world or false perspectives on the world. Desires such as (10) are also directed at perspectival objects in that it is the lack of correspondence between the existing state of the world and the wished-for state that is of psychological significance because it motivates action.

The fact that psychological activities are directed at perspectival objects is important for commonsense psychology. The implication of this fact is that if we want to be able to understand and predict an agent's behavior, we have to pay attention not to the properties of the world but to the agent's perspective on the world. If an agent has a belief about the world that happens to be false then the actual state of the world is irrelevant to the way that agent will behave. The agent's behavior will depend on his or her misrepresentation. Thus, if we want to be able to predict agents' behavior, we would do well to try to establish what they believe.

Psychological Acts

Human beings are entities with various systems of the brain or mind that enable the variety of psychological acts comprising the domain of commonsense psychology. We will concentrate on three general categories of psychological acts, which are broadly similar to the three types of psychological processes identified in traditional scientific psychology (Hilgard, 1980). First, *epistemic* acts are those in which the acquisition, maintenance, or manipulation of knowledge occurs. People are able to perceive objects in the immediate environment, remember objects from the past, and imagine objects that may be fictional or anticipated. Such acts are usually referred to using perceptual terms (e.g., *see, hear*) and cognitive terms (*think, know, remember, imagine*). Second, people also have emotional orientations to objects. They like things, fear things, are proud of things, and so on. Finally, *conative* acts capture the fact that humans are motivated and purposeful—they produce actions directed at objects and they produce these actions because they have intentions to achieve desired goals.

Of course, people do other things as well. Sometimes agents act like any other solid objects—they fall out of trees or bump against chairs. In such cases, we do not interpret the events in terms of commonsense psychology. We say the event occurred accidentally as opposed to intentionally. Part of developing commonsense psychology is learning to distinguish intentional from accidental acts. Other acts do occur in virtue of agents' animacy—people breathe, blink, and pump blood around their bodies—however, these acts are also not the domain of commonsense psychology because they are not relational or directed at objects.

THE CHALLENGES PRESENTED
BY COMMONSENSE PSYCHOLOGY

So far, we have considered some basic characteristics of the conceptual system identified here as commonsense psychology in order to be clear about what this conceptual system entails. Much more can, and has, been said about the characteristics of this conceptual system by psychologists and philosophers (e.g., Dennett, 1987; Perner, 1991b). However, the central question for developmental psychologists is: How is such a conceptual system developed? To a large extent the acquisition of a commonsense psychology may occur in much the same way as the acquisition of any conceptual system, involving the variety of perceptual and cognitive processes responsible for knowledge acquisition or concept formation. I postpone a discussion of general issues to do with knowledge acquisition until chapter 3, when we consider the developmental approach to knowledge. Here I discuss some distinct features of commonsense psychology that present particular challenges with respect to knowledge acquisition by young learners (see Table 2.1). These challenges represent guiding themes for the remainder of the book; indeed, chapters 4 through 10 chart children's progress through early childhood as they find solutions to these challenges.

TABLE 2.1
The Challenges of Developing a Commonsense Psychology

Self-other equivalence	Commonsense psychology assumes that self and others are equivalent in the sense that all are agents of psychological activity, having both subjective experience and objective identity. However, we rarely if ever gain the same kind of information about self and others. Information about the self is different in both quantity and quality from information about others. How do we come to understand that self and others are the same kind of psychological entity?
Object directedness	Commonsense psychology assumes that people have psychological relations to objects, broadly construed. Thus psychological activity is directed at objects, whether these be real concrete objects, or imaginary and abstract entities. However, in most cases the objects toward which people's psychological relations are directed are not directly observable. How do we come to understand that psychological acts are directed at or about things?
Diversity in psychological relations	Commonsense psychology assumes that people may have different psychological relations to the same object and that psychological relations to particular objects may differ within the same person across time. How are we able to understand that our own immediate psychological relation to an object of state of affairs is not the only possible one?
Personal identity	Commonsense psychology assumes that people and, most importantly, the self each have an identity that is continuous over time. How are we able to bind memories of the experiences of our past and imagination of our futures into a self that is deemed not only to persist in time but, in some cases, to warrant preferential treatment compared to our present self?

Self-Other Equivalence

I noted earlier that commonsense psychology applies equally to self and to others. This fact may seem so obvious as to be hardly worthy of comment. However, closer consideration reveals that it is not only worthy of comment, but also presents quite a significant problem for the nature of commonsense psychology. The reason is that the information that is available to us about our own psychological activity is almost entirely distinct from the information that is available to us about the psychological activity of other agents. Thus we might initially suppose that we should develop quite separate bodies of understanding about ourselves and about other people. Nevertheless, we all acquire a commonsense psychology in which self and other are assumed to be essentially equivalent as agents that can engage in psychological activity.

Consider first the experience that we have of our own psychological activity. Our first-person experience is enormously rich, constituted by elaborately complex coordinations of perceptions, feelings, thoughts, and so forth. Take a moment to consider all of your immediate experience. Right now as I write these words, I can see the computer screen with its patchwork of colors and form. More peripherally, I can see the yellow walls of my study, various papers strewn about my desk, and, through the window, the bare trees of my garden, shrouded in winter fog. At the same time, I am aware of my cat scratching herself, my stomach growling, and a pain in my neck from too much computer work. On top of these simple perceptions there is an overlay of mental activity as I try to formulate my thoughts for writing. At the back of my mind I am considering what appointments I have this afternoon and what time I should leave for the university. The latter action will require an exertion of will, as I must relinquish my warm house for the damp chill of this January day. This brief inventory of what philosophers call the *qualia of consciousness* (Block, 1994) barely captures the totality of my experience in one moment, and yet similar inventories could be made for each infinitesimal moment of my existence. Compared to the richness of the direct knowledge of my own experience, what I know of others seems almost negligible.

But it is not only the quantity of what we know about self and others that differs, it is also the quality. Have you ever wondered whether anyone else sees things, either visually or conceptually, the same way as you? How, for example, do I know that the redness I see when I look at a sunset also applies to your experience when you gaze off into the gathering summer night? Admittedly, you may report to me experience that is common with my own; we may both refer to the redness of the sky. But maybe when you say "red," you are actually having the same subjective experience of color as when I look at a green field. If our respective experiences were consistently mismatched in this way, there is no way that language could ever reveal the mismatch to us. A similar argument could be outlined for all of the various aspects of my experience noted earlier. Although there may be overt expressions from others reflecting their experiences—emotional expressions, gestures, and other types of movements—it is always the case that we must infer from those expressions the existence of the experience. The point is that the information we have about our own experience (*first-person information*) can apparently be known directly. However, this information can only be indirectly inferred for others. We never have direct access to the first-person information of others. Rather, we observe others from the outside, from a third-person perspective, and we must infer first-person information.

There is another source of incompatibility between self and other. We know others primarily through what we can observe them do, importantly their verbalizations, facial expressions, postures, gestures, and other movements in relation to the external world, but we typically do not get information about ourselves in the same way. The information we get of ourselves from the outside is quite impoverished. There are a number of avenues for a third-person perspective on ourselves but none provide us with the kind of experience of self as an independent object moving about in a world of objects that we have for others. We can see directly some of our own movements, especially of our limbs. We see photographs of ourselves, but these are static images, capturing a fleeting moment, and reflect little of the flow of our activity. We might get glimpses in mirrors but rarely observe ourselves as others do because to see ourselves in a mirror we typically have to face it, thus limiting our view to only one perspective. Furthermore, we face a mirror to perform certain functions, most obviously grooming, rather than to observe how we appear when we engage in a range of normal activity. These days, mirrors and photographs are commonplace components of Western living and are parts of our material worlds from infancy, so we are quite used to how we look through such media. But try to remember the first time you saw yourself on video (or heard yourself on audiotape). Most people when they first have this experience are somewhat taken aback by how they appear and sound. In contrast, seeing someone who we know well on videotape provides no such oddness of experience. A third-person perspective on self is a strange experience because that is not normally the way we view ourselves. We can call the information that we gain from a third-person perspective *third-person information.*

In short, we know ourselves primarily through first-person information not third-person information and we know others primarily through third-person information not first-person information. Those two types of information are radically different. First-person information is primarily information about the objects of experience, including their various qualities, and about our own attitudes and intentions in relation to those objects. It includes information about self as an actor in only an impoverished form at

best. In contrast, third-person information about others is primarily information about agents and the overt expressions of their psychological activities.
It includes no direct information about the first-person experience of the
agent. Despite this radical difference in the way we experience self and others, we have no problem thinking of others and ourselves in the same
terms—as agents of psychological activities directed at objects. For academic
psychologists and philosophers concerned with how a commonsense psychology is possible, this represents a significant explanatory problem. How
is it that, despite the very different information they provide, both self and
other are equivalently assumed to be psychological agents? There has to be
some way for the information available to us about our own psychological
activity to be understood as equivalent to the information available to us
about the psychological activity of others (Barresi & Moore, 1996).

Object Directedness

We have seen that psychological activity is typically directed at an object,
whether real or imagined. Understanding psychological activity in terms
of psychological relations therefore requires not only that the agent be
known but also that the object to which the agent's activity is directed be
known. However, in many, perhaps most, cases both the agent and the object toward which the agent's psychological activity is directed cannot be
directly known through observation of the world. Traditionally, this problem has been considered for those cases in which the object of the psychological relation is perspectival and thus potentially false. As discussed
earlier, perspectival psychological relations involve an agent having some
psychological relation to a proposition for which the correspondence to reality is of concern. The most commonly considered cases are false beliefs
and desires such as (8) and (9). Because the object of the psychological relation in these cases cannot accurately reflect the current state of the real
world, it stands to reason that such objects cannot be directly known by observation of the real world. Instead, they must be inferred from the activity
of the agent. How this inference is made is the problem. In short,
perspectival psychological relations present a challenge because they require the observer to determine the object of the agent's psychological activity when that object conflicts with reality.

The problem presented by perspectival psychological relations may be
considered to be a special case of a more general problem in determining
the object of agents' psychological activity in relation to all imaginary objects. Clearly, any case in which the object of the psychological relation is
imaginary must also be inferred rather than directly known because imaginary objects are by definition not observable. Thus, imaginary objects also
require some inference on the part of the observer.

However, it is not just psychological relations to imaginary and perspectival objects that are difficult to verify. Even many relatively simple psychological activities that are directed toward real-world objects can present a problem for an observer attempting to resolve the relation. Arguably, the only psychological activities for which all components of the psychological relation (namely, agent, psychological act, object) might be directly available through observation are those activities for which an agent acts bodily on an object, for example, reaching for and grasping an object. Many other psychological relations typically exist at a distance. Refer back to example (1). An observer watching Columbus spying land does not have simultaneous direct observational information about Columbus, his behavior (looking), and the object of his sight. Without such simultaneous exposure to all the components of the full psychological relation from which that relation may be constituted, the observer inevitably has to engage in some inference. So, how is it possible to treat psychological activity as activity connecting an agent to an object, either real or imagined, through some form of psychological relation, when for the large majority of cases all components of the psychological relation are not simultaneously available to observation?

Psychological Relations and Their Diversity

We have already seen how the observation of psychological relations of both self and other yield particular and distinct forms of information even when self and other are engaged in the same psychological relation. Often, however, different people have different psychological relations to the same object. An important aspect of commonsense psychology is the understanding that psychological relations may differ across people even in the same context. Even if I fully understand that you and I are equivalent in respect of our agency, I have to go further and recognize that diversity in our psychological relations may nevertheless exist.

Diversity potentially exists for all types of psychological relations. I may be able to see an object that is hidden from your sight. I may want that last piece of chocolate cheesecake, whereas you could not eat another bite. These cases illustrate that psychological relations to real objects differ across people. Diversity naturally also occurs in relations to imaginary or perspectival objects. Differences of opinion are a routine part of human social experience—I may think that gasoline taxes should be higher to fund public transit systems; my neighbor may believe just as strongly that gasoline is too heavily taxed and those who want to take public transit should pay for it themselves. In such cases, there is no appeal to the truth of the matter; diversity is just a difference of opinion. Sometimes, as when we can make reference to a reality that is indubitable, we are justified in saying that one person's belief is true whereas another's is false. I think that there is a special sale on bestsellers at the bookstore tomorrow but I misread the date in the advertisement. My neighbor did not and he knows the sale ended today. Here diversity in the psychological relations corresponds to different truth values.

Recognizing diversity requires the ability to consider two or more points of view simultaneously. Because we are typically embedded within a particular perspective, it is often difficult to step away from that perspective and recognize that our own point of view is just that—a point of view. To do so, we have to be able to imagine or think about an alternative and potentially conflicting perspective at the same time as we are embedded in our own immediate point of view.

Understanding diversity of psychological relations across agents is a fundamental part of commonsense psychology. However, it is important to understand that diversity of perspective across agents is only one type of diversity. Diversity also exists across other contextual variables, including, most obviously, space and time. Of particular importance to this story is the recognition that diversity exists across time so that a psychological relation that holds at one point of time may not hold at another. I may have a strong desire for chocolate cheesecake when I first see it, but after having gorged myself on a fat slice, the thought of cheesecake may seem quite repulsive. Truth values may also change across time. A child may at one time believe (indeed, she says, "I know") that a whale is a fish, but later in her biological education, she believes that a whale is a mammal. The understanding that psychological relations may change over time also requires the ability to imagine another perspective than the one currently held. Rather than that other perspective belonging to a different agent, however, it is understood to belong to the same agent at a different time.

Personal Identity

Assuming that we can, and we do, solve the problems of self-other equivalence, object-directedness, and relational diversity, we may be in good shape for negotiating the social world of the here and now. However, as I noted at the beginning of this chapter, commonsense psychology is not just about explaining or understanding the current psychological activities of self and others, it is also about explaining people's past actions and predicting their future actions. In the case of predicting future action, the purpose is often to devise and implement plans for our own action that are designed to facilitate or impede the actions of others. But, in order to engage in such future-oriented planning we must assume that people have personal identities that persist through time—that we and others will be, in some essential way, the same people in the future as we are now.

Personal identity is another facet of commonsense psychology that is entirely obvious and probably elicits little further thought in day-to-day life. However, like the epistemic challenges considered thus far, it too presents an interesting problem in terms of knowledge acquisition. Clearly, people change considerably over time—witness how development transforms a baby into a child and then into an adult. Nevertheless, we have a strong sense of people's personal identities stretching from the past through the present and into the future. Thus, I believe my daughter to be the same person now at 5 years of age as she was when she was born, even though in virtually all aspects of her appearance and behavior she is quite different. Furthermore, I have a clear sense that she will continue to be the same person in another 15 years. The assumption that she is the same person across time is why I videotaped her first dance recital and then watched it later and why I put in place a savings plan to cover her university education. So the assumption of personal identity leads us to reminisce about the past and to act in future-oriented ways.

If anything, we each have an even stronger sense of our own personal identity. In some ways I feel I am still the 5-year-old child who forced his mother to listen to him count up to 100 and beyond, and I identify very strongly with the person who will experience the warm glow of pride when (if?) this book appears on the display stand at the next conference I attend. In these and other ways, I treat my present self as essentially equivalent with a person who existed in the past and with a person who will exist in the future—indeed, I call those past and future persons my *self*. Identification with our future selves is an important reason why we tend to act in future-oriented ways. For example, we educate ourselves because we wish to attain the future benefits that such education will yield. It is worth noting that we care so much about our imaginary future selves that we will even go so far as to deny ourselves current pleasures in order to gratify the interests of those future selves, as in dieting or saving. Such prudence is possible because we identify with the person who we will become and we value that person as much as we value our current selves.

But why do we assume such equivalence between our present, past, and future selves? All of us change considerably over time, both physically and mentally. Leaving aside the drastic changes that occur over relatively long periods of time, our interests and tastes often change over quite short periods of time. Furthermore, whereas we directly experience our current psychological relations, we can only imagine those from our pasts and futures. So the epistemic challenge of personal identity is how we are able to see

equivalence between the real experiences of the present and the merely remembered or imaginary ones of a person from the past or future.

The Integration of First- and Third-Person Information

As we have seen, the four challenges in the construction of commonsense
psychology present different issues to the learner. However, a common
theme runs through all four challenges: the need to represent information
pertaining to our own current psychological activity in comparable terms
to information pertaining to psychological activity that is not that of the
current self. In other words, commonsense psychology is built out of a common set of representations that uniformly code our own immediate psychological activity, the observable psychological activity of other people,
and the noncurrent psychological activity of both self and others. We have
seen that information pertaining to our own current psychological activity
has a different form (first-person information) from information pertaining
to others' psychological activity (third-person information). Information
pertaining to noncurrent psychological activity is different again because it
has to be imagined rather than perceived. Nevertheless, commonsense psychology codes psychological activity of self and others, present and nonpresent in comparable terms.

It has been argued (e.g., Barresi & Moore, 1996) that to achieve such a
uniform representational format, the learner has to be presented with information from more than one source on a regular basis and then integrate
those separate forms of information into representations that code both
forms equally. For example, to recognize that the first-person information
pertaining to one's own current psychological activity is of the same kind as
the third-person information pertaining to another person's similar psychological activity, both forms of information have to occur in close temporal proximity and be combined through intermodal perceptual integration.
Similarly, to understand that the information pertaining to one's own current psychological activity is comparable to imagined information about
noncurrent psychological activity, both the current and noncurrent forms
of information must be available in close temporal proximity and then be
combined through an integration of perception and representation.

This solution to the challenges of commonsense psychology makes two
requirements of the information-processing circumstances of learners.
First, learners must be regularly and reliably presented with conditions in
which they are exposed to information pertaining to the psychological activity of self and of others together. Such conditions create opportunities for
first- and third-person information and for current and noncurrent information to be integrated. As we shall see, the social conditions in which
young children develop satisfy this first requirement (see also Carpendale
& Lewis, 2004). Second, learners must be able to construct integrated repre-

sentations from these distinct forms of information. This requirement is met by the suite of information-processing mechanisms with which humans are endowed. We review these mechanisms in chapter 3.

THE ROLE OF COMMONSENSE PSYCHOLOGY
IN THE ORGANIZATION OF SOCIAL BEHAVIOR

I hope that so far this chapter has succeeded in conveying the view that commonsense psychology is an entirely natural aspect of the human conceptual system, even if its commonsense nature hides a complexity that warrants scientific study and explanation. We now turn to a consideration of how commonsense psychology is involved in the organization of social behavior.

Because we tend to value knowledge for its own sake, it is sometimes easy to lose sight of the fact that ultimately knowledge is acquired because it is valuable to us in our lives. This is no less true of the kinds of social knowledge examined in this chapter. Trying to make sense of why people do the things they do is a mostly rewarding, though sometimes frustrating, pursuit. It is even more fun to do it with others, in the manner known as gossip. But commonsense psychology would not have arisen in the phylogeny of our species and would not be acquired through ontogeny if it were not in some way useful. By useful, I mean valuable in allowing us to live our lives successfully. It is axiomatic in psychology that the systems of the brain and mind ultimately function to organize behavior in relation to the environment in which the organism finds itself. Thus, when we look for the function of any particular component of psychology, we must look for the role it plays in the organization of behavior. So what roles might commonsense psychology play in the organization of social action?

Commonsense psychology is a dominant facet of human psychology, and so it is likely that it is involved in many aspects of social and personal life. However, here we focus on two functions that appear in large part to set human beings apart from other animals, and that appear regularly in the pages to come. The first is what has been called *cultural learning* (Tomasello, Kruger, & Ratner, 1993). Human beings are essentially unique in the animal world in their ability to learn from others and for this learning to be incremental over generations. Most of what we learn about the world comes not from direct experience with the environment but from interacting with those around us. More importantly, this learning does not come from simple observation of the actions of others with whom we happen to live (as happens in other social animals), but rather occurs through intentional learning and teaching. This fact of the human condition has led to the accumulation of cultural knowledge—knowledge shared by members of a culture—that characterizes human societies. As we shall see in chapter 6, by the end the first year of life, infants start to use other people to find out about objects and events and such vicarious learning continues throughout life. In concert with this natural tendency to learn from others, human beings intentionally try to teach others and thereby pass on their accumulated knowledge. Teaching comes in various degrees of formality, ranging from the passing on of skills between parent and child to the educational institutions in literate societies, but in all cases, there is an intention of the teacher to increase the knowledge or skill of the learner. When an intention to teach and a desire to learn are combined, the transmission of knowledge is enormously accelerated.

Cultural learning depends on commonsense psychology. In order to learn from another person, the learner must understand that the other has some knowledge about the relevant skill or information and that this knowledge can be shared. In other words, even at its simplest level, learning depends on understanding something about the way other people's and one's own psychological states are directed at objects and can be (or become) equivalent. Similarly, teaching is an intentional activity that is directed at changing and perhaps increasing the knowledge of the learner. So teaching too requires an awareness of people's psychological orientations to the world as well as of the potential to change those orientations.

Although there are clearly explicit forms of learning and teaching, almost all human interactions involve some form of implicit social learning. That is because when people interact, there is nearly always some exchange of information. Information exchange occurs through symbolic means, most commonly through language, but also through other symbolic forms, including visual representations such as pictures and models. As we shall see when we consider the acquisition of language in chapter 8, the ability to use symbols to exchange information is premised on having a commonsense psychology because a symbol is by definition something, such as a word or picture, that is used by one person intentionally to represent something else to another person (DeLoache, 2004).

Although cultural learning and the use of symbols depend on commonsense psychology, they do not necessarily require the full complexity that I outlined earlier in this chapter. In particular, learning through others could probably proceed well enough without any understanding of personal identity through time. So what additional function is performed by the understanding that self and other persist from the past through the present and into the future? The position I take in this book is that commonsense psychology serves to structure an internal mental or imaginative model of the social environment, a model that can be used to test the suitability of potential actions in advance of their execution. As we have seen, the model includes representations of the activities of both self and other and includes representations of activities occurring at multiple locations in time, both in the past and, perhaps more importantly, in the future. The simulation of the social environment involves imagining the kinds of interactions that characterize our social lives, including the psychological relations of both self and others. When we imagine those interactions, we play out in our minds the potential interactions, probing for the one that seems most satisfactory (recall Fig. 1.2). Through such modeling, the individual can compare in imagination different courses of action that may have different implications for the self and for others. Personal identity plays an important role here because the actor in the imaginative scenario must be recognized to be the same person as the self who must make the choice on how to act. The implications of separate outcomes at different points in time may also be considered, so that, for example, a choice can be made between the pleasure of eating the chocolate cake now or the satisfaction of reaching one's goal weight by the end of the week.

Commonsense psychology thereby provides the means by which to make better choices in the social world. It allows us to model in advance social interactions and relationships and it allows us to make choices that will most likely provide future benefit for ourselves and for those for whom we care. The ability to understand and predict others' mental states should benefit both cooperation and competition. For example, if you know what another person is trying to do, you will be able to help them achieve their goal. Alternatively, if that goal happens to be one you desire and both of you cannot have it, you will be in a better position to impede the other if you know more about his of her beliefs, desires, and so forth.

The imaginative model of the social environment is not a static entity. It is not at all like imagining a picture (although we can, of course, imagine pictures) or even a three-dimensional model of the world. Rather, the imagination models the way the world actually works—dynamically. As such, it is more akin to movie clips in which we are thoroughly engrossed, watching the events, but also caring about them, and wishing for events to turn out a certain way. But even the movie metaphor fails because the modeling process is not a fixed program that must play out in a predetermined way, nor is it independent of the self. Instead the environment and our role in that environment is continually being rewritten and tried out as the imaginative scenario plays. It is an active construction or dynamic simulation of the environment, including our own role and the roles of others in that environment.

The result of this dynamic simulation is ideally a decision about what to do, what social act to perform. So how is a decision reached? It is important to appreciate that the simulation is not simply a rich set of representations. When you imagine possible future scenarios involving you and those known to you, you feel the same kinds of emotions as if you were actually interacting with them in real life. The currency of the simulation is the same range of emotions that you experience in response to events that actually occur. Just as when you watch a movie, you experience real emotions through empathy with the characters, when you engage in imaginative simulation you experience real emotions as a result of empathizing with the players in the simulation. Of course in the simulation the players are representations of real people including yourself and those about whom you feel strongly, and this fact yields a considerably greater urgency to the events. Ultimately it is these emotions that determine the choice of action. Potential actions are compared in terms of the emotional significance of their outcomes and the winner is implemented. To use a rather prosaic example, if you are making plans for the weekend and the pleasure anticipated from joining your friends for a good restaurant dinner outweighs the comforting prospect of a quiet night at home, then the reservation will be made.

Whereas commonsense psychology is crucial for planning future social behavior and choice of action, it is often not necessary for the actual implementation of the chosen action. Indeed, sometimes social behavior that looks like it depends on commonsense psychology can occur in a quite automatic manner. Gaze following is a good example. If we observe the scene depicted in Fig. 1.1, we naturally infer that the man wants to direct his friends' attention and that it is this desire that causes him to point. Similarly, it is natural to infer that the success of the gesture results from his friends' understanding that he wanted them to look in that direction because there was something relevant located there. But do these inferences really describe the causes of the behaviors-the man's point and the others' looking? When walking down the street have you ever observed someone looking in a particular direction and found yourself looking in the same direction? This is a familiar experience and yet the thought "I wonder what she's looking at" is more likely a result of your looking in the same direction than what controlled it. In other words, your tendency to follow the direction of gaze is a relatively automatic response to seeing the other's gaze direction. Following another person's pointing gesture is similarly quite automatic.

Because we often plan our behavior with reference to the mental states of others and ourselves, we typically assume that our behavior is directly controlled by our mental states. However, although a plan based on commonsense psychology may provide a reason for an action, it does not necessarily control it. An analogy may make this idea clearer. If you want to make a billiards or pool shot involving striking the target ball lying behind another ball, you may examine the layout of the table and use rough calculations to determine the likely success of different possible bank shots (Fig. 2.1). A commonsense understanding of geometry and Newtonian dynamics (we can call this understanding *commonsense physics*) may well enter into these calculations. However, once a decision is made on which shot to take, this commonsense physics no longer enters into the control of the shot. The action program is simply run off with more or less skill as the player focuses on the goal—striking the cue ball hard enough for it to hit the cushion and bounce off in the direction of the target ball. To put it another way, the

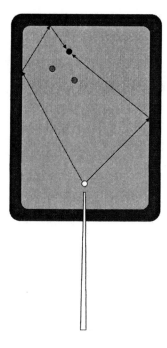

FIG. 2.1. Two approaches to a billiards shot requiring minimal common sense physics.

knowledge that the angle of incidence equals the angle of reflection does not have to be represented for the shot to be made.

Now imagine a game of pool between two novice players with equal physical skill and coordination, one with good commonsense physics and the other with little such knowledge. Who will be the most likely winner? It is reasonable to predict that the player with commonsense physics is more likely to win because he would be able to make better choices of shots even if his implementation was no better than his competitor's. The same logic applies to the application of commonsense psychology to social planning. Social behaviors are recruited in the service of social plans, worked out using commonsense psychology. But once selected, the behaviors themselves may be performed without reference to the psychological understanding. In short, sophisticated social behavior consists of a variety of social acts that are deployed consistent with social plans worked out using commonsense psychology.

SUMMARY

This chapter has described the important characteristics and function of commonsense psychology in humans. We have identified four challenges of commonsense psychology that will provide the main themes for the rest of this book. The first is that the class of agents includes both self and others despite the fact that the information available to any observer about the acts of self and others is qualitatively distinct. This property is referred to as *self-other equivalence*. The second is that commonsense psychology assumes that individual agents are related to objects or events through their psychological activity even though the object to which the activity is directed may often be imaginary or located at a distance. In the remainder of the book, I refer to this as the *object directedness* of psychological activity. The third is that commonsense psychology recognizes that in many cases different agents or the same agent at different times may engage in different psychological activity to the same object. I refer to this as the *diversity* property. Finally, the fourth challenge is that agents experience continuity through time and are naturally interested in their own futures even though there can be no direct knowledge of the future. This aspect of commonsense psychology is referred to as *personal identity*.

Commonsense psychology makes possible two core aspects of human behavior. First, it allows the peculiarly human form of social learning known as *cultural learning*. Cultural learning involves learning about the world through others rather than through interaction with the nonsocial environment. In association with such learning through others, commonsense psychology enables explicit teaching of others. Cultural learning and teaching are commonly carried out using a symbolic mode, and symbol use also depends on commonsense psychology because it involves the use of shared representations to stand for or convey information.

In addition to its role in cultural learning, commonsense psychology has been cast as the material out of which social plans are wrought. Commonsense psychology allows us to negotiate our social interactions over time as we consider in advance the most prudent courses of action. Without it, social behavior would tend to be shortsighted, directed more at serving the actor's own current interests and achieving immediate goals. Devoid of commonsense psychology, we would be less able to consider the interests of others and would be less able to subjugate our own immediate desires to superior future benefits. We would be selfish, here-and-now-oriented beings.

3

The Developmental Approach

In this chapter we take a general look at the developmental approach to conceptual development without focusing in particular on commonsense psychology. As I mentioned in chapter 1, the developmental approach is one general way of understanding the nature of psychological phenomena. By examining simpler forms of abilities and how those simpler forms gradually change, we gain insight into the nature of more mature competencies. Thus, developmental psychology is the study of psychological change with age. Of course, age is just a measure of time since birth, and because time does not cause changes directly, neither does age. Nevertheless change obviously does occur in children and developmental psychology aims to document and explain that change in terms of the variety of influences operating on children.

In popular sources and everyday discussions, explaining how development occurs is still typically cast in terms of the nature–nurture dichotomy. When I first wrote this section, a media frenzy was occurring over the announcement of the birth of the first cloned human. Much of the interest trades on the fear or fascination that such clones will be indistinguishable copies of the parent that donated the nuclear DNA. A recent newspaper headline (*Halifax Mail Star*, December 30, 2002) captured the issues: "Identical Twins Closer Than Clones, Experts Say. Genetic Blueprint Can Be Trumped by Environment." The article went on to explain that even identical (monozygotic) twins who share exactly the same nuclear DNA structure as well as much of their environment are not perfect copies of each other. Therefore, there is good reason to believe that cloned individuals and their donor parent who share DNA structure but relatively little in the way of environmental influence will differ in very significant ways.

Nevertheless, these days the pendulum seems to have swung more toward the nature side. Maybe commonsense psychology just comes with the territory of being human? In the current genomic era this suggestion is often taken to mean something like "built into the human genome." A commonsense genomics answer to the question of where commonsense psychology comes from is that there is a gene or set of genes that causes the expression of commonsense psychology. In fact this is no answer at all and it is important to say a little here about why (for a detailed argument, see David Moore's recent book *The Dependent Gene* [2002]). Leaving aside the difficulty of actually determining what genes are, it is clear that genes do no more than provide some coding information for the construction of proteins. Even for that limited function, they need a complex array of internal cellular environmental machinery. The information provided in the genome is just one influence in an extended cascading process of intricately interrelated influences. The structure of the final product (if there is any sense in which any product is final) depends on information from many sources, of which the genome is one. These influences together produce what we know as development. Inevitably, then, development is the product of an extremely complex set of interactions between characteristics of the organism and of the environment in which those characteristics occur.

Developmental psychology represents the study of a subset of the full set of developmental processes that yield the mature adult. Developmental psychologists tend to focus on the period after birth and the set of influences that can be studied psychologically. As a general rule, we can say that at each and every stage of development further change is a product of psychological processes operating at the existing level of development along with information that is provided in the environment. A critical point is that the information input that is available at any stage of development will depend on the level of understanding at that stage. For example, information relevant to understanding the emotion of pride is meaningless to the child who has not yet acquired a concept of the self as an objective entity because pride is premised on the self as the object of one's own and others' admiration. So the child's level of development constrains the kind of information that can be used for further developmental progress.

DOMAIN SPECIFICITY AND DOMAIN GENERALITY

Before elaborating further on these issues, I address the issue of how commonsense psychology may be connected to other domains of knowledge during development. The field of developmental psychology is divided on the extent to which different aspects of conceptual development occur together. Some authors argue that conceptual knowledge is divided into a number of independent or core domains and that development proceeds essentially separately in these domains (e.g., Spelke, 2000). For example, knowledge of commonsense psychology may be acquired quite separately from, say, knowledge of commonsense physics (i.e., knowledge of the rules governing the physical world) or commonsense biology (i.e., knowledge of the nature of the living world). A strong form of this domain specificity is that for each core domain, the child begins life with a small set of principles that constrain the kind of information the child attends to and that guide how further knowledge is acquired. The psychological processes that are involved in the acquisition of each domain of knowledge are relatively specialized to the domain of knowledge. So, for example, the processes involved in the acquisition of knowledge of psychology are different from those involved in the acquisition of knowledge of physics. The modern grandfather of this kind of view is Chomsky's claim (e.g., 1965) that linguistic knowledge (in particular, knowledge of syntactic structures) is a universal component of the human mental anatomy.

A weaker form of the domain-specific view is that whereas the application of domains of knowledge may be relatively independent so that, for example, commonsense psychology may be acquired and used separately from, say, commonsense physics, the psychological processes that are involved in the acquisition of these different domains of knowledge are essentially common. Another way to put this is that separate knowledge domains are the developmental products of the workings of various domain-general information-processing mechanisms in complexly structured environments (e.g., Karmiloff-Smith, 1992). To see how this might happen we have to recognize that although the psychological processes may be general, they encounter different types and combinations of information in different situations. For example, in early social contexts the visual system encounters regular patterns of features corresponding to faces and quickly builds up representations of faces in general as well as representations of various particular faces; whereas when viewing and interacting with the physical world, the visual system is presented with various forms with overlapping edges and thereby builds up representations of objects and the spatial relations in which they may occur. Before long the visual representations of faces and physical objects are quite distinct. Thus it is information processing in different situations that yields the different domains of knowledge.

The information that is the substrate for the development of commonsense psychology is that provided by the social world. There is no question that for humans the social world constitutes by far the most important part of the environment. From birth to death our worlds are to all intents and purposes our social worlds. Throughout life, the development and maintenance of relationships with others, whether lovers, family, friends, or colleagues, are at the heart of many of our activities. Hardly less motivating is the management of competitive relationships with peers and others with whom we must contend to achieve our goals. Because we are so embedded in a social context, we have an elaborate set of mechanisms to manage the variety of interactions that we encounter. We possess a complex array of social signals, including facial and postural emotional expressions that modulate interactions, and the most extensive and complex communication system known in the natural world—language. As a species, we show by far the most attention to our young, providing massive investment of resources for many years. In concert with this parental tendency, our young are born relatively helpless but possessed of powerful means to recognize and engage potential caregivers. As I show in chapter 4, within days of birth, infants prefer to look at faces than to look at other kinds of stimuli. They produce cries that others try to calm. Within 2 months they smile more at people than at other stimuli. Adults respond by providing attention and by trying to elicit those signs of contentment such as smiling. Once they are engaged with others, infants soon become able to learn from them and within a very few years, young children become sophisticated participants in the networks of relationships in which they are embedded.

Two kinds of social information are of particular significance for the development of the child's commonsense psychology. One is the information available to the child about psychological activity. As we saw in chapter 2, such information itself is available in two forms: information about the child's own psychological activity (first-person information) and information about the psychological activities of those with whom the child interacts (third-person information). Components of both forms of information are available to the infant in the perceptual input from early in life but the extent to which the child can monitor the information clearly changes with age.

The other kind of social information comes from the ways in which first- and third-person forms of information are patterned in the interactions in which the child participates. Social acts typically occur in highly structured sequences. As we shall see, the two forms of information become intertwined in the child's experience very early on in development, certainly before the child has any clear awareness of self or other as independent psychological agents. Within 2 months after birth, infants start to participate in interactions with significant others. These interactions involve both participants signaling emotions, vocalizing, and gesturing. Before long both participants learn to adapt their own acts to the acts of the other so that a rich stream of social information of both first- and third-person forms is available to the infant. With development there is a continual increase in the scope of interactive partners and the sophistication of interactions and so the richness of this coordination of information only intensifies.

Because social information is the substrate out of which commonsense psychology is built, we will need to pay considerable attention to the kinds of social information that are available to children at different stages through infancy and early childhood. The available social information changes as children's social experiences develop from simple face-to-face interactions to language-based exchanges. To capitalize on the increasing complexity of social information, children need information-processing abilities of increasing sophistication. Together the social information present in the children's experience and their information-processing abilities produce the complex conceptual system of commonsense psychology. We now turn to a consideration of the information-processing abilities necessary for this task.

INFORMATION PROCESSING AND DEVELOPMENT

A developmental explanation of the structure of commonsense psychology requires attention to the fundamental psychological processes that enable the elaboration of this conceptual system to occur. We approach this issue from two directions. We first examine the general processes that are designed to coordinate action in relation to available information. Our main interest here is in distinguishing between perceptual and cognitive or representational modes of action control. Then, second, we examine the processes that allow the information available from the social world to become structured into increasingly complex forms in the conceptual system of the developing child.

Controlling Action: Perception and Mental Representation

Like all organisms, humans have a variety of information-processing systems the function of which is to allow them to interact adaptively with the environment. Actions performed in the environment are organized with respect to the information gained from the environment and the interests or goals of the organism. The manner in which actions are organized in relation to environmental information shows substantial variety. Sometimes, as with reflexes, behavior occurs in response to environmental stimulation quite automatically. Of more interest to human psychology is intentional behavior that is directed at consciously represented goals. Goals may be real objects present in the environment and available to perception; for example, there may be a cookie on the table in front of me that I want and so I reach for it. In other cases, goals may be more abstract and require mental or cognitive images to organize action directed toward them. For example, I may have a goal to pay for my daughter's university education. In humans much of our action is in relation to these more abstract goals. Action is organized cognitively rather than perceptually through the use of mental representations in place of perceptual input to guide action. The effect of such mental representations on motivational and emotional states is, however, just as real as it is for perceptual input (Harris, 2000). When I imagine the goal of sending my daughter to University without her having to worry about paying for it, I experience both a desire to achieve that goal and also a form of relief at the thought that she may indeed be fiscally unconstrained during her postsecondary education.

Because the notion of mental representation plays a central role in many of the forthcoming chapters I should say a bit more about it here. For our purposes, mental representation allows an action that was originally controlled by a certain perceptual input to occur in the absence of that input. It is quite literally re-presentation of the input using some kind of mental image. For this to occur there has to be a quasi-perceptual stimulus generated internally that can control action output. Mental representations may be quite similar in character to some original perceptual stimulus, such as a visual or auditory image of an event that was previously perceived. To take a simple linguistic example, as she reaches for the cookie jar, a child may mentally hear her mother say "no" and be thereby dissuaded from indulging. However, mental representations may also combine elements originally derived via perception into novel structures that do not necessarily reflect any particular event that actually took place. Mental language provides perhaps the clearest case. Although individual words and phrases may have originally been learned perceptually, we are able to recombine linguistic elements into novel structures and then use these to control both others' and our own action. In all cases of mental representation, there must be a medium for representation and the representation must link to and potentially control action.

How can we determine when action is being controlled by a mental representation? This turns out to be an extremely difficult question to answer because actions almost never occur without any perceptual input. Rather, there is almost always some perceptual input that acts as an immediate stimulus to action. Indeed this is part of the reason why for many years in the history of psychology (i.e., in the so-called behaviorist years during the first half of the 20th century) mental representations were completely eschewed as explanatory entities. Consider the case where there is a perceptual input controlling action but that input was not the original controlling stimulus as in, for example, Pavlovian conditioning. In the classic case, a dog that naturally salivates when food is presented is subjected repeatedly to events in which the presentation of food is preceded by the sound of a bell. After a number of days of such experience, we find that the dog starts to salivate as soon as the bell sounds and before any food has appeared. Here a response occurs to a perceptual input that has become associated with the original stimulus for the response—the dog salivates to the sound of the bell. It might be tempting to interpret this effect as the bell leading to a mental image of the food and the dog salivating in response to that mental image. If so, then we could reasonably say that the dog has a mental representation of the food. However, this interpretation is really seeing the effect the wrong way around. In fact, it is the bell that allows the response to occur in the absence of the original input (the food) and thus it is the bell that is the representation, albeit not a mental one. Although learning to use such external representations may be a necessary precondition for the use of mental representations, Pavlovian conditioning is not itself evidence of such representation. So, observing an action that is controlled by a stimulus condition, which has been associated with the original eliciting stimulus condition, is not in itself a warrant to speak of the involvement of mental representations. Such control of action may or may not involve mental representation.

A more conservative test for the existence of a mental representation is when the organism can respond to a perceptual stimulus by producing an action that is explicitly different from the original or "natural" response. In this case the perceptual input calls out for one action but the organism produces a different action. Here the only way for the action to be controlled is through an input that is different from what is present in the actual environment, and that input must be internal or mental. Perhaps the most clear-cut example of this in young children is the phenomenon of pretend play (Leslie, 1987). Sometime toward the end of the second year, children will often take an object and use it as if it is something different in a playful manner. For example, a child may hold a banana to her ear and talk as if it is a telephone. It is obviously not the case that the child is simply confused about the object—the child has plenty of experience with both telephones and bananas and they resemble each other only tenuously. Furthermore, the child will mark the pretence with an exaggeration of action and a knowing smile that clearly indicates her awareness of the object substitution. What the pretence demonstrates is that the child's action may now be in relation to an imagined object rather than to the currently perceived one. The imagined object is mentally represented and can trump the real object of perception in the control of action.

A common theme in many developmental theories is that mental representational abilities change substantially over the first few years of life. These changes are held to be at least partly responsible for the behavioral and conceptual changes observed over this period. For many theorists, the period of infancy from birth to about 18 months is characterized by a dependence on a primarily perceptual form of action control (Leslie, 1987; Olson, 1989, 1993; Perner, 1991b; Zelazo, 1996). Jean Piaget (1953) called this *sensorimotor intelligence;* more recent theorists referred to *single updating models* (Perner) or *primary representation* (Leslie) in recognition of the fact that even perception requires that immediately available information in the environment be coded in the mind for it to be acted on. The action that infants may produce in response to perceptual input changes in organization and complexity through infancy, and it clearly is modified by experience. Nevertheless, infants are limited to dealing with information that is provided perceptually.

During the second year, children become capable of mental representational control of action as they are able to imagine or hold in mind one source of information even while attending perceptually to another (Olson,

1989, 1993; Perner, 1991b). As we have seen, pretend play shows this change most clearly (Leslie, 1987). Now action is in relation to some imagined object rather than to the perceived one. The advent of mental representation makes possible a rather different approach to the world—one that admits of vastly more possible responses and is fundamentally more creative. If I am hungry and I have a cookie, I can eat it. But I can also decide to pretend it is a Frisbee and spin it across the room, or crumble it and feed it to my rabbit. Seeing this book in front of me, I can opt to read it; but I can also use it as a doorstop, or tear it up for kindling.

Once mental representation is in place, psychological development becomes in large part the development of the imagination (Harris, 2000). The period from about 2 to 5 years sees efflorescence in children's imaginations as children construct elaborate fantasies in their social and private play. In play, children's behavior is organized largely with respect to a narrative that is internally generated but may nevertheless be coordinated with play partners. Although the imagination sees its most florid expression in play, it is serious business too. The imagination enables the mind to range beyond the here and now to recapture events from the past or consider possible futures as in planning (Suddendorf & Whiten, 2001). It allows a variety of forms of rule-based reasoning, such as drawing inferences from premises and determining whether rules have been violated (Harris; Zelazo, Carter, Reznick, & Frye, 1997). In fact, what is common to all imaginative acts is simply that the events are different from what is true of the immediately perceptible world at the time of the act of imagination.

Once children are capable of mental representation, there may be tensions between perceptual and cognitive control of action. In any particular circumstance, perceptual input may call out for one action whereas cognitive input may call out for another. How, then, is an executive decision to be made about which action to implement? A nice illustration of what is meant here comes from an experimental task known as the Less Is More task, which was conducted with young children and chimpanzees (Boysen, Berntson, Hannan, & Cacioppo, 1996; Carlson, Davis, & Gum, 2005). In the child version of this task developed by Stephanie Carlson of the University of Washington, children are presented with two bowls containing candies. One bowl contains two candies, the other five. The children are also introduced to a puppet, a mischievous monkey who tends to be mean and wants to take the candies. The children are told that they can pick one of the bowls, but that whichever bowl they pick the monkey will take the candies from that bowl and the children will get the candies from the other bowl. Over a series of trials the children get to make the same choice between a bowl with two and a bowl with five. The natural response here is to choose the bowl with the greater quantity—five. However, if the children choose five they lose them and only get two. Instead they need to choose the bowl with two. Here is a case where the perceptual information (five candies) calls out for one action (point to the bowl with five) but to be successful the child has to generate and use a mental representation (something like "two is good") in order to control a different action (point to the bowl with two). Thus there are two sources of information that are in conflict. In order to be adaptive the natural action in response to the perceptual information (choosing the greater quantity) must be rejected in favor of its opposite (choosing the smaller quantity). Children of 3 years or less (and chimpanzees) have enormous difficulty learning to do this. Over multiple trials they continue to choose the greater quantity even though they receive the smaller quantity each time. So it appears that in this conflict situation, what they are not able to do is act on the basis of a mental representation instead of on the basis of the perceptual information.

But if 2-year-olds are capable of using mental representations, why are they unable to solve the Less Is More task? Let us consider the task in more detail. The children are asked over a series of trials which collection they want to pick (two or five candies) and their goal is to get five. Directing the children's action in relation to the perceptual input will lead them to point to the collection of five and they will only receive two. In order to organize the adaptive action, the children therefore have to recode mentally the collection of two as meaning five (i.e., pointing to two will yield five). Now directing their action in relation to the mental representation of two as five will lead them to point to the collection of two. So far, so good. However, the problem is that perceptual input is naturally more immediate and salient and it tends to dominate in the control of action. Even though young children may know that two means five, they may not be able to stop themselves from pointing to the real collection of five. We can think of this as a competition between the strengths of the input-action connections so that, other things being equal, perception-action connections tend to win over cognition-action connections. So, in addition to being able to recode two as five, children have to be able to inhibit acting in relation to the perceptual information. One way to achieve inhibition is to recode the perceptual input in such a way that it does not lead to action, for example, five is recoded as two. In this way the strength of the tendency to point to the collection of five may be attenuated to a level where it now loses in the competition with the tendency to point in relation to the smaller amount. On this account, to succeed reliably on the Less Is More task, children may need to represent mentally both quantities as the opposite value. Simultaneous attention to two mental representations is required to yield the adaptive action—one to implement the action of pointing to the collection of two and one to inhibit the action of pointing to the collection of five. Part of the difficulty young children have with so-called executive problems of this sort is in simultaneously attending to more than one mental representation relevant to the same situation.

The representational limitation that leads to difficulties in the Less Is More task is of quite broad scope. Phil Zelazo, Douglas Frye, and their colleagues showed that in a number of tasks that depend on similar levels of representational flexibility, 3-year-old children do poorly (Frye, Zelazo, & Palfai, 1995; Zelazo et al., 1997). For example, they used a card-sorting task in which a deck of cards could be sorted according to either of two dimensions. On the cards there were pictures of either boats or rabbits and both objects could be either red or blue. The cards could therefore be sorted according to shape (boats go here and rabbits go there) or color (red things go here and blue things go there). Three-year-olds have no difficulty sorting by either dimension alone. However, if children first sort a series of cards according to one dimension (either shape or color) so that they are practiced at it, and then are asked to switch to the other dimension, 3-year-olds typically perform poorly on the second dimension. They tend to perseverate or continue to sort according to the initial dimension because this dimension has become more salient. By 4 years, children have gained the requisite cognitive flexibility and they easily switch to sorting according to the second dimension. Similar results have been found for different tasks that require equivalent levels of representational flexibility (e.g., Frye et al.). Recently it was shown that children's performance on the Less Is More task is correlated with their performance on the card-sorting task (Carlson et al., 2005), supporting the idea that there are quite general developments in representational flexibility occurring from about 3 to 4 years of age.

Earlier I mentioned that imagination requires a medium for the presentation of mental representational input. It is important to recognize the role that symbols, and in particular language, play in mental representation and the control of action. Although the imagination does not depend on language (e.g., mental imagery is more visual in quality), the two soon become inextricably intertwined as we shall see in chapters 8 and 9. Language too gets it start at the end of infancy because it critically depends on the same cognitive advances that make imagination possible—in particular, being able to hold one thing in mind (the meaning) at the same time as attending to something else (the words) in perception. But language quickly becomes the representational medium par excellence. There are likely two main reasons for this. First, language is prodigiously creative, allowing essentially infinite possibilities for thought. Second, it is fundamentally a form of social behavior (Tomasello, 2003) that allows the imagination to be elaborated between people as well individually. I address this issue in more detail in chapter 8.

Symbolic representation becomes an important way of overcoming the tyranny of perception. There is a good deal of evidence that the provision of symbols allows young children to perform better than usual in executive function tasks (Jacques & Zelazo, 2005). For example, providing symbols in place of the real quantities in the Less Is More task improves the performance of both young children and, as it happens, chimpanzees. Boysen et al. (1996) showed that chimpanzees that were previously trained to recognize numerals could learn to choose adaptively (i.e., pick the smaller quantity) if the real treats were replaced on the plates by numerical representations of the quantities—the numerals "2" and "5" written on cards. Now the chimpanzees reliably picked the plate holding the card with "2" on it and were given the larger quantity. What this result shows is that the chimpanzees could use external representations but had difficulty with generating internal or mental representations. Although there is evidence that they too can benefit from the provision of symbols, children easily solve this task without external representations by about 4 years of age (Carlson et al., 2005).

So far this discussion of the nature of mental representation has focused on how environmentally provided perceptual inputs may be replaced by representations in the control of action. But actions do not serve only as the final output of information processing. Actions also serve as input for subsequent actions. In this way, actions are chained into sequences whereby each action in the chain is both the output of prior information processing and an input for subsequent actions. This fact has two very important implications. First, it means that, in addition to monitoring stimuli in the external environment, agents must also monitor their own actions. Just as there are exteroceptive perceptual systems such as vision, there are also interoceptive information-processing systems including proprioception, which processes information about action movements. Proprioception is of particular importance in the control of action because it provides a key source of information about the dynamics and whereabouts of our body parts. This information can then be used in the control of subsequent actions. Proprioception, along with the visceral senses such as hunger and affect, supplies an important part of first-person information.

Second, if perception of action can serve as input, then action too may be potentially represented mentally. We can imagine a prior action in a chain without it actually being performed. With a means to represent both environmental stimuli and action output, we have the potential for the generation of a plan or, in other words, organization of an action in advance of its actual execution.

Pattern Detection and the Construction of Knowledge

We have seen how the control of action changes through development as different forms of information are used. How are these forms of information used to build up knowledge? First, it is important to note that the information that is provided to the child's information-processing system is inevitably structured or patterned in various ways. For example, a sentence spoken to the child consists of speech sounds that vary in pitch, loudness, and rhythm. These variations are not random. Certain sounds reliably follow other sounds and the sounds may co-occur with particular objects in the environment on a regular basis. Second, we should note that infants and children are very motivated and effective pattern detectors. They tune into and pick up on the regularities presented in the input. Certain kinds of regularities seem to be of special significance. In particular, as we shall see in chapter 4, spatiotemporal regularities are of singular importance in infancy. For example, features that occur together in a complex visual stimulus become grouped into a whole. Individual speech sounds that reliably follow each other become combined into wordlike forms.

Patterns are everywhere in the environment. Faces are regular patterns of features with two eyes side by side over a nose and mouth and bordered on the top and side by a hairline. Recognizing this pattern means detecting a face. There are regularities in the ordering of the speech sounds that the infant hears: The infant of English-speaking parents regularly hears [be] then [bi], but rarely if ever [mo] followed by [di]. Before long the infant recognizes and responds to *baby* but not *modi*. It is important to remember that patterns can and do occur across exteroceptive and interoceptive inputs. For example, looking in a mirror and making a face provides an experience of a perfect correlation between the proprioceptive and visual information specifying the facial movement. However, the feeling of making a face and the sight of mom making a face occur together with less regularity. Differences in correlation patterns across proprioception and vision can therefore distinguish the patterns corresponding to the self from the patterns corresponding to others.

Patterns among elements in the information can occur in different ways. John Watson and Gyorgy Gergely (Gergely & Watson, 1999; Watson, 1994) have suggested that infants are particularly adept at detecting patterns of perceptual information that occur in temporal contingency and spatial relations. Temporal contingency refers to the reliability with which one event is located in time with another. Infants pay particular attention to patterns of temporal contingency with high but not perfect reliability (Watson, 1985) and it is interesting that human interactions have exactly that pattern. As we shall see in chapter 5, when adults interact with infants, much, but not all, of the infants' action draws a response from the adults. So the infants' monitoring of the temporal contingency between their own action and that of the other yields a percept that these actions are linked. Objects or events that occur in regular spatial arrangements are also detected as linked. Thus, if two objects regularly occur in the same position relative to each other or if two objects move in the same direction they are associated. Faces provide an important example here. The features of a face, such as the eyes, nose, and mouth, very reliably occur in the same spatial configuration and this configuration is recognized very early in life, as I discuss in the chapter 4.

As commonly occurring perceptual patterns are recognized through these mechanisms, they become integrated and organized into structures: faces rather than features, words rather than separate sounds, and so on. These structures then become the units for subsequent perceptual pattern detection, so that patterns among the structures are detected. Detection of patterns among the structures leads to integration into a higher order set of structures and so on. In this way, developmental change occurs in terms of the highest level of pattern or structure that can be analyzed. As Leslie Cohen (1998, p. 289; see also Cohen, Chaput, & Cashon, 2002) put it, "the infant at one age processes holistic units which become elements in the construction of higher order units at a later age, and those units, in turn, become elements in the construction of yet higher orders at an even later age." When it comes to processing social information, this hierarchical developmental progression will apply as much to patterns detected between exteroceptive (third-person information) and interoceptive (first-person information) sources as it does to patterns detected in information coming from environmental events alone. If particular forms of first-person information reliably co-occur with particular forms of third-person information, then they will become integrated into higher order units. Thus, higher order units of social information may retain characteristics of information derived from both the self and others (Barresi & Moore, 1996).

The perceptual structures that can be acquired through such pattern detection include not just more complex objects, such as faces or words, but also particular kinds of relations between objects. An example from infant development is causality, which involves relations between two or more objects that may be inferred from specific patterns of movements. In particular, if one object moves along a path and contacts another object, which then moves off in the same direction, 10-month-olds, but not 6-month-olds, perceive this event as an integrated pattern of movement (Oakes & Cohen, 1990). Adults viewing the same event describe it in terms of the first object causing the launch of the second object. Relations among objects become of increasing significance in development and are, as we have seen, fundamental to the nature of social understanding.

Detection of patterns in the perceptual input does not simply allow recognition of regularities in the input; it also allows the prediction of future input. Even infants as young as 3 months can use patterns to predict what will happen next. Marshall Haith and his colleagues at the University of Denver (Haith, Hazan, & Goodman, 1988) showed young infants patterns of simple pictures on a computer screen. Pictures were shown briefly on alternating sides of the screen with a short interval between them. Infants' eye movements were monitored in conjunction with the appearance of the pictures. As infants got used to the alternating left-right pattern, they started to move their eyes in anticipation of the next appearance. Using this kind of procedure, Haith and his colleagues were able to show that by 3 months of age, infants were able to detect not just simple alternations between left and right but also more complicated patterns such as two left followed by one right and two left followed by two right (Haith, 1994). Such visual expectations illustrate how pattern detection plays a role in guiding action. Indeed, the future orientation afforded by expectation is a fundamental property of pattern detection processes.

As we shall see in the next few chapters, detection of patterns in perceptual input characterizes development through infancy. However, detecting patterns is a general characteristic of human information processing that continues throughout life. As pattern detection extends beyond perceptual input to include representations, it becomes increasingly more abstract with relations among relations being detected. Analogical reasoning exemplifies this kind of pattern detection. In analogical reasoning, it is the relations among objects that serve as the input, not particular objects themselves. Thus we determine that an analogy holds when we detect that the relations among objects in each of two distinct sets correspond. Detection of such patterns was termed *structure mapping* by Dedre Gentner and her colleagues (e.g., Gentner & Markman, 1997; Gentner & Medina, 1998). A good example comes from work by Gentner and Ratterman (1991). In their study, experimenter and child each had a set of three clay pots of different sizes arranged in a line of increasing size. The experimenter's and the children's sets overlapped in size so that two of the objects were exactly the same size, but the third was different (see Fig. 3.1). Over a series of trials, the experimenter hid a sticker under one of the objects in her set and the

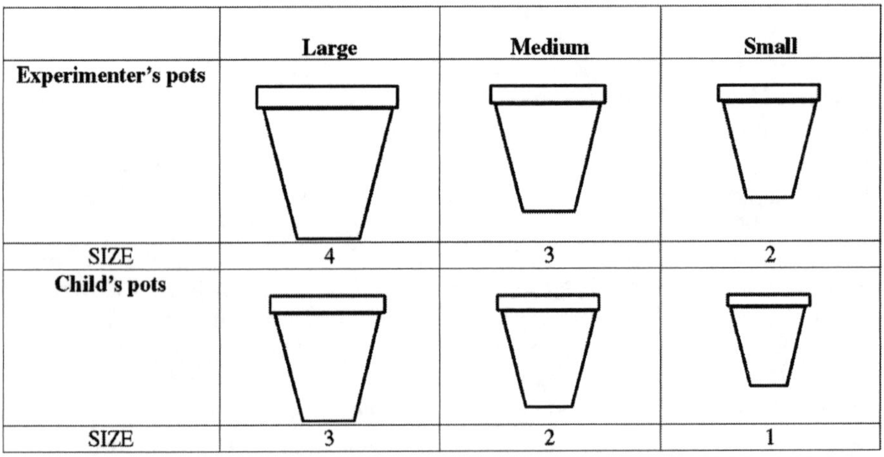

	Large	Medium	Small
Experimenter's pots			
SIZE	4	3	2
Child's pots			
SIZE	3	2	1

FIG. 3.1. Sets of pots arranged in size for experimenter and child as in Gentner and Rattermann (1991).

children's task was to find the sticker under one of their own objects. The sticker was always under the object in the children's set that was of the same relative size as the one in the experimenter's set. This of course meant that it was under an object of different absolute size. In this task, 3-year-olds had considerably difficulty finding their sticker—they tended to look for it under the object that was exactly the same size as the experimenter's. They could detect a pattern across the two sets in terms of the objects themselves, but could not detect the pattern across the two sets in terms of the relations among the objects. Performance improved substantially through the later preschool period, showing that children became better able to detect patterns evident in the relations among the objects in the different sets.

Interestingly, structure mapping is aided significantly by the availability of symbolic representations. Because the same symbol (e.g., a word), may be used for similar relations, the symbol highlights the resemblance of relational patterns. Gentner and Ratterman (1991) repeated their study but implicitly coded the relative size of the three objects by labeling them "daddy," "mommy," and "baby." They then pointed out the location of the sticker in their set using the appropriate label, saying, for example, "My sticker is under my mommy. Where do you think your sticker is?" With this procedure, even 3-year-olds were able to perform well above chance. Thus, in this case, symbolic representation allowed pattern detection to switch focus to more abstract patterns of information.

The Role of the Social World in Facilitating Pattern Detection

There is no doubt that young children are motivated pattern detectors. So far, we have talked as if children go about the task of pattern detection in a solitary way, but of course this is a misrepresentation. The last example illustrates that the patterns that are available in the developing children's environment do not all occur without human intervention. Other people in the children's social world are importantly involved in structuring the perceptual world for the children to aid their pattern detection. They provide much of the information, both social and nonsocial, that children experience and they attempt to provide that information in a way that makes patterns more salient. According to the general developmental approach outlined in this chapter, the optimal conditions for the development of commonsense psychology are those in which parents and others in the children's social world adjust their interactions sensitively to match the children's level of understanding. It is therefore important that they act toward children in ways that reflect sensitivity to children's current level of social understanding.

How is such sensitivity achieved? In their interactions with children, adults generally aim to stimulate the children's attention and interest. As we have seen, children are highly motivated pattern detectors. This motivation means that they both attend to, and get pleasure from detecting, novel patterns. There is also a novelty preference so that once a particular pattern has become familiar it becomes less motivating and children will seek to find novel patterns. Given this set of motivations on the part of children, there are two main ways adults facilitate pattern detection in children. First, adults aim to make patterns more obvious to children. Second, they gradually adjust upward the patterning they provide so that it changes with children's level of pattern detection but is a little more advanced. Children provide the signals adults need to achieve this adjustment. If the adult stimulation is at an appropriate level for the children, that is, at a level that contains elements the children can incorporate into novel patterns, it will elicit attention and often signs of pleasure. In the earliest stages of development such pleasure is clearly evident in smiling, as we shall see in chapter 4. If the adult stimulation is at an inappropriate level, either too complex or too simple, children lose interest and become distracted or otherwise indicate a lack of attention.

Pattern detection is, therefore, a process that generally occurs within the context of social interactions. Children are naturally interested in detecting patterns in the stimulation they receive, and the patterns they detect depend at every point of development on the level of pattern detection they have so far attained. But it is often adults who present stimulation in a way that is tuned to the children's level of development. Cognitive development depends on both the natural propensities of children to try to understand their world and the tendencies of adults to structure that world in a way that it can be more easily understood.

TRENDS IN DEVELOPMENT: STAGES AND UNIVERSALITY

Even a cursory exposure to child development leaves us with some knowledge of developmental milestones: Babies normally take their first step at about 12 months; they become toilet trained sometime around 3 years, and so on. Milestones are valuable because they provide a set of benchmarks for developmental progress. However, when attempting to understand the nature of developmental change, milestones measured in months or years are of little help. As I mentioned earlier, age by itself does not cause change to occur. Furthermore, the age given marks both the endpoint of a complicated developmental process up to that achievement and the starting point of subsequent elaborate developmental events. Thus, in one sense, no age is any more significant than any other because development is continuous and unending. There is no point at which children take a break from development after reaching a milestone to return after they have gotten their energy back.

Nevertheless, there is good reason to believe that certain points in development witness particularly important changes in function, changes that allow further radical differences in psychological organization that in effect create a qualitatively different kind of understanding. By analogy, consider evolution. According to the orthodox Darwinian doctrine of evolution by natural selection, evolution occurred slowly and gradually. Over time cumulative small changes could lead to the evolution of quite different species. But certain events could greatly enhance the prospects for rapid evolutionary change. Moving to a previously unexploited geographical region or environmental niche was a prime candidate. For example, there was enormous scope for further vertebrate evolution once the transition from a purely aquatic environment to a terrestrial environment was made. In the same way, certain events in the development of young children though themselves the product of gradual developmental changes, open up whole new worlds of possibility just as faced the first air-breathing fish that struggled onto land.

In traditional developmental theory, dating to the work of Piaget (e.g., Piaget & Inhelder, 1969), these transition points were seen to mark the boundaries between developmental stages. During transitions between stages there was a significant reorganization in the structure of children's thought such that a qualitatively new way of thinking about and interacting with the world was achieved. The sequence of stages was assumed to be fixed, with each building on the ones that went before, and irreversible. In the chapters that follow, I do not propose a sequence of stages of commonsense psychology in the classic sense. At the same time, I suggest that there are qualitative changes in commonsense psychology during the first 5 years. In the pages to come, we will focus on a number of candidates for important transition points and to some extent our coverage of the development of children's commonsense psychology is structured by these transitions. The first comes early in the first year, at about 2 months of age. It is at this point that infants become alert and responsive enough to be able to engage in extended bouts of face-to-face interaction with another person. The new niche that this opens up is that of social stimulation and the prospect for entering into a relationship with another person. Toward the end of the first year another significant transition occurs when children become capable of interacting with a person over some other object. For the first time, children are able to use another person to find out about the world. Given that this approach to learning essentially characterizes most of the learning that will follow for the rest of life, it is difficult to overestimate the importance of this transition. During the second year, children acquire a new capacity for representation, most obviously through language. Again, it is difficult to overemphasize the significance of this achievement when we consider the role that linguistic communication plays in human functioning. Further significant transitions characterize the preschool period, but this brief synopsis of the major transitions during infancy should illustrate the way in which radically new worlds of opportunity are opened up by certain achievements.

Finally, I should say a few words about norms in development. In this book, we follow the development of commonsense psychology from an idealized, normative perspective. The typical developmental trends are presented. This should not be taken to mean that all children fit these trends or that there is no influence of individual differences. It is commonly observed that there is considerable variability in the ages at which children reach various milestones. Some start slow and catch up, others show the reverse pattern. Not only do rates of development differ, but there are also individual differences in patterns of development. Some paths of development are so atypical that they lead to serious difficulties in social functioning. Children with autism may present particularly tragic cases where, from an early age, social behavior and commonsense psychology are severely disrupted (Hobson, 1993). Within typically developing children, there are also variations in the ways that children respond to social information that may have profound importance for their social lives. Initial temperamental differences among children can translate through development into functionally meaningful differences in mature social responsiveness. Across cultures, there may be profound differences in patterns of social interaction. Nevertheless, we assume that the form of commonsense psychology outlined in chapter 2 is developed by all children within the normal range and that its development follows the same pattern across the first 5 years.

SUMMARY

The study of development provides an understanding of the nature of psychological structures by examining how they progress through different forms in the life span of the individual. A comprehensive developmental account requires a clear articulation of the structures to be understood as well as an answer to how change in those structures occurs, and what points in development are of particular significance. In this chapter and in chapter 2, I provided an outline of these issues. In particular in this chapter, I argued that development occurs through general-purpose information-processing mechanisms operating on information provided through children's participation in the social environment. Development proceeds both through change in the way action is controlled and through change in the complexity of the knowledge structures available to control action. Action is initially tied to perceptual input but later becomes controlled through mental representations that become increasingly elaborated in the imagination. Knowledge structures become increasingly complex through detection of regularities or patterns in the available information. Patterns are used to construct not only more complex concepts of objects in a hierarchical fashion but also relations among objects. Armed with this general approach to the nature and progress of development, we can now turn to the facts of early social experience.

4

The Origins of Social Action
in Early Infancy

Having considered the nature of commonsense psychology and of developmental psychology in a general way, I now begin on the task of describing the development of commonsense psychology. In this chapter we examine the earliest phase of development after birth. Our main goal in this chapter is to examine when and how the infant first gains exposure to the social information that will be important in the development of commonsense psychology. We will consider social information in both third- and first-person forms. Third-person information is largely derived from other people, who start to become involved in the infant's life at birth. First-person information is derived from the infant's own activity. As we shall see these two forms of information are available from the beginning of life outside the womb.

Of course, development in general does not begin at birth. Birth is the culmination of 9 months of intense developmental change. During the prenatal period a single fertilized egg cell is transformed into a baby with essentially all the body parts it will ever need, including a brain already possessed of billions of neurons. Although some learning in response to social stimuli does occur prior to birth (e.g., DeCasper & Spence, 1986), it is clear that the transition from the intrauterine environment to the outside world presents the opportunity for massive exposure to social information. The neonate's perceptual and action systems are designed to respond without prior postnatal experience to certain properties of environmental stimulation. Much of this stimulation just happens to be provided by other people in the new baby's world. And even at birth much of the limited range of behavior that the baby produces is well suited to recruiting parental attention. This attention from others provides further social stimulation.

In this way, first-person and third-person information become intertwined very early in life. In this chapter, we will examine how the newborn infant starts to make sense of social information and how the infant succeeds in encouraging others to continue to provide such information. We start by considering the kinds of social acts that newborn infants produce.

SOCIAL ACTS

Social acts may be defined as individual acts that are either produced in response to stimulation provided by others or that are treated as such by others. Social acts constitute the building blocks or elements out of which more complex forms of social behavior are built. From birth, infants produce a variety of acts that can be considered social in one or both of two ways. Some infant acts are in response to stimulation provided by adults. Perhaps the simplest, but in many ways the most important is orienting. Orienting is the overt behavioral manifestation of attention, or what we might call *interest*, and infants come into the world interested in information that is provided by the social world in both the visual and auditory modalities. For example, as we will see, they prefer to look at human faces compared to many other visual stimuli, and they prefer to listen to the sound of a human voice compared to many other kinds of sounds.

Other acts that infants perform, such as crying and smiling, serve to recruit social attention. Adults in the infant's environment respond to these acts and their responses typically involve rich streams of social stimulation—comforting, facial expressions, vocalizations—as well as attention to the infant's physiological needs. We will see soon how important these acts are for establishing the right kind of informational input for the hungry information-processing systems with which the infant comes into the world. Together these social acts serve to embed the infant in a world of rich social experience right from birth.

Let us look at some examples of how these different forms of social acts develop over the first few months. We will first look at how infants respond to social information from the world and second examine certain acts that serve to recruit adult attention.

RESPONDING TO THIRD-PERSON INFORMATION: FACES AND VOICES

Face Perception

The human face is the source of an enormous amount of social information. It is first and foremost the mark of the bearer, allowing us to identify and recognize the individual. It also provides information about the characteristics of the person, such as age and sex. To the extent that we need to respond to different people differently, we must distinguish and categorize them. The face is the primary means of doing this. The face also carries information about the psychological relations of the person. Emotional expressions, both as broad categories such as happiness, sadness, and anger and also in the exquisite subtlety of their variation, can be read in the face. The actor's goals and intentions can be partially discerned from eye direction.

So when are infants able to perceive faces? To answer this question, I should say a little about what we mean by perception of a face. Perception here may mean discrimination of a face from other visual stimuli but it may also mean discrimination of information given in the face such as identity and expression.

In any case, the key to determining what infants can see is to test whether they can discriminate one visual stimulus from another. Since the pioneering work of Robert Fantz (1961, 1964), developmental psychologists interested in studying the visual capacities of young infants have relied primarily on visual attentional preferences to discern what infants can see. In the typical visual preference procedure, two static stimuli are presented to the infant, either simultaneously side by side or sequentially, and the infant's responses to the displays are measured. To show a preference the infant has to spend more time looking at one stimulus than another. If the infant does indeed prefer to look at, or fixate on, one stimulus over another, then we can conclude that he or she must be able to tell the difference between, or discriminate, them.

Visual preferences can also be assessed by presenting infants with stimuli that move across their field of vision. When moving stimuli are presented, infants tend to move their eyes in order to keep looking at the stimulus. Importantly, they track some stimuli further than others and so we can determine which stimuli they prefer to track. It is worth noting that these two types of response—visual fixation and tracking—are controlled by different brain systems and that the system controlling tracking develops earlier than the system controlling fixation (Bronson, 1974). This means that, at least for the first few months of life, evidence of discrimination using eye movements can often be obtained developmentally earlier than evidence of discrimination using looking time.

It is important to note that discrimination can only be as good as the infant's eyesight allows. Measures of infants' acuity show that the ability to detect detail in stimuli is quite poor at birth, but develops rapidly over the first few months. It has been suggested (e.g., Bremner, 1994) that newborns' perception of a human face could at best resemble the right panel of Fig. 4.1 compared to the average adult's perception in the left panel. However, even to an infant with such limited acuity, faces are still discriminable from many

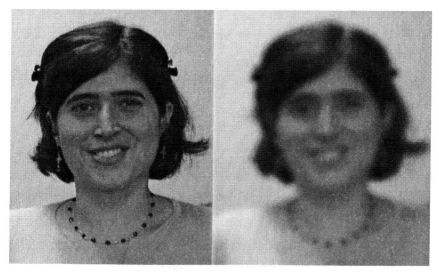

FIG. 4.1.   Sharp and blurred photos of a female face.

other stimuli given their characteristic configuration of two patches of high contrast centered over another area of high contrast, all circumscribed by an external high-contrast contour.

Discriminating Facelikeness.   Researchers interested in exploring the origins of face discrimination in young infants have used simplified schematic facelike stimuli such as those in Fig. 4.2, as well as abstract patterns assumed to correspond to the contrast configurations approximating the appearance of a face to infants with low acuity (see Fig. 4.3). In such experiments it is critical to choose a set of stimuli that differ in only the facet for which we want to assess infants' preferences. Infants' interest in the facelike stimulus must be compared to their interest in an equally complex stimulus that does not resemble a face. If the infants then prefer to look at the facelike stimulus we can conclude that it is not because they like to look at things that have a certain level of complexity quite independent of whether they resemble a face.

There is now good evidence that by 2 months infants reliably prefer to look at pictures resembling faces compared to pictures that are similar in terms of various other properties such as complexity and symmetry (Maurer & Barrera, 1981). It is assumed that this discrimination is achieved by the infant visually exploring the details of the stimuli and being more interested in the stimulus resembling a face. But where does this preference for faces come from?

FIG. 4.2.   Examples of a schematic face and a symmetrical scrambled schematic face.

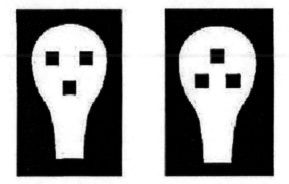

FIG. 4.3.   Facelike and nonfacelike stimuli. From "Face Preference at Birth: The Role of an Orienting Mechanism," by V. Cassia, F. Simion, and C. Umiltà, 2001, *Developmental Science, 4*, p. 104. Copyright 1996 by the American Psychological Association. Reprinted with permission of the authors.

Recent evidence has shown that even newborns show a preference for facelike stimuli under certain conditions. First, if a schematic face is moved across newborn infants' visual field, the infants track the stimulus by shifting their eyes with the movement of the face (Goren, Sarty, & Wu, 1975; Johnson, Dziurawiec, Ellis, & Morton, 1991). Johnson et al. (1991) tested infants as young as 40 minutes and found that infants tracked a moving facelike figure further than a stimulus that controlled for complexity and symmetry. Second, although newborn infants are not very good at maintaining a fixation to a static image in the center of the visual field, they do make eye movements to stimuli presented toward the edge of the visual field. Viola Cassia and her colleagues (Cassia, Simion & Umiltà, 2001) presented the high-contrast configurations of Fig. 4.3 to newborns such that each stimulus was presented to the edge of the visual field. Under these conditions, the babies shifted their eyes more often to the facelike configuration than to the comparison.

These results with moving or peripherally presented stimuli show that visual stimuli that share certain pattern properties with faces lead to orienting eye movements in infants even from the first few hours of life, before much experience with the meaning of faces could have occurred. Some researchers have therefore proposed that infants come equipped with an innately provided perceptual template for face perception. For example, John Morton and Mark Johnson (1991) proposed that infants begin life with such a template, the function of which is to control eye movements so that when presented with faces in the periphery of, or moving across, the visual field infants tend to orient toward and fixate those faces. They argued that this capacity would significantly increase infants' exposure to faces and thereby allow them to learn about faces much more quickly.

Other researchers still doubt that the early preference for facelike stimuli is actually specific to faces. In fact, even the simplified stimuli that control for complexity and left–right symmetry have not controlled for up–down symmetry. Chiara Turati and her colleagues (Turati, Simion, Milani, & Umiltà, 2002) presented newborns with stimuli that differed in up–down symmetry (see Fig. 4.4) and found that similar preferences to those found for facelike configurations were found for "top-heavy" stimuli that did not resemble faces. So apparently infants come into the world with a visual system that directs eye movements to top-heavy stimuli whether or not these stimuli look like faces.

FIG. 4.4. Top-heavy and bottom-heavy nonfacelike stimuli. From "Newborns' Preference for Faces: What Is Crucial?," by C. Turati, F. Simion, I. Milani, and C. Umiltà, 2002, *Developmental Psychology, 38*, p. 877. Copyright 2001 by Wiley. Reprinted with permission of the authors.

Although these issues are important for understanding the mechanics of early visual perception, whether or not the infant has a face-specific perceptual bias at birth matters little from a functional point of view. Even a preference for top-heavy visual stimuli means that very young infants tend to look at faces when they are available, for example, when the mother is close by. The extra attention to faces means that within a very short space of time, babies become able to discriminate not only faces from other objects, but also different kinds of faces based on identity and different facial expressions.

Perceiving Information in the Face: Identity and Emotion.   One of the earliest feats of facial discrimination that babies achieve is to recognize their mothers. Research has now shown that very early in life, infants are able to discriminate their mothers' faces from matched female strangers' faces and indeed prefer to look at their mothers' faces. Bushnell, Sai, and Mullin (1989) and Bushnell (2001) reported that within 4 days newborns prefer to look at their mothers' faces compared to a female stranger's. In this work, newborns were presented with their mothers and a female stranger side by side. Odor was masked by using air freshener and the babies' looking time to the two women was measured. More often than not, the babies spent more time looking at their mothers than at the strangers.

Although this result appears quite robust (Pascalis, De Schonen, Morton, Deruelle, & Fabre-Grenet, 1995), it is not clear on what basis the preference is initially established. Olivier Pascalis and colleagues reported that when the external contour of the faces and the hairlines were masked by pink scarves, neonates no longer showed a preference for their mothers. It is possible, therefore, that the initial preference that infants show is acquired through familiarity with the mothers' hair and face shape. However, as with the preference for top-heavy stimuli, this early familiarity tends to ensure that the infant looks at the mother.

Not surprisingly, the mother is a special stimulus for babies. Her face is the one that tends to accompany the good things in early life—comfort and nourishment. So it is no surprise that even newborn infants very quickly prefer her appearance to that of strangers. This early preference for the mother's face records the fact that infants become integrated into a social network essentially from birth, not just because that social network surrounds them but also because they actively seek it out.

Discriminating among other faces for which there may be no early preference is also possible within a few months of birth. When there is no intrinsic preference for one stimulus over another, researchers must try to create one in order to investigate infants' discrimination. Preferences are best created by taking advantage of infants' tendencies to lose interest in highly familiar stimuli, the process of *habituation*. If the same stimulus is presented repeatedly to infants they initially orient toward it but over time lose interest and look away. At this point a new stimulus that differs in the experimentally critical way can be presented. Because infants prefer to look at new things, they start looking again if they can discriminate the new from the old stimulus, so such recovery of looking evidences discrimination.

Discriminating among faces can be done in different ways. We may notice that two faces differ in terms of a particular feature of the face—perhaps one face contains a large nose and the other a button nose. As adults, there is good evidence that we can tell faces apart not with reference to a particular feature or features (i.e., featural processing) but with reference to a more holistic representation of the face, including the various parts and their spatial arrangement. The latter form of facial perception is called *configurational*, relying as it does on the configuration of the facial features. One piece of evidence that older children and adults use configurational processing is the fact that it is much more difficult to recognize individual faces when they are viewed upside down (or inverted) than when viewed right side up (Carey & Diamond, 1977). Inversion disrupts the configuration even while keeping the individual features intact.

Studies of infant face perception have explored not only when infants can tell faces apart but also how they do it (e.g., Barrera & Maurer, 1981; Cohen & Cashon, 2001). Maria Barrera and Daphne Maurer used the habituation approach to show that infants as young as 3 months of age could discriminate photographs of unfamiliar adults. This study did not allow any conclusions to be drawn on how the infants made their discriminations. However, Leslie Cohen and Cara Cashon (2001) specifically investigated the issue of whether infants use featural or configural processing when perceiving faces. They habituated 7-month-olds to photographs of two unfamiliar adults. They then tested for recovery of looking to one of the original photographs, to a blended photograph that contained features of both of the habituation faces, and to a completely novel face. The pictures were presented in both upright and inverted orientation. If infants were processing the faces configurally, then they should show more interest in both the novel and blended faces in the upright orientation in the test period because both faces would be perceived as different from the original. In contrast, only the completely novel face should garner more interest when the faces were presented upside down because only featural information could be used here and the blended face shared features with the original face. In fact, they found that when viewing pictures in the upright orientation the infants showed significant recovery of looking to both the novel and blended pictures. In contrast, when the pictures were presented in inverted orientation, only the completely novel pictures elicited significant recovery of looking. These results show that at least by 7 months of age, infants can tell faces apart from their overall configurations and not just from their differing features.

Faces convey a great deal of information about individuals beyond their identity. The face is the most obvious marker of a person's psychological states. As with the perception of identity, facial expressions of psychological states can be read from individual features (e.g., the upturned mouth corners of a smile) or more holistically from the configuration of the whole face. Although it is likely that infants of a few months of age can discriminate emotional expressions based on particular features, such as mouth shape, discrimination using configurations of features has not been demonstrated before about 5 months of age (Bornstein & Arterberry, 2003). Roberta Kestenbaum and Charles Nelson (1990) provided a good example. They habituated 7-month-old infants to photographs of three different models all posing with a happy expression. Two conditions were used. In one all photos were presented upright and in the other they were all presented in inverted orientation. After habituation, the infants were presented with three different expressions—happy, fearful, and angry—all of which were similar to the habituation expressions in having a similar toothy appearance of the mouth. The results showed significant recovery of looking to the fearful and angry expressions but not the happy expression for the infants who viewed the stimuli in upright orientation. The infants who viewed the stimuli in inverted orientation did not show recovery of looking to any of the expressions. These inversion effects imply that the emotional expressions were being perceived as configurations of features rather than individual features.

This evidence of perception of configurations of features in infant face perception illustrates an important general principle of infant learning that we addressed in chapter 3. Across many different areas of infant learning, it is clear that infants are sensitive to the patterns among different features in the stimuli to which they orient (Cohen, 1998). In face perception, those patterns exist among the different facial features that make up the face. Features that reliably occur together form meaningful wholes that are more than the sum of the parts. These new units can then be used in the detection of higher level patterns and relations.

Voice Perception

In the auditory domain there is no doubt that the most important social information is that carried by the human voice. Perceiving and responding to the human voice provides the typical route into language. We shall see later in the book how important language is for developing commonsense psychology. It is also worth noting at this point that the voice can carry information about the speaker's identity as well as the speaker's emotional state and so in many ways the information available in the voice mirrors that available in the face. So what can infants discern from the sounds they hear around them?

Infants are not only interested in visual stimuli; they are also interested in certain sounds, although demonstrating that interest presents more of a challenge to the researcher. Although visual orienting provides a clear overt manifestation of even young infants' interest in certain forms of visual information, auditory attention does not have as obvious a behavioral manifestation as seeing. We know that babies can hear from birth because they startle in response to sudden sound onsets. We also know that they can determine the direction of origin of a sound because they turn in the direction of a sound. But, what about the discrimination of different sounds? To investigate auditory discrimination, researchers have experimentally conditioned infants' behavior by associating an overt behavior to the presentation of specific sounds. For example, in the nonnutritive sucking procedure, infants suck on a pacifier that is connected to a device that measures changes in air pressure. This device is connected in turn to a tape recorder (or other sound-generation equipment). Through electronic intervention, the tape recorder can be made to turn on when the rate of air pressure changes meets some threshold and turn off when that rate falls below threshold. Infants soon learn that by sucking on the pacifier in the required way (by sucking at a faster or slower rate) they can make the sound turn on or off. If listening to the sound is rewarding, infants maintain a sucking rate to keep the sound on. Once this relation has been established it is possible to use both preference and habituation recovery (or novelty preference) to assess auditory discrimination.

This approach has been enormously valuable in helping to map young infants' auditory discrimination and preferences. For example DeCasper and Fifer (1980) showed that even from birth, infants prefer to listen to the sound of their mother's voice compared to a novel female voice. When both were available to the infant depending on whether the infants modified their sucking rates either up or down, infants tended to change their sucking in order to maximize the amount of their mother's voice that they heard. DeCasper and Prestcott (1984) demonstrated in subsequent studies that this preference appeared in babies before a similar preference for their father's voices. Furthermore, it could well be due to intrauterine learning. We know from intrauterine recordings that the mother's speech is audible within the womb (Richards, Frentzen, Gerhardt, McCann, & Abrams, 1992). DeCasper and colleagues (1994) showed that at 37 weeks of gestation, reliable fetus heart rate changes were observed to a short rhyme that had been repeatedly recited by the mothers-to-be over the previous 4 weeks. Furthermore, DeCasper and Spence (1986) showed a preference in a group of newborn infants for a particular story that their mothers had read repeatedly to them during the last trimester of their pregnancy.

Such work has shown that infants like to listen to the sound of the human voice, in particular that of their mother. However, infant speech perception research has gone much further in showing that infants come into the world with basic auditory abilities that are fundamental to the perception of the components of speech (Jusczyk, 1997). As I now discuss, infants rapidly come to grips with many of the very intricate aspects of speech perception such as perception of individual speech sounds (called *phonemes*) and word segmentation.

Spoken language is quite different from the written form you are now reading. The sounds produced in speech are not nicely segmented into individual letters, words, sentences, and paragraphs. In spoken language the sounds mostly run together and what gaps in the speech stream there are often do not correspond to the ends of words or sentences. Recall the experience of hearing someone speak a language that is completely foreign to you. It is almost impossible to discern any kind of structure in the stream of sound. In spoken language, even the individual building blocks, or phonemes, which approximately correspond to the letters of written language, depend much more on their contexts than do written letters. For example, the /t/ sound in *tap* is actually rather different from the /t/ in *pat*, the former being aspirated and the latter unaspirated. Yet this distinction plays no meaningful role in English (although it does in Thai). More troubling yet is the fact that, even within a language community, speech is produced by many people who possess vocal tracts that vary widely. Men have longer vocal tracts than women and adults have longer vocal tracts than children. The length of the vocal tract, as well as the size of the vocal chords, affects pitch, which is why on average men have lower voices than women, who have lower voices than children. Differences among speakers in the condition of the mouth, tongue, lips, and vocal chords can also affect the way any particular speech sound is produced. And yet, despite these differences, infants need to learn to recognize phonemes spoken by any speaker.

These facts about spoken language might seem to present an insurmountable difficulty to infants in perceiving speech sounds as speech. However, it is also a plain fact that within a year of birth infants can already understand some of the language used around them. How do they achieve this feat? Just as the infant starts life with a visual system that responds to social sights, so they start life with an auditory system that responds to social sounds. We have already seen that from birth infants like to listen to the sound of human voices. They also prefer to listen to higher pitched voices, and in particular, their own mother's. This means that infants tend to attend to voices just as they tend to attend to faces. Other properties of the auditory system allow the parsing of the speech stream to occur.

A large body of research on infant speech perception abilities has shown that from birth infants can discriminate many of the phonemes that occur in natural languages (see Jusczyk, 1997). For example, by using habituation methods, it has been shown that infants can tell the difference between the sounds /b/ and /p/ and between the sounds /d/ and /t/. These two pairs of phonemes differ only in what is called *voicing* (or voice onset time). The first phoneme in each pair is voiced because in speaking the sound the vibration of the vocal chords occurs along with the bringing together of the lips and the subsequent release of a puff of air through the lips. For the two unvoiced phonemes, /p/ and /t/, the vibration of the vocal chords occurs slightly after the release of air through the lips. In all other respects the two sounds in each pair are identical to each other. Using artificially synthesized speech sounds it has been shown that not only do young infants discriminate these pairs, they discriminate them in exactly the same way as adults do. Thus both infants and adults perceive the transition from voiced to unvoiced phoneme at about 35 milliseconds voice onset time (Eimas, Siqueland, Jusczyk, & Vigorito, 1971).

What is particularly interesting about these findings is that not only can infants discriminate speech sounds in the same way as adults; they are actually better at these discriminations than are adults. Adults can typically only discriminate the phonemes that are used in the language (or languages) that they speak fluently. Infants, however, are able to discriminate phonemes from any language. The initial ability, therefore, appears not to depend on any exposure to language. Rather, development in this case consists of learning to ignore the phonemic distinctions that are not relevant to the particular language that the child learns. Studies of the developmental changes in this ability (e.g., Werker & Tees, 1984) have shown that this tuning out of phonemic distinctions that are not part of the infant's own linguistic community starts in the second half of the first year of life, exactly the time when infants are starting to understand their first words. Thus the developmental changes in perception of speech sounds may well be tied to the growing appreciation of the meaning of speech.

Although it was originally suggested that the ability to discriminate phonemes from birth was a particularly human adaptation for speech (e.g., Eimas et al., 1971), this now appears not to be the case. In fact, a variety of other mammals ranging from rodents (in particular, chinchillas) to primates show similar performance when tested for their abilities to discriminate human speech sounds (e.g., Kuhl & Miller, 1975; Kuhl & Padden, 1982). It therefore seems more likely that phonemic discrimination reflects basic properties of the mammalian auditory system that were capitalized on during human language evolution.

Phonemes represent one level of the structure of spoken language. They are the building blocks of language that are not meaningful in themselves but may be combined according to a set of phonotactic rules to yield meaningful units such as words. As noted earlier, discerning these units in the speech stream presents another challenge to the infant because the speech stream is not segmented like written text. Recent research has pointed to how this segmentation is made possible in infancy.

Using sequences of nonsense syllables, researchers have shown that infants are able to learn sequences that tend to occur together on a reliable basis. This ability, called *statistical learning*, may well be related to the perception of temporally patterned features considered in chapter 3, and is probably of rather general significance in infant development (e.g., Aslin, Saffran, & Newport, 1999; Kirkham, Slemmer, & Johnson, 2002). However, it was first demonstrated clearly in the area of speech segmentation. Jennifer Saffran and colleagues (Saffran, Aslin, & Newport, 1996) familiarized 8-month-old infants with sequences of simple consonant-vowel (CV) syllables, for example, [bidakupadotigolabubidaku ...]. These strings were played to the infants for 2 minutes in a continuous stream to resemble natural speech. The number of presentations of each individual syllable was held constant within the overall speech stream, but the way in which different syllables were combined was varied. Some syllable combinations, such as [bida], occurred with high frequency so that whenever [bi] occurred, [da] always followed. Other combinations, such as [kupa], occurred much less frequently, with [pa] following [ku] only one third of the time. This pattern approximates that of natural speech, where words contain sound combinations that occur with high probability whereas transitions or gaps between words involve sound combinations with low probabilities. Learning was assessed using novelty preference by presenting the infants with different three-syllable sequences. Some of these test sequences contained the "words" from the familiarization phase, (e.g., [bida]) and others contained the gaps (e.g., [kupa]). The results showed that the infants preferred to listen to the three-syllable sequences that contained the gaps and that they therefore perceived these sequences as novel. This finding showed that the infants had not only become familiar with the highly frequent combinations but also that these combinations in some sense stood out or had been extracted from the continuous speech stream. The familiarity of these combinations meant that they were no longer as interesting to the infants as the combinations that had been relatively rare in the original stream of speech sounds.

These results show that in principle infants can learn the sound sequences that occur in regular combinations even after only a few minutes of exposure. In the case just described the familiarity of the commonly heard combinations led them to be of less interest to the infants because nothing else was associated with these common combinations. But in the case of natural language, certain commonly occurring sound sequences are associated with important events and so the ability to detect these sound combinations and what they may imply is of some significance. Indeed there is evidence that even young infants have already learned at least one very commonly occurring speech sound sequence. Mandel, Jusczyk, and Pisoni (1995) presented 4.5-month-old infants with repetitions of their own name and of names of other infants with equivalent stress patterns. They found that the infants listened significantly longer to the recordings of their own names. Similar results were not found for other commonly occurring words like *mommy* or *baby* (Jusczyk, 1997), so it would appear that the extraction of sound sequences at this young age is extremely limited and depends on a very high degree of familiarity. But notice in this case, the infants paid more attention to the familiar sound sequence perhaps because it indicated maternal attention.

There is of course no suggestion that Mandel et al.'s (1995) results mean that infants know the referent of their own name. However, just a couple of months later it appears that the initial steps of linking familiar sound sequences to referents are being taken. Tincoff and Jusczyk (1999) showed 6-month-olds videotapes of their own parents or male–female stranger pairs in a preference procedure while either the word *mommy* or *daddy* was played repeatedly in a synthesized gender-neutral voice. They found a significant looking-time preference in these infants for the named parent but not for the same-sexed stranger. So, by the middle of the first year infants are starting to recognize the patterns in auditory and visual information that will allow them entry into the world of language. I take up this story again in chapter 8.

MONITORING THE SELF

So far the findings we have considered relate to young infants' attention to, and perception of, information originating from others, or what I termed in chapter 2 third-person information. In other words, it is all information that is available to any observer of another person. Even in the early months of life, infants are also exposed to information about the self and their own activity. Some of this first-person information is completely private or exclusively available to infants as actors. For example, the proprioceptive information available from posture and movements is a type of information that is only presented to the actor and uniquely specifies the self. Haptic or touch information may also uniquely specify the self in the sense that if we touch ourselves, haptic information is available from both of the parts that are in contact (called *double touch*), whereas if we touch something else, or if we are touched by someone else, haptic information is only available from one part. In contrast, some information, such as visual information about our movements or auditory information about our vocalization, overlaps with similar information available from others, and thus has third-person characteristics. However, when such information relates to our own action or appearance, it has a certain characteristic, fixed, and egocentric perspective, and as such also specifies the self.

Monitoring first-person information plays a critical role in the performance of intentional action. When we perform an action, the proprioceptive information about that act is compared to the information available through the other perceptual modalities. The detection of a correspondence between these two sources of information essentially specifies that any observed change in the information available was self-caused. In contrast, observed changes in the information available that do not have a match in proprioceptive information are attributable to events in the world. To illustrate, suppose an object appears to move across your visual field from left to right. Such observed motion can be caused in two ways. First, the object may be actually moving from left to right in the world while you maintain a direction of gaze fixed in space. Second, the object itself may not have moved, but rather you may have moved your eyes from right to left. Proprioceptive information from the muscles controlling eye movements allows the discrimination of these two cases. If the observed movement of the object is correlated with appropriate proprioceptive feedback from your eye movements, then the movement of the object is unconsciously recognized to be caused by those eye movements. In this situation, the apparent movement is canceled and instead the object appears to be stationary. It is important to note that the two cases of apparent movement differ fundamentally in that the apparent motion caused by eye movements is repeatable, whereas the apparent motion resulting from real object movement may not be. What this means is that the same experience can be generated through repetition of the action. This kind of repetition of action is the elemental building block of intentional action (Russell, 1995, 1996).

There is evidence that even from birth, infants are sensitive to first-person information. Rochat and Hespos (1997) examined the rooting reflex in babies in the first day of life in response both to external stimulation (a gentle stroking of the infants' cheek) and to self-stimulation when the infants spontaneously touched their own cheek. They found that infants were much more likely to turn with their mouths open in the case of external stimulation, indicating that even at birth, infants discriminate single-touch information from information characterized by double touch and proprioception.

Rooting is of course considered to be a neonatal reflex in that it has a particular form, namely, turning and sucking, produced in response to a particular type of stimulation, normally from a nipple. Effects observed with rooting may not therefore have general relevance to more intentional action. The more general investigation of infants' proprioception presents two challenges to the researcher. First, unlike most other forms of sensory information, proprioceptive information cannot be directly controlled by the experimenter. Second, like audition, proprioception does not have a clear-cut overt behavioral concomitant. The solution is to examine proprioceptive and visual information together and use infants' preferential looking as a measure of their sensitivity to the correspondence between vision and proprioception.

Lorraine Bahrick and John Watson (1985) were the first to hit on this solution. They dressed infants in long, striped socks and sat them in a highchair opposite two TV screens. They then videotaped the infants' legs while they

were free to kick and showed this videotape live to the infants on one of the
TVs. At the same time, a videotape of another infant's legs similarly
dressed was presented on the other TV screen (see Fig. 4.5). As the infants
moved their legs they would see one video that moved in precise correspondence with them and one that did not. Five-month-old infants preferred to look at the TV that showed the video of the other infant rather than
the one that was a live video of themselves. Because the infants' own legs
were hidden from direct sight, this result shows that the infants must have
been picking up on the correspondence between the proprioception of their
own leg movements and the visual information provided on the TV
screens. Interestingly, 3-month-olds did not, in general, show the same pattern of preference. At this age, some infants preferred to look at the video of
their own legs and others preferred to look at the video of the other infant's
legs (as did 5-month-olds). Nevertheless, both of these patterns show that
the infants discriminated between the two videos. As a result, Bahrick and
Watson concluded that infants from at least 3 months can detect the temporal correspondence between their own proprioceptively perceived
movement and the visual appearance of that movement.

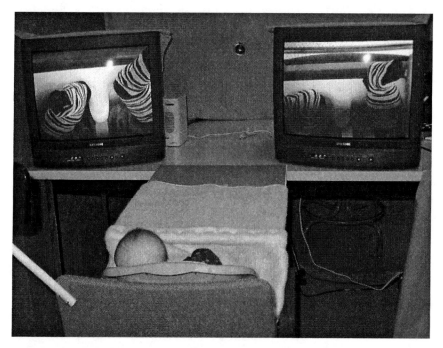

FIG. 4.5. Visual-prorioceptive intermodal preference paradigm (courtesy
Shana Nichols).

Proprioception allows perception of the temporal relation between our own movement and events in the world. But proprioception also allows perception of the spatial relation among our own body parts and between our body and the external world. Other investigators extended Bahrick and Watson's (1985) approach to study the detection of such spatial relations. For example, Philippe Rochat and Rachel Morgan (1995) presented their 3- to 5-month-old infant participants with a TV with a split screen showing two live videos, both of their own legs and feet. One of the displays was derived from a video camera opposite the children, the other from a video camera looking down at the children's legs from above. In this way the two displays both showed live videos of the babies' legs, but one looked as it would from the babies' perspective and the other looked as it would from someone else's perspective. The infants preferred to look at the video that showed their legs as they would appear from someone else's perspective. Not only did the infants look longer but when they looked at the observer's view, they also tended to move their legs more. Further experiments showed that the source of the infants' discrimination appeared to be the movement directionality. That is, infants looked longer when the direction of the movement on the visual display did not match the proprioceptively perceived movement of their legs, as would be the case when people look at their own legs directly. These results show that infants are not only sensitive to the temporal relations, but also to the spatial congruence, between proprioceptive and visual information.

Temporal and spatial information are examples of what are called *amodal* properties of stimulation. By amodal, we mean that the information is not tied specifically to one perceptual modality such as vision. For example, temporal information can be specified through vision, as the rate at which visual events occur in time; through audition, as the rate at which sounds occur in time; and through proprioception, as the rate at which muscle feedback occurs in time. Because the same type of information may be available through different perceptual modalities, the detection of amodal properties is critical for detecting correspondences across different information sources.

This fundamental perceptual capacity to detect amodal properties is of profound significance for the development of social understanding. It allows infants to detect patterns of information that are evident in the interaction between self and world. I have already mentioned how events that depend on the self may be differentiated from events that are independent of the self on the basis of the correlation between proprioceptive and visual information. In the infant's world much of the available information originates from other people. People stimulate infants through every available means—they provide sights, sounds, touches, smells, and tastes. With the ability to detect patterns in the correspondence between the first-person information provided by their own activity and the third-person information provided by the activity of others, infants are in a position to learn how they are linked to the social world. They can develop expectations for the kinds of social information that reliably follow their own activity, and they can learn to act in particular ways to achieve particular forms of social stimulation. As we shall see in chapter 5, these abilities provide the foundation for social interactions. Before that, however, I should address the kinds of acts that infants can produce in the early months and the ways in which these acts serve to provide social stimulation.

ACTS THAT RECRUIT SOCIAL ATTENTION

We now turn to the social acts in infants' behavioral repertoire that serve to recruit adult attention. Infants are born into a social world. From the beginning they are immersed in an ocean of adult interest. Some of this adult attention needs little incentive. Adults spontaneously look at, caress, kiss, and talk to young infants. Nevertheless, young infants are not designed to rely only on the natural interests of adults; rather, they have a variety of actions that spur adults into care and stimulation. The first and most obvious of these actions is crying. Crying starts at birth and remains the most salient social behavior for the first few months of the infant's life. Crying is a vocal expression of distress and parents are strongly motivated to alleviate that distress. In the process they try various things, including feeding, diaper changing, and comforting. These adult responses are clearly aimed at rectifying a potential physiological or emotional disturbance, but they also serve a valuable social purpose. They bring the adult close to the infant and provide the infant with visual and auditory information about the adult. They also provide the first context for social interaction and perhaps an early opportunity for the infant to detect the responsiveness of people.

Within two months, a set of behaviors that are more pleasing to adults enters the infant's repertoire. In addition to crying, which is produced when in distress, infants start to make vocalizations when they are relatively relaxed and when they are positively aroused. These vocalizations include elements of speech sounds that are later incorporated into vocal language and so they sound completely different from the grating noise of crying. Because these vocalizations involve extended vowel-like sequences such as [u]s and [a]s, this form of vocalization is sometimes referred to as *cooing*. Adults find these sounds pleasing as they are much easier on the ears than crying and they show that the infant is content. Adults also behave as if these vocalizations are meaningful by responding with vocalizations of their own. As a result, the infant's early vocalizations become embedded in interactions with others.

In addition to vocal acts, young infants also produce a range of facial expressions of which by far the most significant is smiling (Sroufe & Waters, 1976). Rudimentary smiles may be observed in infants from shortly after birth, but these early smiles, which involve a simple upturning of the corners of the mouth, are not elicited by social stimulation (see left panel of Fig. 4.6). They may occur spontaneously during sleep or be elicited by a light touch or blowing on the infant's cheek. The first waking smiles are typically produced by light tactile stimulation such as stroking or by gentle moving of the arms or legs. Within a month, infants are producing smiles that involve both the mouth and the eyes. The best elicitor of such smiles is the sound of a human voice, in particular the mother's voice. Shortly thereafter, smiles are produced in response to dynamic visual stimulation, such as a nodding head, and soon the stationary human face becomes the most effective elicitor. Now smiles appear as clear grins and may often be accompanied by cooing vocalizations (see right panel of Fig. 4.6). By 2 months of age, then, infant smiling clearly seems to be social.

Researchers still do not have a full understanding of why infants smile, but the account that seems to be most acceptable is the tension release hypothesis, first proposed by Sroufe and Waters (1976). This hypothesis is an attempt to pull together the different developmental phases of smiling and laughing into a single process. In essence, smiling is believed to accompany an increase of tension or physiological arousal above a certain threshold and then a relaxation of that arousal. As perceptual learning and cognitive development proceed, the complexity of the stimulus re-

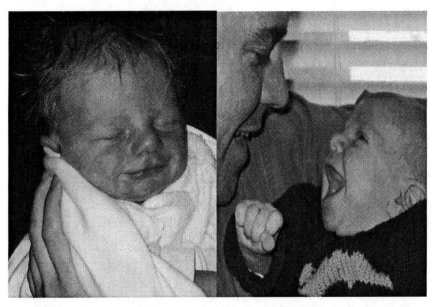

FIG. 4.6.   Neonatal (left) and social (right) infant smiles (courtesy Lindsay Outread and Philip D. Zelazo).

quired to produce the threshold level of arousal gradually increases. What was once sufficient, such as a light touch at 2 weeks, later is insufficient, and a more complex stimulus is required. In this way, smiling is produced in reaction to progressively more complex forms of stimulation through early development.

Another manifestation of smiling illustrates this process further. The mastery smile is also produced from about 2 months when infants detect a reliably contingent environmental effect of their action. For example, in a classic study, Watson (1972) arranged crib mobiles to turn whenever infants made head movements on their pillows. Over a period of days, infants increased the amount of head turning they did as they learned to activate the mobile. In contrast, a control group of infants for whom the mobile was activated independently of their behavior did not show an increase in their head turning. Whereas it was expected that infants would learn to activate the mobile, it was less expected that the infants in the contingent group not only produced more head turning, but also smiled much more than those in the control group during the mobile activation. These results show that, by 2 months, infants can process the temporal relations between proprioceptive and visual events and smile when they are able to detect a reliable contingency. As we will soon see, this relation between contingency learning and smiling is of profound significance. It means that a highly social signal is tied to the perception of a natural characteristic of human interactions—that they have a contingent structure.

Somewhat later in infancy, smiles are produced in intentionally communicative ways. Even young infants smile after they see their mothers, but by about 9 months infants also smile in anticipation of seeing their mothers as they turn to face them from an initial position facing away (Jones & Hong, 2001). Such anticipatory smiling is coincident with the use of other communicative gestures and shows that infants are starting to use smiles to regulate the social interactions that serve as the focus of chapters 5 and 6.

Whatever the underlying reason for early infant smiling, there is no doubt that it has a profound effect on adults. When parents experience their infants' smile for the first time, it is as though their baby finally recognizes and loves them. In addition, the smile is an indicator that all is well with the infant. The smile, therefore, is a powerful motivator and parents work hard to reproduce it. Other adults too, even if they are encountering an infant for the first time, often try to elicit a smile and try different tactics until they succeed. Now the smile comes into its own as perhaps the single most important tool the infant has for generating social stimulation. Parents soon learn that smiling is most easily elicited by a pattern of stimulation that has them placing their faces quite close to the baby's and providing regular touch and sound. In line with the tension release hypothesis, a pattern in which such stimulation builds slowly before full exposure releases broad smiles and laughter after 2 months. Hence peek-a-boo soon becomes a favorite game for both parent and infant. Just through regular attempts, the parent learns that responsiveness to the infant's acts is especially effective at producing smiles. As I describe in chapter 5, these patterns of contingent acts soon lead to extended sequences of emotionally aroused interaction.

But the true brilliance of the smile is in its progressive nature. As I mentioned, the kind of stimulation required to elicit smiling becomes ever more complex. What this means is that adults gradually increase the complexity of the stimulation they provide so as to keep the child happy. Under optimal conditions, therefore, the smile elicits a stream of social stimulation from adults perfectly suited to the infant's information-processing needs. In this way the infant's smile serves to tune the complexity of the adult's stimulation to the infant's needs.

This brief review illustrates how multifunctional the smile is. The smile serves to bring and keep adults close. It leads adults to engage with infants in structured contingent interactions that lead in short order to the establishment of the patterned interactions that provide the context for learning about the world and for the development of the first relationship. And, perhaps of most importance, the smile modulates the quality of the social stimulation that adults provide to match the infant's own needs.

SUMMARY

In this chapter, we have seen that infants start life with simple responses that quickly immerse them in a world of social stimulation. They orient preferentially to the sights and sounds of people and thereby are in a position to learn more about those people. So, the lifelong task of making sense of social information starts right at birth. Within days of birth infants' preferences are even more specifically tuned to individual people in their social worlds. Within a few short months, infants have built relatively complex patterns out of the information with which they are provided. They recognize familiar faces and facial expressions. They have started to discern words in the speech they hear around them. At the same time, infants start to detect the correspondence between their own actions and events in the world. And along with all this, infants produce social expressions that not only serve to draw adults close but also encourage those adults to provide further stimulation ideally suited to the infants' learning needs.

Given all this, what can we say about how far the infant has come toward solving the challenges involved in building a commonsense psychology that I outlined in chapter 2? Commonsense psychology needs information not only about other people and their activity but also about the self. The evidence discussed in this chapter shows that infants begin life outside the womb sensitive to perceptual information that is relevant to both third- and first-person information. Faces and voices are the primary sources of third-person information relevant to commonsense psychology. First-person information is also available to infants, through proprioceptive monitoring of their own activity and through their perceptual and emotional experiences. Together, these different forms of information start to be coordinated in the sense that infants can detect correspondences between first- and third-person sources of information. These aspects of early social experience provide the information-processing foundation for commonsense psychology.

But it is important to note the limitations. As seen in chapter 2, commonsense psychology involves psychological relations to objects. The social information that infants are exposed to in the first few months is not yet about either other people's or the self's relations to objects. Much of the third-person information is derived from others' actions toward the infant not toward objects. In a similar vein, although they can certainly attend to different objects in their worlds, infants are not yet acting on or manipulating objects. So there is only a very limited sense in which infants can be said to have psychological relations to objects in their worlds. In addition, to develop a commonsense psychology that recognizes the equivalence of self and other, infants need to experience the same psychological relations from both first- and third-person points of view. And this requires experience with situations where the infant and others participate in patterns of social interaction in which their own and the other person's activity are bound into regular and predictable patterns. Such patterns are set up through the next few months of life as the infant becomes embedded in interactive contexts in which first- and third-person information regularly co-occur. It is to the development of these interactions that we turn next.

5

From Social Interaction
to Social Relationships

By approximately 2 months of age the kinds of social acts reviewed in chapter 4 have become well enough established that infants can participate in social interactions. In early development, social interactions may be defined as sequences of social acts performed by the infant and an interactive partner that are contingently structured. As such they involve the two participants acting socially in response to the social acts of the other. The sequences need not be very long or very smooth initially. The critical feature is that each participant responds to the acts of the other by producing acts that themselves tend to elicit further social acts. Because the mother is the most common participant with whom the infant interacts, I typically refer to the mother as the other participant. It should be understood, however, that early interactions can occur with any other person who is willing to engage the infant appropriately.

In normal development the phase of interaction starts by about 2 months of age, when infants become clearly responsive to social stimuli such as faces and voices. Initially the interactions are rather uncoordinated but as mother and baby gain more experience with each other, the interactions acquire greater fluidity. By 3 to 4 months, mothers and infants know each other well enough that both have expectations of the other (Kaye & Fogel, 1980; Tronick, Als, & Brazelton, 1980). Mothers can read their infants' signals so that they know when their babies are ready to interact and when they are out of sorts. At the same time, from their accumulated experience with their mothers, infants acquire expectations about how their mother will behave and they may get distressed when she does not act as expected. This coordination between infants and their mothers has been described as a dance (e.g., Stern, 1977).

In this chapter we will review what is now known about the nature and development of early social interactions. Before doing so, however, a number of features of these early mother-infant interactions should be emphasized. First, the interactions involve a significant emotional component. The interactions show a pattern of increasing and decreasing arousal modulated by actions that serve to regulate that arousal. The exchange between infant and mother often centers around smiling, with the mother trying to produce smiling in her infant and showing positive emotional gestures to her infant. To the extent that the interaction proceeds successfully in this direction, both participants get more aroused. If the infant's arousal gets too high, with a consequent loss of physiological control, either or both participants may try to calm things down by backing off somewhat. The result is a shared experience of pleasure, which usually stays within acceptable limits of arousal. The emotionally arousing nature of these interactions provides the beginnings of a bond between the infant and mother, which serves as the context for subsequent learning both about people and about the world of objects.

Second, the early interactions are face-to-face engagements between the two participants and are not yet about anything else (see Fig. 5.1). Because early interactions involve only the two interacting participants, they are sometimes called *dyadic*. From an outside observer's point of view, dyadic interactions bear a certain resemblance to the interactions

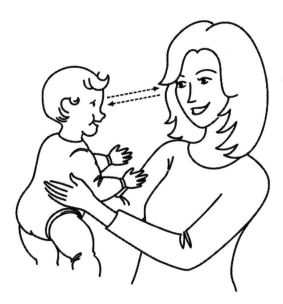

FIG. 5.1. Dyadic interaction.

that characterize many social exchanges throughout the rest of life. Most importantly, there is an apparent turn-taking structure with both participants acting in response to the other. Because of this turn-taking structure, these interactions have also been termed *protoconversations* (e.g., Bateson, 1975; Trevarthen, 1979). However, they differ fundamentally from the large majority of interactions, including true conversations, involving older children and adults. Interactions between older participants typically involve a topic or a point to the conversation. As we will see in chapter 6, it is only in the second half of the first year that interactions gain a focus on some third thing and become *triadic*.

Dyadic interactions serve to bring infant and adult together to allow them to engage with the other in an emotionally positive way. As such they are the most primal and the purest form of human social connection. Sometimes interactions between adults function simply at this most primal level. For example, romantic exchanges between new lovers may involve no words and need not be about anything, and yet they serve to allow the lovers to connect at an emotional level. Many other interactions between adults share this function even though there may be an overlay of discourse on a topic of common interest. Imagine meeting a close friend after a few years apart. Although you may talk endlessly about events since you were last together, in large part this talk serves not just to educate you both about your experiences but also to reestablish the emotional connection between you.

These examples from adults show how social interactions are intimately connected with social relationships and in this chapter we will also review how relationships become established for the first time in infancy. In general, positive social interactions that occur repeatedly with the same person and through this experience acquire familiarity and predictability provide the basis for social relationships. Those with whom we have made a connection at this fundamental level become special to us such that we can speak of having a relationship with them. In a superficial sense, a relationship may be considered to be a patterning of interactions between the same two people over time. But often what provides the opportunity for a series of interactions over time is a desire to continue the emotional connection established in a previous interaction. We know that when we interact with that certain individual we will again experience the pleasure associated with a smooth interaction. Such a process also occurs for the first time in the first year of life as infants establish a relationship with their mother.

Relationships are not just about sharing positive emotional closeness, they are also about supporting the other in times of stress. Whereas the sharing of positive emotions is a two-way street in infant-mother interactions, the handling of negative emotion is one way: The mother ameliorates her infant's negative emotion. There are two fundamental ways in which this happens. First, from birth, infants cry and mothers actively respond to their infants' crying by trying to find ways to soothe their child. Second, by about the middle of the first year, as infants are becoming more mobile and oriented to the world, they start to experience fear reactions, in particular to strangers and novel situations. Now mothers serve as a haven to which the infants can retreat when fearful. This latter component of the infant-mother relationship is fundamental to what is known as *attachment* (Bowlby, 1969)—the process by which infants start to use the mother to enhance their feelings of security in relation to the outside world.

DYADIC INTERACTIONS

In chapter 4 we saw how by 2 months, infants respond to social stimuli with acts that themselves appear social (e.g., smiles). Parents respond enthusiastically to their infants' growing social sophistication and attempt to engage with them in bouts of simple play. These interactions have been the focus of a considerable amount of research over the last 30 years. The standard approach to their study is to bring a mother and her infant into a laboratory setting where each participant can be videotaped. The mother is asked to play with her baby "as you would normally do at home." The two videotapes are then combined into a single picture showing how both participants would appear to each other (Fig. 5.2). The combined tape is carefully

FIG. 5.2.   Split-screen video still showing infant and mother face-to-face interaction.

coded for various behaviors. This research shows that the typical form of these bouts is as follows (e.g., Brazelton, Koslowski, & Main, 1974; Tronick, Als, & Adamson, 1979). With the infant supine, supported on her lap, or in a baby seat, mother brings her face quite close to her infant's and gives a big smile with eyes wide open, looking into the infant's eyes. She also typically talks and manipulates the infant's hands or feet and maybe bounces the infant gently. This multimodal stimulation gets infants aroused and they commonly gaze back at the mother and may smile, vocalize using extended vowel sequences (cooing), and move their limbs. As the infants get aroused, they may increase the intensity of their signals, smiling more broadly, vocalizing more loudly or in burst-pause patterns, and thrusting legs and arms out more vigorously. Mothers continue the interaction by responding contingently to the infants' signals. They may comment on something the infants do, change expressions from smile to surprise, manipulate again the infants' limb, or touch the infants' cheek or tummy. Mothers also have a tendency to imitate the infants' facial and vocal expressions (Moran, Krupka, Tutton, & Symons, 1987; Stern, 1985). These responses lead to further smiling, vocalization, and movement from the infants. In this way mother and infant become engaged in an interaction in which each person's action depends on the actions of the other (Cohn & Tronick, 1988).

Not only do both participants engage in an active way in the dyadic exchange, they also respond to signs that all is not right. For example, if the infant appears happy, engaged, and controlled, the mother continues her stimulation. If the infant appears distressed, the mother backs off so that she is not so close to the infant and reduces the intensity of her behavior—she may soften her vocalization and tactile stimulation. If the infant appears distracted with a loss of mutual gaze, the mother may work harder to try to engage her infant. In these ways, she tries to encourage the infant back into the interaction. Her attempts may or may not be successful. If they are, the two can continue with their exchange of social signals; or if they are not, then the interaction tends to wind down into another state.

For their part, the infants also have means to control the interaction. Because successful interaction occurs within a window of arousal, infants modulate arousal using gaze and other signals. If arousal gets too high, infants typically avert their gaze from the mother, thereby removing from sight the most arousing source of stimulation (Brazelton et al., 1974). As arousal falls to within the acceptable range, they may again look toward the mother and reengage with her. As infants develop from 2 to 6 months, they also learn that their signals can elicit more stimulation from their mothers. For example, if the mother is too passive, infants increase the intensity of their signals as if to elicit more response from the mother.

In some cases of interactions, the form of the social act is matched across the infant and adult. Such cases are called *imitation*. Imitation can occur when the adult responds to the infant's act or when the infant responds to the adult's act. Although there is some evidence that infants are capable of imitating another person's behavior, in particular some facial expressions such as tongue protrusion, from birth (Meltzoff & Moore, 1977, 1983; for reviews see Anisfeld, 1991, 1996), it is not clear what role such early infant imitation plays in social interaction. Examination of the form of natural face-to-face interactions has provided no evidence that young infants imitate their mothers' behavior (e.g., Moran et al., 1987). In contrast, it is well established that mothers imitate their infants' vocalizations and facial expressions in early interactions (Malatesta & Haviland, 1982; Moran et al.; Stern, 1985). In imitating their infants, mothers provide a form of feedback that displays not only temporal contingency but also sensory relations and spatial information. As such it may be a particularly rich kind of feedback for infants' learning of the relations between their own action and effects in the world (Gergely & Watson, 1999).

Although mother-infant interactions may involve a variety of different behaviors—mutual gaze, emotional expressions, vocalizations, arm and hand movements—they are normally characterized by two overarching properties: warmth and contingency. It is just these properties that have been assumed to be of greatest significance for social and emotional development.

Warmth refers to the fact that these interactions have primarily a positive valence. Mothers smile much of the time they are interacting and try to elicit smiles from their infants (Cohn & Tronick, 1987). Although infants do not spend as much time smiling in these episodes as their mothers, it is nevertheless clear that a successful dyadic interaction is one in which the infant produces a regular stream of smiles (e.g., Cohn & Tronick; Kaye & Fogel, 1980; Yale, Messinger, Cobo-Lewis, & Delgado, 2003). Indeed, as smiling wanes in the interaction, it is a signal that both infant and mother will soon wind up the exchange. The mutual enjoyment of the dyadic interaction is important because it reflects the origins of the affiliative emotions including love (MacDonald, 1992). Dyadic interactions can therefore be seen as the initial hothouse for the growth of love in the infant.

Although young infants presumably experience pleasure in interacting with the mother, there is likely no sense in which infants understand that their pleasure is the same as what the mother is feeling. Infants experience the first-person characteristics of pleasure (i.e., their own internal feeling of happiness or joy), but observe the third-person characteristics of pleasure in the mother (e.g., smiling). Dyadic interactions fundamentally involve emotion that is shared across two participants without being attributable by the infants to either. Nevertheless, dyadic interactions may provide the first context in which both first- and third-person characteristics of the emotion are available simultaneously to infants. This patterning of emotional information allows infants to detect how first-person emotional information is correlated with third-person information.

Contingency refers to the likelihood that within dyadic interactions each participant responds reliably to the other's actions. The key issue here is timing: For there to be contingency, one partner must produce a social act shortly after (say within a second or two) the other partner produces one. The acts do not have to match in form (although they may, as in the case of imitation) but they do have to be linked in time.

There is no doubt that, under normal circumstances, mothers respond relatively reliably to their infants' acts. For example, during dyadic interactions, the most likely time for mothers to perform some social act, such as a smile or vocalization, is when infants shift from having their gaze averted to gazing at the mother (Kaye, 1979). It is worth noting that the degree of contingency provided to infants in their interactions with their mothers is not the perfect contingency available as, for example, between proprioception and vision when infants observe their own limbs moving. Because of this difference the contingent feedback that mothers provide has sometimes been called *imperfect contingency* (e.g., Bigelow, 1998). As noted in chapter 3, infants find high but not perfect contingency particularly interesting (Watson, 1985). There is also evidence that by 4 to 5 months infants prefer to interact with an unfamiliar woman who previously interacted with them in a contingent fashion compared to an unfamiliar woman who previously interacted in a noncontingent fashion (Bigelow & Birch, 1999). At this same age infants are also most responsive in interaction with strangers whose particular level of contingent feedback resembles that of the infants' own mothers (Bigelow). So we can conclude that infants develop a preference for the particular level of contingency that their mothers provide.

Provision of such contingent feedback by mothers is likely important for infants' social learning. Through monitoring of the contingent relations among their own actions and events in the world, infants can learn about the relations between their actions and their effects. As we see later in this chapter, such learning is important in the development of social relationships. There is also evidence that infants' experience with social contingency can under some circumstances affect their attention to completely unrelated nonsocial information (Dunham, Dunham, Hurshman, & Alexander, 1989). In particular, Philip Dunham and his colleagues at Dalhousie University exposed groups of 3-month-old infants to interactions with a female experimenter. For one group the experimenter responded to particular infants' actions (vocalizations or leg kicks) with a contingent vocalization combined with touch to the infants' belly. For another group, the experimenter performed exactly the same number of infant-directed actions but they were not contingent on anything the infant did. All the infants were then given the opportunity to watch a slowly flashing light combined with a repeated tone. This audiovisual stimulus was presented only if the infants fixated a light in front of them in the testing room, so that the amount of stimulation was infant controlled. The authors reported that infants who had received the contingent interaction fixated the light significantly more than infants in the noncontingent group. This result means that infants in the contingent group were able to handle a greater amount of stimulation in the subsequent test than infants in the noncontingent group. So contingent responsiveness from mothers probably plays an important role in infants' information processing in general.

Whether infants act similarly contingently in relation to their mothers' actions has been the source of some debate. Some authors have argued on the basis of the appearance of dyadic interactions that even young infants do respond with a high degree of contingency to their mothers' acts (e.g., Reddy, Hay, Murray, & Trevarthen, 1997; Trevarthen, 1979), and that they are effectively equal partners in controlling the organization of the interaction. An alternative view is that although infants' social acts certainly increase in general within dyadic interaction, they are essentially distributed randomly within the interaction. The appearance of a reciprocally contingent interaction is created by mothers structuring the pattern of their infants' social acts by appropriate insertion of their own acts in their infants' random stream (Schaffer, 1984).

The truth, not surprisingly, is probably somewhere in between and depends somewhat on the age of the child. Three-month-old infants' expressive acts are more likely to occur after their mothers', and in this sense the infants are responding contingently (e.g., Cohn & Tronick, 1988). However, there is evidence that 4- to 6-month-old infants, but not 2-month-olds, recognize the extent to which the interaction they are engaged in has a contingent structure. Philippe Rochat and his colleagues (Rochat, Querido, & Striano, 1999) compared infant reactions to an interactive partner who either played a contingently structured peek-a-boo game with them or played the game in a disorganized, random way. Whereas 2-month-olds gazed and smiled equally in both play conditions, the older infants gazed and smiled significantly less in the disorganized game. In addition, there is evidence that by 6 months, infants have developed into much more autonomous interactants who produce their expressive gestures at appropriate times within a dialogue of interaction. For example, 6-month-olds attend to the mother and produce facial and vocal expressions toward her without her first eliciting the attention (e.g., Kaye & Fogel, 1980).

Disruptions in Dyadic Interaction: The Still Face Effect

The findings reviewed so far were all derived from studies of relatively unconstrained seminaturalistic face-to-face interactions between mother and infant and show clearly how sensitive infants are to their mothers' behavior. A particularly fruitful experimental approach to this issue has been to observe the effects of disruptions in the typical quality of these interactions.

The procedure used most extensively was first developed at the Boston Children's Hospital Medical Center by Ed Tronick and his colleagues (e.g., Tronick, Als, Adamson, Wise, & Brazelton, 1978; see also Adamson & Frick, 2003). They arranged a session in which mothers would first interact normally with their infants for a few minutes, then sit passively and unsmiling for 2 minutes, and then interact normally again. The results with 3-month-old infants were very clear-cut. Infants showed a dramatic decline in smiling and eye contact during the "still face" period compared to both the initial and final normal interaction phases. These results were interpreted by the authors as demonstrating that infants had definite expectations about how their mothers should behave in interaction. When those expectations were violated, the infants became upset.

As we have seen, normal maternal behavior in dyadic interaction has many action components (smiles, gaze, vocalization, touch, etc.) as well as a particular form of temporal contingency. Because the original still face procedure involved removing all of these components from the maternal behavior, it was not clear what components were most important. A number of researchers (Muir & Hains, 1999) have now systematically investigated the effects of removing different components of the maternal multimodal stimulus using the same basic design as Tronick et al. (1978). The standard procedure is to present an impoverished maternal stimulus sandwiched between two periods of normal maternal interaction. In reviewing these studies it is worth separating out the studies manipulating specific behavioral components, including emotional expression, and the studies manipulating contingency per se. It is also particularly informative to compare the effects of the different manipulations on infants' smiling and gaze.

First, with respect to the behavioral components of maternal interaction, research has manipulated touch, vocalization, gaze, and emotional expression. It has been found that removal of touch or vocalization from the maternal stimulus has a relatively neutral effect on 3-month-old infants' responsiveness so long as contingency and smiling are maintained (Gusella, Muir, & Tronick, 1988). This is not to say that these components of the stimulation are unimportant, and indeed, Stack and Muir (1992) showed that active maternal touch can ameliorate the effects of a full still face. However, these components do not seem to play the most important role in maintenance of the interaction. Second, providing fully active, contingent interaction, but with eyes averted, leads to a significant reduction in both gazing and smiling in 5-month-old infants (Hains & Muir, 1996b; Symons, Hains, & Muir, 1998) so maternal eye contact appears to be important for interaction at least by 5 months. It is not known whether a similar effect would be present in younger infants. Finally, conducting the experiment with a contingent, interactive puppet in place of the mother has no effect on infant gaze but leads to a large reduction in infant smiling through all phases of the experiment (Ellsworth, Muir, & Hains, 1993).

Studies manipulating maternal emotional expression have examined the extent to which the posing of different emotional expressions while remaining passive affects infants' responses. Removing maternal activity during the manipulation phase but maintaining a smiling face leads to as much of a decrement in gaze as with a full still face in infants older than 4 months (D'Entremont & Muir, 1997; Rochat, Striano, & Blatt, 2002), showing that infants of this age expect their mothers to show more than just a smiling face. Interestingly, there is evidence that with 2-month-olds, having the mother sit still while maintaining her smiling face does not lead to a decrease in infant's gaze (Rochat et al.). In addition, although there is also a decrement in infant smiling in this condition, it is not as large as for the full still face (D'Entremont & Muir). Together these results show that infant behavior, and in particular smiling, is most affected by the removal of the eye contact and positive emotion provided by the mother.

Second, manipulations of contingency have been conducting typically using a delayed video feedback procedure. This approach was first implemented by Lynn Murray and Colwyn Trevarthen (1985). Through the session, mothers and infants interacted via video. This was achieved by placing the two interactants in separate rooms. Each faced a TV monitor and a video camera. Each video camera relayed a live image to the TV facing the other participant. In this way, each interactant could view and respond to the live behavior of the other. At the same time a recording was made of each interactant's behavior. Studies with mothers and infants as young as 2 months show that a relatively normal interaction can proceed in this manner (e.g., Murray & Trevarthen). After an initial period of normal interaction, the live video signal was halted and the tapes of the just completed interaction were rewound. The tape of the mothers' behavior was then played back to the infants. In this way, the exact same pattern of maternal behavior as before was provided to the infant, however that behavior was no longer contingently related to the infants' own behavior.

Using this procedure, Murray and Trevarthen (1985) reported that 2-month-olds showed decreased gaze and smiling and evidence of distress during the replay period. Although this result has been taken as evidence of 2-month-olds' sensitivity to contingency, the study had some shortcomings. In particular, only four infant-mother pairs were tested, there was no control condition in which the second phase involved continued live feedback, and the procedure had an unfortunate order confound whereby the noncontingent phase always followed the contingent phase without a subsequent return to contingency in a third phase. As a result, it is possible that Murray and Trevarthen's results were due to fatigue. A number of authors attempted to reproduce the effect while including larger sample sizes and a three-phase design. These studies have had mixed success and the evidence that 2-month-olds differentiate the contingent and noncontingent conditions is not strong. Philippe Rochat and his colleagues (Rochat,

Neisser, & Marian, 1998) carried out two experiments with 2-month-olds and their mothers and completely failed to replicate the original effect, finding no difference in infant behavior between live and replay phases. Ann Bigelow and her colleagues (Bigelow, MacLean, & McDonald, 1996) found similar results to Murray and Trevarthen with 4-month-olds in that both infants' gaze and smiling decreased significantly from an initial live phase to a subsequent replay phase. However, there was an even further decrease in gaze and smiling in a third, live, phase, and without a control group it was not possible to determine if the effect was due to fatigue. Sylvia Hains and Darwin Muir (1996a) reported no effects of replayed maternal behavior with 5-month-olds compared to live interaction with their mothers. However, they did find that similarly aged infants in interaction with strangers gazed and smiled less during the replay phase compared to the live phase. It is possible that by 5 months, infants are familiar enough with their mothers' patterns of interaction that the replay is not disturbing. In contrast, when they try to interact with someone whose behavior is unfamiliar, noncontingency in the adult feedback seriously undermines the infants' ability to engage in a turn-taking interaction.

The Origins of the Dance Between Self and Other

We have seen that, with the onset of social smiling, infants are equipped to engage their mothers in social interaction. The latter are of course willing participants and so the stage is set for interaction to develop. Within interactions, each partner's acts depend on those of the other. Over the next few months, individual infants and their mothers forge their own patterns of social interaction. They learn the ways in which their partner responds and become able to predict their partner's behavior. It is this behavioral attunement in the context of dyadic interaction that Daniel Stern (1977, 1985) likened to a dance.

Two key properties of dyadic interactions are worth emphasizing. First, they are generally characterized by positive emotion. This positive valence is important because it means both partners will be motivated to engage with the other. As a result, their interactions continue to become refined and this enables a raft of later social developments, including, as we shall shortly see, the development of the first relationship. Second, dyadic interactions are by nature contingent and reciprocal. Even if the mother is initially responsible for structuring the turn-taking nature of the interactions, the infant soon begins to share that responsibility. With the infant's and mother's actions occurring in close temporal proximity, dyadic interactions provide the infant with regular patterns of information involving input from both participants. Not only is there close temporal proximity between the infant's and the mother's acts but there may also be close similarity in form of the two participants' action when vocal, facial, and even manual imitation takes place. As we will see, these are the first situations in which information relevant to the construction of commonsense psychology is available.

THE ONSET OF ATTACHMENT

Through the middle of the first year, as infants become more attuned, and more skilled, in their interactions with their mothers, they start to show evidence that they are developing a relationship with her. Recall that a relationship may be defined as a series of positive interactions over time between the same two people maintained by a desire to continue the pattern. By the middle of the first year, infants start to show a clear preference for interacting with their mothers over strangers and even over familiar others, such as their fathers, with whom they are typically less attuned. This preference reflects the fact that infants have learned the interactional patterns that are well coordinated and pleasurable and that infants can anticipate the occurrence of such interactions with certain individuals. Infants' positive emotional experiences engendered in these interactions form the basis for their growing love for their mothers (MacDonald, 1992; Stern, 1985). It is also worth noting that whereas love is the dominating emotion in this growing relationship, anger may also be involved, particularly in the case of infants who have experienced a history of interactions characterized by inconsistent or unreliably contingent maternal responsiveness (Isabella & Belsky, 1991; Sullivan & Lewis, 2003).

During their first 6 months of life, infants also experience considerable distress. Distress has many sources, including physiological states such as hunger and pain, and psychological events, such as sudden intense stimulation like loud noises. Distress also results when infants' arousal increases without alleviation (Sroufe, 1995). In chapter 4, we saw that smiling results when infants' arousal reaches a certain threshold and then is released. When release does not come, crying rather than smiling may result. This effect can occur when infants are presented with a source of stimulation that is both attractive but also too different from the infants' current way of processing such stimulation. By the middle of the first year, interactions with strangers can have this effect. Whereas between 2 to 4 months, infants show relative equanimity in interacting with familiar and unfamiliar people, thereafter they start to show more negative reactions to strangers. Strangers, being people, have an intrinsic interest to infants. However, because they typically do not behave in a way that fits the infants' acquired pattern of interaction with their mother, they can also be a source of distress. What this means is that infants may start to cry when strangers try to interact with them.

As infants move into the second half of the first year, they become able to anticipate those objects and events that may cause pleasure or distress. In the case of anticipating distress, a new emotion—fear or anxiety—emerges. Anxiety is often seen very clearly as a response to strangers, so that infants may shy away from the approach of strangers and seek contact with their mothers. Stranger anxiety appears in a range of intensities, so that whereas some infants become very distressed at the approach of a stranger, others may show a slight wariness but no more. When infants clearly prefer interacting with certain individuals over others and indeed exhibit contrasting emotional reactions to different people, we can reasonably say they have entered into relationships.

At about the same time, infants start to show anxiety to separations from their mothers. If the mother leaves the vicinity of the infant, especially if she goes out of sight and especially if the environment is novel, the infant shows signs of distress and cries or otherwise attempts to bring the mother back. Separation anxiety is another clear-cut sign that infants have formed a relationship with their mother. In fact, it is particularly telling in this regard because the infant is now showing a pattern of behavior brought on by the absence of the mother, thereby indicating that in some sense the infant's emotional orientation to the mother endures even when she is not actually present.

These emotional reactions also coincide with significant changes in infants' mobility (Campos et al., 2000). Crawling begins typically by 7 to 8 months of age and with it comes a massive expansion of the practical world. Infants can now move away from or toward the mother or other objects in the world. This ability exposes the infant not only to many more opportunities but also to many more potential threats, such as strangers or heights.

These various developmental changes come together to herald the onset of attachment. Attachment is a particular pattern of infant behavior characterized by use of a loved person—the mother—to alleviate fear or anxiety (Bowlby, 1969; Goldberg, Grusec, & Jenkins, 1999). When infants feel comfortable or secure, for example in a familiar environment like the home, they are content to be left alone and to explore the environment. Anxiety may be induced when infants are taken to an unfamiliar environment, or a novel and potentially threatening person or object is present. In such circumstances, infants will have much less tolerance for being left alone. They try to stay close to the mother and, if the mother leaves, they typically become distressed and cry out for the mother. When the mother returns, infants either call, or if mobile, move toward the mother. As infants' anxiety becomes alleviated through closeness with their mother, they may become more willing to explore the novel environment. In this way, the mother is used by the infant as a secure base from which to explore the world.

The standard approach to assessing attachment is the Strange Situation, first used by Mary Ainsworth and her colleagues (Ainsworth, Blehar, Waters, & Wall, 1978). The Strange Situation is a structured observation session that consists of seven 3-minute phases during which infants are observed as they respond to different forms of social stress. In the first phase, the mother and infant are left in a laboratory room that contains chairs and various toys. In this period the mother sits in a chair and the infant is given the opportunity to explore the room. In the next phase a stranger enters the room, remains silent for 1 minute, then talks to the mother for another minute, and finally approaches the infant. The mother then leaves and the stranger comforts the infant if necessary or sits in a chair. This is the first separation episode. After 3 minutes or less, if the infant remains too upset, there is the first reunion episode when the mother returns and the stranger leaves. The second separation episode then occurs as the mother leaves the infant alone in the room. Separation continues into the next phase as the stranger enters and comforts the infant if necessary. Finally, the mother returns for the second reunion episode and the stranger leaves. Through this series of episodes, the Strange Situation offers the opportunity to observe different manifestations of the attachment relationship. Separation anxiety and associated protest behaviors are typically observed during the separation episodes. Proximity-seeking or contact-avoiding behaviors are observed particularly during the reunion phases. Stranger anxiety and secure base behavior may be observed in the other episodes. In this way a relatively rich assessment of the quality of the infant's attachment can be gained.

Studies using the Strange Situation have repeatedly shown that infants differ in the quality of their attachments to their mothers. The traditional approach to describing these differences has been to place infants into a small number of categories (Ainsworth et al., 1978), although dimensional approaches have also been adopted. In the categorical approach, there are assumed to be three main types of attachment relationship. First, most infants show appropriate levels of distress when their mothers leave, contact seeking when they return, and use of their mothers as a secure base from which to explore the environment. These infants are classified as "secure." "Avoidant" infants show relatively little separation distress and little interest in establishing or maintaining contact with their mothers during reunion episodes. They may or may not actively explore the environment. "Resistant" infants show a mixed pattern of initially clinging to their mothers with little exploration, distress on separation, but then angry or rejecting responses to their mothers in the reunion episodes. They appear to be more preoccupied with their connection to their mothers than with exploring the environment.

Although many researchers value the categorical approach to attachment quality, it has been claimed that these categories actually reflect two underlying dimensions (e.g., Fraley & Spieker, 2003). So, for example, as we have seen, attachment has components that relate to the emotional bond between the infant and mother (e.g., behavioral reactions motivated by love or anger) and also a component relating to how infants use the mother to manage security and anxiety. Infants may vary on these different dimensions in different ways.

The fact that secure attachment is in part an implementation of the love, trust, and effectance acquired initially through early experience of interactions with the mother is evidenced by research that has examined longitudinal relations between early interactions and security of attachment. John Bowlby (1969) and Mary Ainsworth (Ainsworth et al., 1978), the originators of modern attachment research, suggested that the establishment of attachment toward the end of the first year should depend on how the mother and infant interact earlier in the first year. In particular, their claim was that sensitive mothering should lead the infant to be more willing and able to use the mother as a secure base. Because attachment security involves the infant using the mother to modulate distress and anxiety, it is surprising that very little research has examined the relation between maternal responsiveness to crying and attachment. What research has been done has provided mixed results (Bell & Ainsworth, 1972; Belsky, Rovine, & Taylor, 1984; Del Carmen, Pederson, Huffman, & Bryan, 1993; Van IJzendoorn & Hubbard, 2000), although there is some support for a link. For example, Rebecca Del Carmen and colleagues (1993) found that the effectiveness of mothers' management of their infants' distress at 3 months was significantly related to security of attachment measured in the Strange Situation at 12 months. This finding is consistent with the idea that maternal sensitivity to distress early in infancy leads to more secure attachment. In contrast, Marinus Van IJzendoorn and Frans Hubbard found that mothers of infants classified as avoidant in the Strange Situation at 15 months were more likely to have been particularly prompt in their responsiveness to their infants' crying during the first year. These authors interpret these somewhat counterintuitive findings in terms of these mothers being overintrusive due to a very low tolerance for their infants' expression of distress. Such maternal overintrusiveness has been shown in other studies to be related to avoidant attachment (e.g., Isabella & Belsky, 1991; Smith & Pederson, 1988).

Considerably more research has examined the relation between maternal behavior in face-to-face interactions and later attachment (e.g., Isabella, 1995). A comprehensive review of this literature carried out by Marianne DeWolff and Marinus Van IJzendoorn (1997) provided clear general support for the existence of a link. Maternal sensitiveness (or promptness of response), contingency, and physical contact during the period when their infants are 2 to 6 months are all quite strongly related to strength of attachment security by the end of the first year. More recently, it has been shown that the warmth and contingency characteristics of early interactions may contribute differently to the development of attachment. Susanne Völker and colleagues (Völker et al., 1999) observed a sample of mother and 3-month-old dyads in face-to-face interaction. They then assessed the same pairs in the Strange Situation when the infants were 12 months old. Measures of warmth or affection and contingency or responsiveness were derived from the observations of the face-to-face interactions. Similarly, two kinds of measures were derived from the observations in the Strange Situation: *overall security*, which relates to how the infant uses the mother to buffer anxiety, and *contact seeking versus avoiding*, which relates to the physical and emotional closeness between the infant and mother. The results showed that maternal warmth at 3 months was correlated with infant contact seeking at 12 months, but not with overall security. In contrast, maternal contingency at 3 months was related to overall security of attachment but not contact seeking. Thus, whereas the growth of love seems to be related to a history of warmth in interactions, the use of the mother to manage fear is related to the regular experience of contingent maternal responsiveness.

What we see in attachment is the culmination of social and emotional development in the first 6 to 8 months of life. Through regular interaction, infants develop a connection to the mother involving intense emotions and expectations about how the mother will respond to them. In the majority of cases, this connection is characterized by love and trust. These expectations become part of the way the infant reacts to the wider world so that when stressed, infants are able to use the mother to alleviate their own anxiety in relation to the world. In this way, attachment to the mother represents the origins of infants' use of another person to mediate their own reaction to the world.

I should not end this section with the impression that only mother-infant relationships are important. The primary caregiver, who is most often the mother, enjoys a special relationship with the infant. However, other relationships are also important from an early age. When infants are given regular interactive experience with others, they quickly develop strong emotional relationships with them also. Infants may enter into relationships with fathers, older siblings, extended family members, and unrelated regular caregivers such as nannies or day-care workers. Most infants enjoy a network of relationships and all can be used to some extent to modulate their emotional orientations. Compared to the mother-infant relationship, it seems that these other relationships are less likely to be used for the protective, or anxiety modulation, function of attachment, perhaps because infants typically have not experienced the same degree of contingent interaction with others as they have with their mothers (Goldberg, 2000). However, the experience of warmth in interaction and the consequent desire to interact may characterize a wide range of relationships.

COMMONSENSE PSYCHOLOGY
IN DYADIC INTERACTIONS AND ATTACHMENT

So what progress has been made toward the development of commonsense psychology as the child becomes a participant in social interactions and then relationships? We have seen from the various approaches to studying dyadic interactions considered in this chapter that infants become attuned to the quality of the interactions with their mothers during the period from about 2 to 5 months. Within dyadic interactions, the infants' and mothers' actions become increasingly coordinated. Mothers attempt to respond contingently to their infants' actions and infants progressively do the same. Gradually therefore, the first-person information provided by the infants' action and the third-person information provided by the mothers' action are coordinated in time. As the regularity of this coordination increases, infants are able to detect and recognize the persistent patterns of information created by combining both kinds of information. In effect, infants' participation in dyadic interactions comes to involve integrated representations of combined first- and third-person information.

These integrated representations are a first and necessary step on the way to meeting the challenge of self–other equivalence that was considered in chapter 2. Recall that as adults we recognize that both self and others are equivalent in the sense that we are all agents of psychological relations to objects. This recognition of self–other equivalence occurs despite the significant differences in the quality and quantity of the psychological relations of ourselves and others. Self–other equivalence depends, then, on a set of representations of psychological agents that integrate first- and third-person information. It is the participation in dyadic interactions that first allows infants to acquire integrated representations involving both first- and third-person information. These representations incorporate information from both self and other and so provide the basis for self–other equivalence. However, there is not yet true self–other equivalence because infants do not yet attribute psychological states independently to self and other. As adults, we understand that others have first-person characteristics and that we have third-person characteristics. For infants, self and other are not yet independently identified.

In dyadic interactions, infants' focus is entirely on the mother, but in the attachment relationship, infants use the mother to regulate their anxiety about objects or events in the environment. The warmth experienced in the relationship buffers the uncertainty experienced in unfamiliar circumstances. In this way, infants' emotional orientation to the outside world can be modified by the mother's orientation. Now the focus of the interaction is in part outside the two-person confines of the dyadic interaction. This shift in focus of the interaction from within the dyad to external objects and events is a critical step in the development of commonsense psychology. It means that, for the first time, there is the potential for infants to appreciate that people's emotional states are directed at other objects. As seen in chapter 2, understanding the object directedness of psychological states is a core feature of a mature commonsense psychology.

So far, I have concentrated on the emotional properties of the attachment relationship as it becomes established during the middle of the first year. The emotional nature of the bond between infants and mothers is important because it serves to maintain an association between the infants' exploration of the world and their experience of the mother. In this way, attachment acts as a kind of glue to ensure that infants' first-person experience in relation to objects remains combined with their third-person experience of the mother's social actions. Thus, when infants experience a novel object or event from a first-person point of view, they typically also experience in close temporal proximity the third-person information available from their mothers' expressions. So first- and third-person information remains associated even as the infants' focus shifts to objects outside of the infant-mother dyad.

Although it is the emotional connection between infant and mother that enables the correspondence between first- and third-person information to be maintained as the focus shifts away from the dyad, other forms of psychological information are involved. As we shall see in chapter 6, information pertaining to what I have called epistemic relations becomes central. Epistemic relations are first evident in actions that involve interest or attention, such as looking at something. Imagine an unfamiliar person enters a room where an infant is playing with his mother. The infant may look toward the stranger and feel some uncertainty or anxiety. At this point, the infant tends to look toward and approach the mother, and then may look again at the stranger from the safety of the mother. At the same time, the mother may acknowledge the infant's approach with a smile and then become engaged with the stranger, perhaps smiling, looking, and talking to the new person. In this episode the infant's initial interest in the novel person is combined with mild anxiety. The attachment relationship allows the infant to reduce the anxiety so that he can perhaps indulge his interest from a safe vantage point. In close correspondence, his own emotional and attentional orientation to the stranger is combined with his awareness of his mother and her emotional and attentional expressions. Together, the infant is presented with both first-person and third-person information of both an emotional and attentional (epistemic) kind.

SUMMARY

In this chapter, we have reviewed how the child's social activity becomes intertwined with that of others. Reciprocal patterns of social acts—emotional expressions, vocalizations, gestures—begin within a few months of birth and quickly develop into specific patterns for particular partners. We have seen that through their participation in dyadic interactions infants become attuned to the psychological states of their mothers. Repeated experience with these interactions yields expectations about how the mother will respond to their social overtures. Armed with this trust, infants can face the wider world, knowing that should threats arise, they can recruit their mothers' aid.

Despite this growing social sophistication, there is not yet any clear evidence that infants have a commonsense psychology. Dyadic interactions do not involve objects and so there is no apparent sensitivity on the part of infants in the first 6 months to the object directedness of others' activity. There is also no clear sign that they recognize the similarity between self and other. And yet, the developments discussed in this chapter are as crucial to the development of commonsense psychology as those reviewed in chapter 4. With the growth of social interactions and relationships, two important components necessary for the development of commonsense psychology are set in place. First, through regular experience interacting with their mothers, infants participate in coordinated behavioral patterns in which their psychological states and those of their mothers are closely matched in time and even form. What this means is that infants regularly experience together first-person information pertaining to their own psychological states and third-person information pertaining to the psychological states of another person. This close association between the first-person characteristics of their own activity and the third-person characteristics of their mothers' activity allows the detection of information patterns involving both kinds of information. First- and third-person information become combined in infants' processing of social information.

Second, infants' entry into the first relationship involves their use of another person to regulate their psychological orientation to the world. When infants experience anxiety in the face of unfamiliar and potentially threatening circumstances, they turn to the mother for the comfort her actions provide. The use of the attachment figure in this way soothes the anxiety and enables infants to more readily explore the environment. Infants have now learned that mother is a source of comfort and calm in the context of the wider world. Although this is not yet the use of another person to gain information about the world, it is only a short step from using the mother to calm distress to using her to find out something about the unfamiliar circumstances.

Thus, dyadic interactions and early relationships are critical to the development of commonsense psychology. However, before infants can truly be said to be addressing the challenges of commonsense psychology, one further piece must be put in place: They have to combine an interest in objects with their interest in people.

6

From Interest in Objects to Sharing Intentions

Until the age of about 4 months, infants find social stimulation particularly appealing. As we have seen, faces, voices, and the contingent patterns of social interaction dominate the infant's experience during the first phase of life. In part, this is due to natural preferences—preferences for faces, speechlike sounds, and so on. However, it is also in part due to the infant's limited motor capabilities. Social stimulation comes to the infant, rather than the other way around, and so even though young infants have very little control over their bodies and limbs, they can still benefit from the willingness of adults to stimulate them. Between 2 and 4 months of age infants gain considerable control over their torso and neck muscles, so that by 4 months infants can generally sit with support and can hold their heads steady. Postural control is important for a significant new development: visually guided reaching (Fontaine & Pieraut le Bonniec, 1988; Thelen & Spencer, 1998). Even though they cannot yet locomote, infants can now start to move out into the world and bring objects to themselves. Even if most of what infants grasps quickly finds its way to their mouths, they are still expanding their range of experience.

Between 4 and 6 months, infants refine their reaching and grasping. Objects that are available within reach result in infants opening their hands while reaching to anticipate contacting the object. Now, objects that are grasped are not just brought to the mouth but may also be manipulated by one or sometimes both hands while the infant watches. Infants become interested in the visual and tactile properties of objects and before long objects with attractive attributes become worthy competitors with people as attention getters and keepers. Indeed the proportion of time that infants make eye contact in face-to-face interactions is reduced quite considerably by 6 months (Kaye & Fogel, 1980), because other objects are now distracting attention away from faces. Mothers typically recognize this change and introduce objects such as toys into their interactions with their infants.

We saw in chapter 5 that early interactions between infants and adults differ from those between two adults in that they do not have a focus—they are not about anything. By 6 months infants have become interested in things but at first they do not share this interest with others. In contrast to adults who typically like to share their experiences of the world, young infants' exploration of objects is initially a quite solitary exercise. So although mothers may be successful in attracting their infants' attention with toys, this does not yet lead to social interactions with toys as their focus. If infants are offered a toy, they will typically take it and concentrate on it alone—manipulating it, mouthing it, banging it, and often finally dropping it. At this point, the infant's attention may return to the mother, but as soon as the infant retrieves the toy, the infant's interest is again consumed by it. What is happening here is that the infant is able to act on the toy or with the mother in different phases of the game, but is not able to put the two together. The infant is not able to use the toy to further the interaction with the mother, or to use the mother to find out more about the toy.

Nevertheless, mothers understand that toys are now an important way to their infants' hearts and, not wanting to give up on the pleasures of the face-to-face interactions they have been enjoying, they incorporate toys into their play. Toys become a means to enrich their interactions, and mothers repeatedly present a toy that their infant takes, manipulates, and then drops or pushes away. Such sequences evolve into simple turn-taking games that may involve elements of routine. The infant is intent on manipulating an object but then drops it out of reach; mother picks it up and returns it to the infant and the cycle is repeated. Rolling or pushing a toy repeatedly is also common. Mother rolls an object into the infant's reach; infant grasps and manipulates for a while, and then haphazardly pushes it away; mother rolls the object back.

Initially these object games are supported entirely by the mother. Mothers engage their infants with objects using an exaggerated form of action that Brand, Baldwin, and Ashburn (2002) at the University of Oregon called "motionese," to mark the idea that this form of action has characteristics that resemble the kind of speech (motherese) that mothers use with infants. These researchers compared how mothers of infants engaged in object-centered interaction with their own 6- to 13-month-old infants and with an adult to whom they were close. The mothers were given five novel objects with different properties that could be demonstrated. For example, one of the objects was a red suction cup that could be attached to the table and that made a popping sound when it detached. In general, the mothers' action with their infants was characterized by greater enthusiasm, interactiveness, and repetitiveness among other things than with the adults. In addition, the amount of time spent in joint action, where both mother and infant manipulated the objects, was much greater than with adults. So mothers work hard in these object-centered interactions to keep the interaction around the toy interesting for their infants.

One way in which mothers keep the object-centered interactions interesting may have important implications both for how infants learn about objects and for how they learn about people. Shana Nichols (2005) found that mothers also provide opportunities for object-directed imitation by their infants. In a study of 9-month-olds and their mothers in free play with toys, Nichols found that most mothers did not directly imitate their infants' actions on toys. This contrasts with earlier dyadic interactions where mothers often did imitate. Instead almost all mothers provided setups whereby mothers took a toy, demonstrated an action with it, and then handed the toy to the infants. In so doing, mothers provided for the infants the opportunity to learn something about what can be done with the toy. If the infants then tried to repeat the event, they were likely to reproduce the actions the mother used and therefore end up imitating the mothers' actions on the toy. Such imitative episodes may be an important way in which infants are provided with contingent and corresponding first-person and third-person information pertaining to actions on objects.

Initially, the infants' role in these object-centered interactions is confined to manipulating and then rejecting the object. Gradually and almost imperceptibly over the next few months the interactions become reciprocal. Rather than simply pushing the toy away, infants push it towards the mother. And somewhere along the way a profound change in attention happens. Rather than simply concentrating on the object, infants take their turn and then, miraculously, look up at their mother's face, as they anticipate the mother's turn. Through their experience with interaction involving toys, infants learn the regularities of the game and can predict that mother will do something interesting subsequent to their own action on the toy. From now on, social interactions involving objects are characterized by infants switching attention rapidly and flexibly from object to partner's face, and back again, continuously monitoring both. Infants have now entered the period of joint engagement and have, in a very fundamental way, crossed a watershed into a new phase of life.

It is interesting to compare the nature of social interaction in this new phase of life with those forms established earlier and reviewed in the previous chapter (see Fig. 5.1). From now on, interactions are primarily triadic (Bakeman & Adamson, 1984; see Fig. 6.1) because they involve three components—infant, adult, and object—where previously they were dyadic— involving infant and adult only. However, despite a difference in number of participants, and therefore attentional requirements, triadic interactions often retain the structure of dyadic interactions in that they involve mutually contingent patterns of actions produced by both partners (Dunham & Dunham, 1995; Striano & Rochat, 1999). In addition,

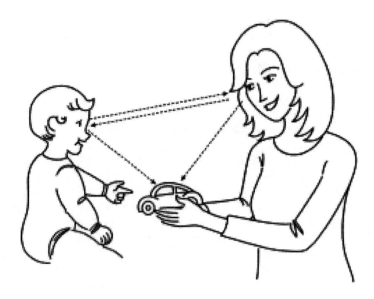

FIG. 6.1.   Triadic interaction.

triadic interactions retain the primarily positive, cooperative tenor of dyadic interactions. This key emotional characteristic is seen best by contrasting the kind of attachment behavior I described in chapter 5 with triadic interaction. We saw that when infants experience anxiety, perhaps in response to a novel situation, they approach the mother and use her to gain comfort. Attachment behavior then is primarily a withdrawal from the world to the security of the mother. The reduction in anxiety may then allow infants to become more exploratory. In contrast, triadic interactions also involve the use of the mother but now in a more outward-looking manner. As infants explore the world of objects, the mother is used to regulate the infants' intrinsic interest in that world.

The phenomenon of emotional social referencing illustrates this transition nicely (Baldwin & Moses, 1996). Social referencing occurs when infants are confronted with a mildly threatening object or situation, for example, a toy spider located across the room. The typical reaction is for infants to look at the spider, next look at the mother's face, and then use the mother's emotional reaction to guide their own behavior. So, if the mother looks at the toy and smiles, infants are more likely to approach the toy. However, if she looks fearful, infants are more likely to approach the mother. In this situation, infants are teetering between interest and anxiety and the mother's expression tips the balance. If mother expresses fear, then the attachment behavioral system wins out; if she expresses positive interest, then exploration wins out.

The incorporation of an object into a triadic interaction where the dominant motive is interest allows for the first time the possibility of solution to one of the epistemic challenges posed in chapter 1. We have seen that commonsense psychology involves psychological relations that are directed at objects. The challenge is: How can infants develop an understanding that people's psychological acts, especially those that occur at some distance from their target object, are in fact directed at objects? Clearly, it is necessary for infants to be able to attend to both the person who acts and to the target object. With the transition into triadic interactions, infants can now attend to both adult and object and thus can, in principle, determine that the adult's action is object directed or intentional. In this chapter, we will review evidence on how infants begin to appreciate the intentionality of others' action—first in situations involving direct object contact and later moving on to situations of psychological action at a distance. First, it will serve us well to review briefly developments in triadic interactions at the end of the first year (see Carpenter, Nagell, & Tomasello, 1998).

THE DEVELOPMENT OF TRIADIC INTERACTIONS

As mentioned, triadic interactions start sometime between 6 and 9 months with the infant and adult cocoordinating their activity with respect to the same object. Early coordinations tend to be on objects that are in the immediate space between the two participants. The act of giving is an early action-based form of triadic interaction in which an object is exchanged between the participants. Mother hands a toy to the infant and then holds out her hand and asks for it back. The infant places the toy in the mother's hand and mother says, "Thank you!" Such an exchange may be repeated and in the process, infants become able to coordinate their actions on an object with those of the mother. These sequences of reciprocal actions on an object may gradually change. Vasudevi Reddy (1991) described how giving can evolve into teasing. The infant holds out an object to the mother but then pulls it back. The mother reacts as if aggrieved, but then smiles and the infant has learned a new game in which breaking the previous routine is a novel way to enhance the quality of the interaction.

Interactions also occur over objects without an exchange. Infants commonly hold an object up for the adult to see. Such showing also reliably elicits an enthusiastic adult response such as "Oh wow, isn't that neat!" or "You've got a rattle!" At other times, the adult shows the infant things—real objects or pictures—and they share attention to a common focus. Sharing attention in this way, whether infant or adult initiated, involves the coordination of another psychological relation—both participants are looking at the same thing.

In order to share attention efficiently, infants have to be sensitive to behaviors like gaze and pointing that indicate that the interactive partner is attending to an object. Responding to gaze direction shows a relatively pro-tracted development during the first year. Barbara D'Entremont and her colleagues (D'Entremont, Hains, & Muir, 1997) found that even 3- to 6-month-olds turned in the same direction as an adult when there were attractive toys visible right next to the adult. However, such young infants do not follow gaze when there is no target simultaneously present (Butterworth & Cochran, 1980; Corkum & Moore, 1998; D'Entremont, 2000). Such early gaze following is probably best explained as the adult's movement stimulating a shift in the infant's attention in a relatively reflex-ive way (D'Entremont; Moore, 1999a). The movement of the adult's gaze shift leads the infant's attention in the same direction as the movement and the infant's attention is then captured by the most interesting object in view. In any case, this early form of gaze following is not yet incorporated into triadic interaction. By about 9 to 10 months, infants are able to respond to gaze even when there is no target object simultaneously in view. If a 10-month-old and adult are in face-to-face interaction and the adult turns to the side to fixate a target toy a few feet away, the infant turns in the same di-rection, thereby finding the target (Corkum & Moore). This difference in age of onset between gaze following to targets in view versus out of view is important because it shows that only at 10 months does the infant's obser-vation of the change in gaze of the adult lead to an expectation that there is something interesting to be seen in the location to which the other turned. Such gaze following shows that infants are now able to coordinate their gaze with others' gaze in situations involving possible rather than actual objects. To put it in the terms introduced in chapter 2, the third-person information of the other's gaze is coordinated with the expectation of the first-person information corresponding to seeing an object.

Whereas gaze tends not to be used intentionally to clearly indicate a shift in attention, other actions are designed to indicate attention and to direct others' attention. Perhaps the most obvious example is index finger pointing. Pointing is used for a variety of communicative functions, such as requesting or showing, but trades on the fact that it serves to shift the perceiver's attention to the object of interest. Infants' tendency to follow the direction of pointing gestures develops slightly later than following gaze, but is typically well established by 12 months (Carpenter et al., 1998). This difference in age of onset between gaze and pointing following is interesting because it illustrates the different origins of these two forms of attention. As seen in chapter 5, infants are sensitive to gaze direction from early in life in the context of dyadic interaction. The disruption in face-to-face interaction caused by shifts in gaze becomes integrated rela-tively early into triadic interactions as the break in face-to-face interaction is recognized by the infant as a signal to shift attention from the adult to the object. Pointing, involving index finger extension, however, is a more conventional directive gesture without a history in dyadic exchanges—it is used by one person to direct the attention of another. It is not surprising, therefore, that following pointing requires the consolidation of shared attention in triadic interaction.

The coordination of psychological relations between infants and adults during this period is genuinely reciprocal. Sometimes, as in gaze following, infants use the adult's action to find out about the world. Sometimes they use an object to elicit a reaction from the adult and thereby enhance the interaction. We have seen already that showing objects is an early form of triadic interaction. By the end of the first year, showing has often been joined by pointing as a means of eliciting adult reactions to objects. The development of the production of pointing enjoys a special place in accounts of early communicative development because of its apparently transitional role in the development of language. Elizabeth Bates and her colleagues (e.g. Bates, O'Connell, & Shore, 1987) argued that the acquisition of pointing marks the infant's entry into a genuinely purposeful form of communication that will soon be supplemented and then superceded by language. Pointing sometimes starts as object exploration; for example, younger infants touch objects with the index finger extended. As triadic interactions become well established, however, pointing assumes the role of showing, at first to objects that are in the space between infant and adult, and, typically by the beginning of the second year, to objects that are at some distance from the infant (e.g., Leung & Rheingold, 1981; Zinober & Martlew, 1985). By then, pointing has often taken on at least two communicative functions (Bates, Camaioni, & Volterra, 1975): to show something (called the *protodeclarative* function) and to demand something (called the *protoimperative* function).

During this same period, imitation of actions also occurs readily. Infants copy both arbitrary or conventional actions, such as waving "bye-bye," and instrumental actions on objects, for example, banging a stick on a pot to make a noise (Meltzoff, 1988; Piaget, 1962). Imitation reveals that infants can coordinate and match their own action with that of an interactive partner. When the action is object directed, imitation provides a powerful means for acquiring novel modes of using objects (Tomasello et al., 1993).

This brief review shows that by the beginning of the second year, infants are participating with others in object-centered interactions in which a range of psychological relations to those objects is coordinated. Both infants and adults exhibit and respond to each others' action, perception, and emotion relations to objects. In the process, infants shift their attention flexibly between object and person. They may follow someone's gaze to find an object but then look back to check what the person is doing. They may reproduce an action that the adult has just performed while looking at the adult's face. The joint engagement that characterizes these interactions provides an envelope within which both infant and adult feed off each other's actions toward objects. All the while, infants are learning the regularities that bind their action to that of others.

One-year-old infants' participation in coordinated bouts of triadic interaction, in which they share intentional activity with others toward objects, looks strongly like they have a basic commonsense psychology. If infants follow another person's gaze surely they must understand that that person can see something that they cannot? And if they look to the mother when unsure about how to react to something, then surely they must appreciate that their mother may like or dislike that thing? As a result, some authors (e.g., Bretherton, 1991; Tomasello, 1995) argued that the period from 9 to 12 months represents a watershed not only in social interactive behavior but also in commonsense psychology. Tomasello (e.g., 1995, 1999a, 1999b) made the case most explicitly. He argued that the complex of triadic interactive abilities that emerges from about 9 months reveals that the infant has developed a new understanding of people as intentional agents like the self. According to Tomasello (1999b, p. 302):

> [Nine-month-olds understand that] intentional agents are animate beings with the power to control their spontaneous behavior.... [They] have goals and make active choices among behavioral means for attaining those goals. Importantly, intentional agents also make active choices about what they pay attention to in pursuing those goals.

In this view, infants respond appropriately in triadic interactive contexts because they now understand the interactive partner as an intentional agent—someone who can attend to things and pursue goals when acting on objects.

Tomasello's (1999a, 1999b) account articulately characterized the infant at the end of the first year as having a commonsense psychology that includes an understanding of both self–other equivalence and the object–directedness of psychological activity. Importantly, he argued that it is this commonsense psychology that makes possible the range of triadic interactive behaviors we observe by the end of the first year. In short, he suggested that commonsense psychology enables infants to show triadic interactive behavior. The idea that some general understanding of people as intentional agents underlies developments in triadic interactions is consistent with the fact that the different elements of triadic interaction—gaze following, social referencing, communicative gestures, imitation—all emerge within a relatively short space of time (Carpenter et al., 1998). However, it should be noted that studies of these interactive behaviors have not necessarily found them to be correlated with each other (e.g., Slaughter & McConnell, 2003). That is, if we look at the development of these interactive behaviors in individual children, it is not the case that children show either all of them or none of them. In fact, whether infants show one type of behavior, such as gaze following, appears to be unrelated to whether they also show other behaviors, such as social referencing or pointing. Such findings imply that these behaviors are perhaps not all based on the common foundation of commonsense psychology.

An alternative account that is in line with the theoretical and developmental arguments outlined in previous chapters, is that from about 9 to 12 months, infants start to recognize the patterns of information associated with triadic interactions. Most importantly, they start to detect the difference between patterns in which object-focused interactions can proceed and patterns in which such interactions cannot proceed. For example, infants have learned that, in order for an episode of joint engagement to proceed, the other person's gaze must be directed toward an object of interest. When the conditions for joint engagement are not in place, perhaps because the partner is looking elsewhere, the infant attempts to establish those conditions, perhaps by following the other's gaze or attempting to redirect the other's gaze. Notice that the patterns of information associated with object-focused interactions are ones involving both first- and third-person information. The patterns involve the coordination of first-person information pertaining to the infant's own psychological orientation to the object with third-person information pertaining to the interactive partner's action in relation to the object. So, like the dyadic interactions reviewed in chapter 5, triadic interactions involve a combination of first- and third-person information, but now, unlike dyadic interactions, the information also includes the object that is the focus of the interaction.

This account assumes that infants understand something about the object directedness of others' activity. In order to detect whether the object-focused interaction can proceed, infants must be able to detect whether the partner's activity is directed at an object of interest. However, the account does not require that infants understand that their own experiences are equivalent to those of others. As we have seen, understanding self–other equivalence entails understanding that others have first-person experience like the self and that the self is an objective agent like others. Nor does the account require that infants understand that self and other may have different psychological relations to the target object. For infants to understand this kind of diversity in psychological relations they have to understand that another person's psychological relation to an object may differ from their own. Thus, though self and other are both agents, they can have different and independent psychological relations to the same object, for example, I can see the toy and you cannot or you like the carrots and I do not. In chapter 7, we will focus on evidence that infants come to understand these two aspects of commonsense psychology between 12 and 18 months of age. In the rest of this chapter we will review evidence of how infants begin to grasp the object directedness of psychological activity. As we saw in chapter 2, understanding object directedness is a foundational element of commonsense psychology. All intentional activity from the most abstract thoughts to the simplest purposeful actions on objects share this feature. We have now reached the point where infants truly are beginning to grasp this property of psychological activity.

EXPERIMENTAL INVESTIGATIONS OF THE UNDERSTANDING OF OBJECT DIRECTEDNESS

In order to try to get a clearer understanding of what infants know about object directedness and other aspects of psychological activity, researchers have turned to experimental investigation. Two main approaches have been adopted. The earlier approach involved placing the infant in a triadic interactive setting with an adult—either the mother or an adult—and then manipulating the adult's behavior with the infant. A more recent approach adopted the habituation method used to study infant perceptual discriminations, and examined how infants discriminate among demonstrations of psychological activity. In this way, the habituation approach has been used to provide a window onto infants' knowledge of commonsense psychology.

Interactive Approaches to the Study of Infants' Commonsense Psychology

Gaze Following and Pointing.   Because of its central role in triadic interactions, gaze following has attracted considerable interest among researchers. Research has examined both the accuracy of infants' target localization and the cues that infants use when following gaze. In these studies, infants are typically placed opposite from, and a short distance away from, an adult. The adult interacts with the infants in a face-to-face manner and periodically turns to one or other side to fixate a target picture or object in the room. In the research on target localization, target objects such as toys are placed in different locations around the room with some in the infants' visual field and some outside the visual field (e.g., Fig. 6.2). During the experimental session, the adult turns to fixate the different targets on different trials. Such experiments have revealed that when infants first start to follow gaze to the correct side, they do not fixate the particular target that the adult is looking at. Rather, they look at the first object that happens to be on their scan path (Butterworth & Cochran, 1980). In other words, although they can use the adult's head turn to look to the correct side, they do not seek to find which object the adult is looking at. Looking for the particular object that the adult is attending to develops during the first half of the second year (Butterworth & Cochran; Carpenter et al., 1998). Another sign of the developing specificity of gaze following that develops between 12 and 18 months is seen in the fact that if the adult looks at a target, such as a picture, that is located on a barrier facing to-

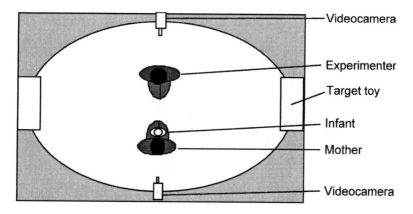

FIG. 6.2.   Schematic showing typical laboratory setup for gaze-following studies.

ward the adult and away from the infant, infants try to look on the adult's side of the barrier (Dunphy-Lelii & Wellman, 2004; Moll & Tomasello, 2004). So, during the first half of the second year, there is evidence that infants can use others' gaze to determine quite precisely in the three-dimensional world where an interesting object may be located.

Other experiments have manipulated the cues that are used to signal gaze. As adults, we know that in order to see something, the eyes must be directed at it. However, gaze is often associated with head orientation because we typically turn our heads in the direction we want to look. So what aspects of an adult's gaze behavior do infants use when they turn in the same direction as their interactive partner? A number of researchers have examined infants' gaze following in situations where the orientation of the adult's head and eyes are independently shifted (Brooks & Meltzoff, 2002; Butterworth & Jarrett, 1991; Caron, Butler, & Brooks, 2002; Corkum & Moore, 1995; Lempers, 1979; Moore & Corkum, 1998). For example, Valerie Corkum and I (1995) showed infants various types of cues, including head turns with eyes moving in the direction of the head turns, head turns with the eyes remaining straight ahead and focused on the infant, and eye turns without the head turning (see Fig. 6.3). We found that when infants first started to follow gaze to targets outside the immediate visual field at about 9 months, they only paid attention to the head turn. That is, they followed head turns whether or not the eyes were moving in the same direction and they did not follow the eye turns without head turning. Infants do not appear to recognize the significance of eyes turns alone until the middle of the second year when they will follow eye turns without a head movement (Butterworth & Jarrett; Moore & Corkum). Nevertheless, prior to this point

FIG. 6.3.   Photos of different gaze direction cues for gaze following.

infants may know that the eyes are important in the context of head turns because 12-month-olds typically fail to follow head turns if their eyes are closed or covered with a blindfold (Brooks & Meltzoff; Caron et al.).

Together these results on gaze following show that when they first start to follow gaze, infants have a pattern of responding to gaze direction that differs from that of older children or adults. Nine-month-olds respond primarily to head orientation and they do not look for the particular target that the adult is looking at. This pattern is consistent with infants following gaze because they have acquired an expectation that when people turn in a certain direction something interesting may be found there (Moore & Corkum, 1994), not because they understand that people look at, and see, things.

Over the next few months, infants develop a more mature pattern of responding whereby they pay attention to the orientation of the eyes and they do attempt to determine exactly where in three-dimensional space the adult is attending. This pattern more closely resembles what we would expect if infants understand that gaze is directed at objects. However, it is still the case that infants are acquiring an increasingly more accurate model of how adult gaze behavior predicts where interesting objects will be located in space. As such, all gaze-following behavior can be considered to be a matter of infants coordinating third-person information about others' gaze activity with their own first-person intention to locate a target.

Gaze following involves infants using others' attention to find out about objects in the world. We have also seen that infants use objects to enhance their interaction with adults as, for example, when they show things to others. Experiments examining under what conditions infants show things are relatively rare. Moore and D'Entremont (2001) examined infants' pointing under different conditions of adult attention. Infants interacted face to face with a female adult experimenter and periodically during the session an interesting sight appeared on one or other side of the pair. The sight was a stuffed dog that was illuminated and rotated. For some infants, the adult with whom they were interacting simultaneously turned and looked at the toy as it was activated. For other infants, the adult either turned and looked in the opposite direction or continued to face forward as the toy was activated. The results showed that 14-month-old infants were more likely to point at the toy when the adult was either looking at the toy or was looking at them, and least likely to point when the adult was looking in the wrong direction. In contrast, 24-month-olds pointed more when the adult was either looking in the wrong direction or looking at them, and less when the adult was looking at the toy. Because the younger infants pointed more when the adult was either looking at the toy or looking at them, these results suggest that when infants first start to point they point more to maintain the triadic interaction with the other than to redirect the other's attention to an interesting sight. In contrast, by 2 years, the infants recognized when the adult was looking at the wrong toy and gestured to try to get her to focus on the one that was more interesting to them.

It is important to recognize, however, that pointing is a truly triadic interaction—it serves to facilitate sharing of experience toward an object or event. This fact is demonstrated by a recent study by Ulf Liszkowski and his colleagues at the Max Planck Institute for Evolutionary Anthropology in Leipzig (2004). In their study, pointing was elicited from 12-month-old infants in response to a variety of interesting events, such as moving toys or flashing lights. An interactive adult then responded in one of four different ways. The adult looked at the event and commented on it, looked at the infant and commented on the infant, looked at the event and did not comment, or looked at the infant and did not comment. The condition in which the adult both looked at the event and commented was the most effective for maintaining infant pointing across trials. These results show that the infants used pointing as a means to establish or enhance the triadic interaction with the adult. They recognized that for the triadic interaction to proceed successfully, the adult had to be both attending to the target object and responsive to them.

Emotional Social Referencing. As I mentioned earlier, by the end of the first year, infants show social referencing whereby they look toward their mothers when confronted with a novel ambiguous object or situation and respond based on the emotional expression displayed by the mother. Social referencing appears to depend on infants' understanding that people have emotional orientations to objects. However, it is also possible that social referencing works by infants empathically catching the emotional experience that the adult expresses and then reacting on the basis of that emotion to whatever is novel in their environment. It is likely that when infants first start to use others' emotion to guide their own behavior to novel objects, it is not because they understand that others have emotional orientations to objects. Donna Mumme and Ann Fernald (Mumme & Fernald, 2003) showed 10-month-old infants two novel toys and then had an adult look toward one of them and emote either positively or negatively using both vocal and facial expressions. The toys were then both presented to the infants and their reactions observed. They found that rather than infants extracting an emotional message about the particular toy toward which the adult had attended, the infants showed a corresponding change in their own emotional state as evidenced by their facial expressions. This change in disposition led to a more global reaction to the toys so that they were more interactive with both toys when the adult emoted positively and less interactive with both when the adult emoted negatively.

Other research by Lou Moses and his colleagues (Moses, Baldwin, Rosicky, & Tidball, 2001; see also Mumme & Fernald, 2003; Repacholi, 1998) showed that before long, infants do respond to the object directedness of others' emotional expressions. They also presented 12- and 18-month-old infants with pairs of novel toys. In a series of trials one of the toys in a pair was handed to the infants. While the infant was attending to this toy, the experimenter either vocalized pleasantly ("Oh," "Nice") or disgustedly ("Ew," "Yecch"), and looked at either the same toy as the infant or the other toy in the pair. The infants responded to the expressions by following the adult's gaze to whichever toy she was attending to. Both toys in the pair were then presented side by side to the infants and the infants' affective reaction and interest in the two toys was assessed. The results showed that infants showed less approach and more negative reactions to the toy that the adult was looking at after they heard the disgust expression. In contrast, they showed more approach and more positive reactions to the toy that the adult was looking at after they heard the pleased expression. This work shows that by 12 months infants respond to the emotional expressions of others. But, more importantly, they did not just respond in a global way, avoiding everything that was present when the adult expressed disgust and approaching anything that was present when the adult sounded pleased and interested. Instead, the infants used the adult's gaze to determine the particular object that the adult expressed affect toward and that they modulated their own behavior depending on the valence of that affect—avoiding it if the adult showed disgust and approaching it if the adult expressed interest.

But do infants learn anything about the object toward which the adult emotes? Interestingly, Matt Hertenstein and Joe Campos (2004) found a significant difference between 11- and 14-month-olds in a similar procedure to that just described when the infants were given an opportunity to play with the toys either immediately or 1 hour later. They found, like Moses and colleagues (2001), that when the opportunity to interact with the toys was provided immediately after the emotional exposure, infants at both ages interacted more with the toy that the adult had been positive toward and less with the toy that the adult had been negative toward. However, when the infants were removed from the test scene after emotional exposure and then brought back 1 hour later, only 14-month-olds showed differential responding to the toys. In short, the two groups of infants learned something different from the emotional displays. The 11-month-olds responded emotionally to the emotional displays of the adult and the emotion they experienced guided their immediate reaction to the toys. However, once their emotion was no longer present after the 1-hour delay, they had no way to differentiate the toys. In contrast, the 14-month-olds, having witnessed the adults' emotional displays, transferred the emotional meaning to the toys themselves and therefore responded appropriately on both the immediate and delayed tests.

Together these results on emotional social referencing show that as they approach 1 year of age, infants respond in kind to certain emotions expressed by others and they can combine this emotional response with gaze following. As a result, infants are able to connect adults' emotional expressions to particular objects through their own response to the adults' actions. As such, for the first time emotional expressions observed in others may be understood to be directed at objects in the world.

Imitating Actions On Objects. Psychological relations involving attention, such as gaze and pointing, and emotions, as seen in social referencing, might be considered to present a particular challenge to the development of commonsense psychology because the psychology activity is displaced in space from the object toward which it is directed. As I mentioned earlier, after about 6 months of age, infants also start to engage in social interactions involving actions that occur directly on objects, for example, giving and taking. These object exchanges also appear to evidence the coordination of object-directed intentional actions between infant and adult. However, they do not clearly show that infants understand that the actions involved are object directed. Evidence of infants' sensitivity to the object-directed nature of intentional actions is best seen in imitative interactions. Infants start to imitate actions on objects between about 6 and 9 months of age (Meltzoff, 1988; Piaget, 1962). Meltzoff had an adult model a variety of simple target actions on objects that resulted in interesting effects. These actions included shaking a hollow plastic egg containing metal nuts, and pushing a button on a box to activate a beeping sound. Nine-month-old infants observed these actions and then they were given the various objects and allowed to manipulate them. Now it was possible that the infants would produce the target actions without any observation of the model. So, to rule out the possibility that apparently imitative actions might simply be spontaneously produced actions, control groups of infants were used. For example, in one control group, the adult merely touched each object and in another, the adult performed different actions on the objects. In all conditions, the number of target acts that the infants produced was assessed. The results showed that the infants were much more likely to produce the target actions when they had observed the adult perform them compared to when they had not seen the adult perform those particular actions. These results confirm that 9-month-olds can use their observation of others' object-directed actions to guide their own actions on objects. Such imitation is of considerable importance for the acquisition of novel actions on objects.

However, it is unclear what exactly infants learn in such imitative interactions. It is possible that the observation of the adult's action on the object teaches infants about the affordances of the object and not about the relation between the adult's action and the effect it produced. That is, the children might learn from observing the model what each object can do, but not actually learn anything about the action that was used to produce the effect. Elsner and Aschersleben (2003) addressed this issue using an innovative design in which they independently manipulated the link between two adult actions and two effects. They built an apparatus that had had an easily manipulated ring attached to a box (see Fig. 6.4). Infants of 9, 12, 15, and 18 months of age were divided into three groups. One group (the self group) saw no demonstration. Another group (the obs same group) saw a demonstration in which the adult pressed the ring to make the sound occur and pulled the ring to make the light go on. The third group (the obs diff group) saw the reverse contingency—pulling the ring made the sound and pressing the rings made the light go on. Infants were then allowed to play with the ring box that was always set up so that pressing the ring led to the sound and pulling the ring led to the light. Thus, the contingencies between the actions and effects were set up for the infants in the exploration phase as they were in the demonstration phase for the obs same group. This design allowed the authors to examine whether the infants had only learned the effects that were possible with this novel box or whether they had learned about the connection between the possible actions and the possible effects.

Infants at all ages and in all conditions enjoyed manipulating the ring to experience the effects, but the 9-month-olds showed no difference across the three conditions—they pressed and pulled the ring whether they had seen the adult do likewise or not. At this age, therefore, there was no evidence of imitation in that the infants were no more likely to manipulate the ring in the two demonstration conditions (the obs same and obs diff groups) than in the no-demonstration condition (the self group). However, given that there was little else for them to do with the apparatus in the no-demonstration condition, it is not surprising that they performed the target actions at quite a high level in this condition. The results for the older groups were different. The 12-month-olds performed more target actions in the two demonstration conditions than in the no-demon-

Adult demonstration	Infant exploration (120 s)
Group "Self" No adult demonstration	
Group "Obs same"	

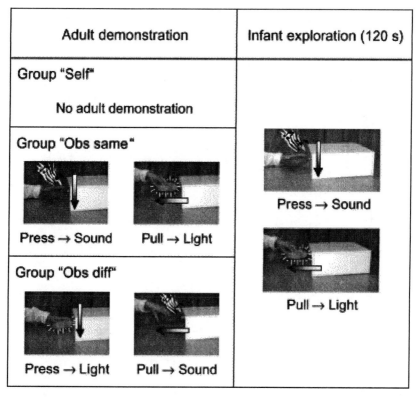

FIG. 6.4. Design of Elsner and Aschersleben's (2003) study of infants in which action and action effects were independently manipulated. From "Do I get What You Get? Learning About the Effects of Self-Performed and Observed Actions in Infancy," by B. Elsner and G. Aschersleben, 2003, *Consciousness and Cognition, 12*, p. 738. Copyright 2003 by Elsevier. Reprinted with permission of the authors.

stration condition. These infants had learned from the demonstration that manipulating the ring produced interesting effects. However, the number of target acts did not differ across the two demonstration conditions. Thus, it seemed that although they had learned that the actions produced interesting effects, they had not learned the particular effects of the two actions. Only at the oldest ages of 15 and 18 months did the infants in the obs same group produce more target acts than those in the obs diff group. These older infants clearly demonstrated an understanding of the relation between the observed actions and their effects. When that relation was maintained from demonstration phase to exploration phase as in the obs same group, the infants produced many imitative acts, but when the relation was disrupted as in the obs diff group, the infants were confused and produced fewer imitative responses.

The various experimental studies on interactive behavior show that the period spanning the end of the first year is an energetic time for the elaboration of early commonsense psychology in the context of triadic interactions. By early in the second year, triadic interactions are well practiced and infants can use adults' object-directed action to locate and find out about objects in the world. They also use objects to enhance their interactions with others and together these two motives structure the social experiences infants enjoy. During this period, there is evidence that infants are gaining an understanding of the object directedness of a wide variety of psychological acts. They treat attentional acts like gaze and pointing as having a focus on an object: they combine this understanding of gaze with their sensitivity to emotional expressions to respond appropriately to the particular objects toward which others express positive and negative emotions: and they can start to use the observed relations between others' manual actions and the effects those actions achieve in their attempts to reproduce those effects.

Habituation Approach to Infants' Commonsense Psychology

Studies of how triadic interactions develop are an important source of information on infants' developing commonsense psychology. However, with such studies we are necessarily left to draw inferences about commonsense psychology from social interactive behavior and, as we saw in chapter 1, this is a risky enterprise (Moore & Corkum, 1994). These studies do not unambiguously inform us about the nature of the infants' commonsense psychology. Because infants do not communicate through language we cannot ask them directly what they understand about those with whom they interact. An alternative approach is to try to examine the structure of the infants' representations of social events using methods derived from infant perception.

The logic of the visual habituation approach to examining infants' commonsense psychology is consistent with the general logic of the habituation approach to studying infants' perception (see chap. 4). Infants are presented with one stimulus repeatedly until their initially high interest wanes. They are then presented with test stimuli that differ in critical ways from the initial habituation stimulus. Because commonsense psychology involves intentional relations between agents and objects, different representations of such relations can be presented to see how infants respond. In an early study, Woodward (1998) examined how 6- and 9-month-old infants responded to representations of the action of reaching for an object. Infants saw a display with two objects. A hand extended from the side of the display and grasped one of the objects (Fig. 6.5). This action was repeated until the infant habituated. The position of the two objects was then

Fig. 6.5. Illustration of the habituation and test stimuli for the study of infants' understanding of the object directedness of reaching and grasping. Adapted from "Infants Selectively Encode the Goal of an Actor's Reach," by A. Woodward, 1998, *Cognition, 69*, p. 6. Copyright 1998 by Elsevier. Reprinted with permission of the author.

switched and two test events were presented in counterbalanced order. In one test event the hand reached for and grasped the same object as before (old object). In the other test event the hand reached for and grasped the other object (new object). Note that the old-object event involved a reach with rather different spatiotemporal properties even though the same object as before was grasped. The new-object event involved exactly the same reach and grasp as before but now a different object was contacted. So both test events were in some sense different from the habituation event but only the new-object event was different in terms of the intentional relation between the reach, the grasp, and the object grasped. Given that infants generally attend more to novel information as opposed to information to which they have habituated, if they perceive these events in terms of an intentional relation between the action and the object, they should show greater recovery of attention to the new-object event than to the old-object event. Alternatively, if the infant only processed the habituation event in terms of the arm movement, then they should show greater recovery to the old-object event because the form of the movement was rather different. The results showed that infants as young as 6 months of age showed greater recovery to the new-object event thereby indicating that they had processed the earlier event as a reach to a particular object, rather than just as a reach. In terms of the example illustrated in Fig. 6.4, after habituation to the arm reaching for and grasping the ball, the infants showed greater recovery to the test event in which the arm reached for and grasped the teddy bear.

In a subsequent study using this "switch" procedure (Woodward, 1999), performance of 5- and 9-month-old infants was examined for displays in which the human hand reached and grasped an object or extended toward the object and touched it with the back of the hand without grasping. The latter action was used as an example of an act that was human but not purposeful. In this study, infants at both ages again showed evidence of representing the reach and grasp as object directed. However, the infants did not differentiate between the old-object and new-object test trials for the back-of-the-hand touch. Interestingly, if infants are shown during habituation that the back-of-the-hand action can be used in an apparently goal-directed way, for example, to sweep an object from one place to another, then 8- and 10-month-olds but not 6-month-olds appear to represent the action as goal directed (Király, Jovanovic, Prinz, Aschersleben, & Gergely, 2003). Together these results show that by the middle of the first year, infants have a fairly well-differentiated representation of the familiar action of reaching and grasping as object directed. Of course, infants themselves are capable of visually guided reaching by 5 months, so it appears that representing others' reach and grasping as object directed develops at about the same time as infants are capable of producing similar conative acts. A few months later they appear to be able to generalize such object directedness to more unfamiliar actions.

Studies using the switch procedure to investigate infants' representations of epistemic acts such as looking and pointing have found that representing such epistemic acts as object directed comes rather later than for reaching and grasping. Woodward (2003) reported experiments in which infants were shown displays of an actor looking toward one of two toys. After habituation, the position of the toys was switched and the actor gazed at the same toy as in the habituation trials or at the other toy. The results showed that when gaze was the only cue, 12-month-olds but not 7- or 9-months-olds recovered attention more to gaze to the new toy than to gaze to the old toy. This result supports the idea that by 12 months, infants represent gaze as object directed. It is important to note that this positive result occurred despite the fact that infants at all ages in the study followed the actor's gaze during both habituation and test events and spent more time looking at the toy toward which the actor was gazing. So the representation of others' gaze as object directed appears not to coincide developmentally either with infants' own looking behavior (obviously, infants have been looking at things since birth) or with infants' ability to follow the gaze of others.

In an attempt to examine the possible correspondence between infants' production of social acts and their perception of the same acts, Amanda Woodward and Jose Guajardo (2002) used the switch procedure to investigate the representation of pointing in infants of 9 and 12 months of age on the grounds that infants often start to point themselves between these ages. Because infants often do not follow points to objects located some distance away at this age (e.g., Carpenter et al., 1998), the pointing gesture demonstrated was one in which the pointing finger actually contacted the target object. Their results showed that as a group, only the 12-month-olds recovered attention to the new-object events during the test trials. In a follow-up experiment, Woodward and Guajardo showed that for infants between 8 and 11 months, whether the infants were pointing themselves was a strong predictor of their tendency to represent pointing as object directed.

Using similar switch procedures other researchers examined infants' representation of pointing when the gesture did not contact the target object. Claudia Thoermer and Beate Sodian (2001) tested a group of infants at 10 and 12 months of age and found that at neither age did the infants recover more to the new-object event than to the old-object event. Indeed in their study, 12-month-old infants showed greater recovery of looking to the old-object event, in which the form of the pointing gesture changed, even though it was directed at the same toy as in the habituation event. This result suggests that infants at 12 months do not represent pointing gestures that at are some distance from their target objects as object directed, despite the fact that when tested for their ability to follow points, the large majority of the infants participating in the study succeeded by 12 months. Infants understanding of such noncontact points probably develops quickly, however. Using essentially the same procedure as Thoermer and Sodian, Moore (1999b) found that 13-month-olds did represent noncontact points as object directed.

The studies using the habituation procedure reviewed so far presented infants with isolated actions, repeatedly. But psychological acts do not typically occur in isolation—they are part of an ongoing stream of behavior. At about the same time that infants start to understand psychological activity as object directed, they also start to recognize the sequencing of psychological activity. When we as adults observe the behavior of another person, we naturally parse that behavior into combinations of intentional actions. Imagine watching someone in a grocery store. A man may push his cart in one direction, reach and pick up a bunch of bananas, lean to put them in his cart, look at the piece of paper in his other hand, turn his cart, and head off in another direction. Adults all typically agree on the units of intentional action contained within such streams of behavior (Baldwin & Baird, 2001). Thus, we would all recognize that the vignette just outlined contains a series of intentional actions—moving to the bananas, choosing a bunch, checking the shopping list, moving to get the next item. To examine infants' parsing of such streams of behavior, Dare Baldwin and her colleagues (Baldwin, Baird, Saylor, & Clark, 2001) presented 10- to 11-month-old infants with videotaped sequences of everyday intentional actions. For example, in one sequence a woman in a kitchen notices a towel on the floor, reaches to pick it up, moves toward a towel rack, and places the towel on the rack. Although the sequence involved four different intentional components, the movement was continuous throughout the sequence, so that there was no clear break in the action. Infants were habituated to the videotapes and then presented with test videos that included segments of the original sequences. These segments were stopped showing a still frame that either corresponded to the completion of an intentional act (e.g., grasping the towel) or occurred just before or just after the completion of an intentional act (e.g., leaning down toward the towel but not yet grasping it). The former are viewed by adults as showing a completed intentional action whereas the later are viewed as showing an incomplete or interrupted action. Infants showed significantly more recovery of attention to the interrupted-action videos than to the complete-action videos. These results provide evidence that infants parse the stream of behavior into intentional units much like adults.

The work on parsing the stream of behavior shows that by the end of the first year, infants parse action sequences in much the same way as adults, but it does not tell us whether infants understand anything about the connections among actions in these sequences. To illustrate, as adults we know that the actions in the grocery store vignette described earlier are connected because each provides a basis for the next: Satisfying the intention to get the bananas sets up an intention to find the next item on the list, and so on. To examine infants' understanding of the relations among particular intentional acts, other researchers examined whether infants understand that emotional orientations toward an object should engender an appropriate action toward that object. Thus, for example, if we look excited about one of two objects, then we should go on to reach for that object rather than the other one. Ann Phillips and her colleagues (Phillips, Wellman, & Spelke, 2002) presented infants with a display in which an adult looked and smiled toward one of two objects located side by side in front of her. After a brief pause during which the display was screened, the adult was shown holding the toy she had previously smiled at. This sequence was shown repeatedly to the infants until they habituated. They were then shown two test displays. In one, the adult performed a sequence of acts intentionally compatible with the habituation display but now both directed at the second toy. In the other, the adult performed a sequence of acts incompatible with the intentions showed in the habituation display—she looked and smiled at one toy and then held the other toy. Infants of 12 and 14 months, but not 8 months, showed greater recovery of attention to the incompatible display than the compatible display, indicating that they saw the former but not the latter as different from the habituation display. In subsequent research, Sodian and Thoermer (2004) used the same design to show that 12-month-olds also appear to expect that a person who looks and grasps one of two toys will later hold that toy rather than the other one.

Together, the evidence from habituation approaches to the representation of intentional action shows that by about 12 month of age, infants understand that a range of psychological acts are directed at real objects but that this understanding is not an all-or-none achievement. It appears first for manual actions, for example, reaching and grasping, as early as 5 to 6 months of age. By 9 to 10 months it is evident for epistemic actions that involve direct object contact, such as pointing. Finally, by the beginning of the second year, infants represent epistemic and emotional acts as object directed even when the target object is more distally located. Furthermore, they can recognize intentional acts from an ongoing stream of behavior.

CONSTRUCTING AN UNDERSTANDING OF PSYCHOLOGICAL RELATIONS

Both interactive and habituation studies of infants' commonsense psychology indicate that 1-year-olds have solved the first challenge discussed in chapter 2—that psychological acts are relations to objects. So how is the understanding of the object directedness of different psychological acts achieved? The evidence is consistent with the general approach to knowledge building introduced in chapter 3. As infants participate in interactions with others, they start to detect the patterns connecting objects to the actions of self and others that are evident in the structure of these triadic episodes. It is likely that a variety of aspects of experience go into the construction of these representations. First, infants observe both their own and others' purposeful acts in a similar way, for example, as arms reaching for, grasping, and otherwise transforming the arrangements of objects in the world. That adults reach for, grasp, and hold objects is a relatively straightforward combination of actions to observe in the social world and so it is no surprise that it is learned first (Woodward, 1998). Understanding other psychological acts such as gaze and emotion is more problematic because they occur at a distance from their objects. However, relevant patterns are available in experience. In particular, as discussed earlier, actions tend to occur in regular sequences and so actions that do not contact objects directly are often accompanied by actions that do. Take the case of gaze. People tend to gaze towards things they are reaching for and holding, so gaze could become linked to objects by its regular association with actions that directly contact objects (Woodward, 2003).

Observations of our own or others' independent object-directed activity can perhaps go some way toward the construction of an understanding of psychological relations. But notice that the type of information infants would gain from such observation would necessarily be restricted to only one kind: either first- or third-person information. Therefore, simple observation of the object-directed action of either self or others would provide a limited understanding of such action. The experience of interactivity may well be more important for the acquisition of an understanding of object-directed action, which integrates both first- and third-person information. As we have seen, during the second half of the first year, infants participate in object-centered interactions during which they share psychological relations with others toward objects—they share attention and emotions to the same objects, they imitate each others' actions on objects, and they otherwise communicate about objects. It is during these interactive experiences that they regularly experience both the first-person characteristics of their own psychological relations and the third-person characteristics of others' psychological relations in recognizable patterns. For example, as they follow gaze reliably, they become exposed to sequences of experience whereby other people's gaze behavior is linked to objects via the infants' own contingent gaze toward the objects. The regular participation in interactive episodes involving such sequences of actions means that infants can construct representations of these episodes that combine both first-person and third-person information about the actions involved. These representations capture the object-directed nature of psychological activity, but they do it in a way that is not specific either to the self or to other people. The representations characterize the interactions, not the individual actions of either of the interacting participants.

It is important to recognize, however, that the understanding of the object directedness of psychological acts is likely built up in a relatively piecemeal way initially. There are a number of pieces of evidence that point to this interpretation. First, infants' performance in different situations involving object-directed actions is initially not correlated. I mentioned earlier that Virginia Slaughter and Danielle McConnell (2003) found that triadic interactive behaviors, such as gaze following and pointing, initially occurred somewhat independently. Furthermore, when infants between 9 and 12 months are tested on their understanding of the object directedness of both pointing and gaze (Woodward & Wilson-Brune, 2003), there is no correlation. Those infants who appear to understand gaze as object directed are no more likely to understand pointing as object directed than those who do not understand gaze as object directed.

Second, infants' understanding of gaze and pointing in habituation contexts is not related to whether they actually follow gaze or pointing respectively in triadic interactive situations. So, for example, some infants follow gaze but do not appear to understand gaze as object directed (Woodward, 2003). This finding implies that infants are not building a general understanding of these actions that guides their behavior in all circumstances. Rather, the scope of their understanding is initially relatively limited.

Third, infants' understanding of psychological relations in others is inconsistently related to their own engagement in these psychological relations. For example, understanding reaching as object directed develops at about the same age as the ability to perform reliable object-directed reaches. As seen earlier, Amanda Woodward and Jose Guajardo (2002) found that infants who had started to point spontaneously were more likely to understand pointing as object directed. However, the same is not true for gaze or emotions, as infants do not appear to represent these psychological acts as object directed until late in the first year and well after they have been looking at and feeling emotions toward objects for many months. These findings all suggest that infants' early understanding of the object directedness of psychological activity initially develops for particular actions performed either by the self or other.

If infants detect the patterns of first- and third-person information corresponding to different types of psychological relations in an initially case-by-case way, then this means that early psychological representations are not linked up as part of a more general conceptual understanding of people as psychological agents. According to some accounts (e.g., Tomasello, 1999a, 1999b), 9-month-old infants have a general concept of goal-oriented agent that includes both self and other. However, the evidence reviewed here is more consistent with an approach to early intentional understanding that characterizes infants' initial attributions of intentionality in terms of object-directed psychological acts rather than in terms of goal-oriented agents. Two main characteristics differentiate these two theoretical proposals. First, understanding intentional relations at the level of object-directed actions means that intentionality is not yet attributable to individual agents such as self and other. In short, infants do not yet have a commonsense psychology that recognizes individual agents as centers of intentional activity. Second, if intentionality resides in actions rather than agents, then it is not yet true that infants understand goal directedness. Goals are more abstract psychological objects that agents have and toward which those agents can implement a variety of actions. Only as infants start to detect the correspondences among the variety of intentional acts that individual people perform do they move to attributing goal-directed intentions to people independently of the particular acts they perform.

Although infants' understanding is initially action based, this does not prevent them from entering into triadic interactive episodes with other people. Action-based intentional representations can guide action toward successful triadic interaction, including object-centered play, social referencing, and the like. The criterion of success remains the extent to which the pattern of the interaction conforms to the infants' interactive goals, including the sharing of interest in, and feelings about, objects. By monitoring the patterns of correspondence between the first-person information about their own psychological relations to objects and the third-person information about their interactive partners' psychological relations, infants are capable of determining when psychological relations are or are not shared, and they can adjust their own action to achieve such sharing.

It is important to note that the argument outlined in the last few paragraphs is fundamentally consistent with a developmental sequence enabled by the kinds of hierarchical pattern detection processes we have encountered before. Infants first build representations of particular object-directed action such as reaching and grasping as early as 6 months of age. These are actions that they have commonly observed in others but also in themselves as they become adept at visually guided reaching. But these representations are of very limited scope. They likely apply only to actions that directly contact objects (such as grasping) and they are not linked to other actions. Over the next few months, infants start to participate in triadic interactions with others and are thereby exposed to interactive episodes in which their own actions on objects are coordinated with the actions of others on the same objects. It is these interactive episodes that likely allow them to start to construct representations of attentional and emotional actions that they cannot see themselves perform and that do not directly contact objects. Through these interactive experiences that involve gaze following, emotion sharing, and so on, infants are exposed to reliable patterns of correspondence between the first- and third-person forms of information pertaining to attentional and emotional actions. As a result, they are able to build more sophisticated representations of intentional actions—representations that combine first- and third-person forms of information. By the end of the first year, infants represent a range of actions, including manual actions that contact objects as well as attentional and emotional actions, as object directed. It is at this stage that we can say that infants' representations involve object-directed actions. But pattern detection continues unabated. Armed with these action representations, infants are then able to pay attention to the patterns that occur among them. Within interactive episodes, various actions are naturally sequenced, for example, gaze is followed by an emotional expression, which is followed by a reach. The detection and representation of these sequences is what constitutes the more abstract commonsense psychology representations of goal-directed agents. As we shall see in chapter 7, this work is completed during the second year.

SUMMARY

In this chapter, we have seen how infants' growing interest in objects becomes incorporated into their interactions with others to yield interactions in which both infant and partner are focused on the same object. Interactions are now about something, and both participants coordinate their interactive behavior with respect to the object that is their shared focus. Although intuition may lead us to think otherwise, we have seen that infants do not need a full-blown commonsense psychology to show triadic interactive behaviors. They attend to and learn the patterns of information, including both first-person information of their own psychological activity and third-person information of the activity of other, that correspond to coordinated interactions. They learn to use a variety of actions to maintain and enhance these interactions.

However, although infants do not need a commonsense psychology to participate in triadic interactions, these interactions are of profound importance to the subsequent development of commonsense psychology. Through repeated interaction with others over objects, infants become experienced in coordinating their own intentional activity with that of others. In the process they detect the reciprocal patterns between their own and others' actions that occur in these interactions. They learn the contingent relations that specify how others' actions depend in part on their previous actions and they learn how to act in relation to objects in response to others' action. Detecting and recognizing these patterns involves constructing knowledge of how others' action is related to real objects and how the first-person information provided by the infants' own intentional activity is coordinated with the third-person information provided through the observation of their interactive partner's intentional activity. As infants gain more experience with both their own and others' object-directed actions, they construct representations of the object directedness or intentionality of these actions. In these representations, the intentionality is initially tied to the particular actions rather than being a property of individual agents. Nevertheless, these representations serve as guides for the achievement of coordinated object-centered interactions between infants and their interactive partners.

In this chapter, we have seen how infants rise to meet the challenge of developing a commonsense psychology that I have referred to as object directedness. Their growing understanding of self and others does not yet recognize, however, the equivalence of self and other. Although both first- and third-person information enter into the initial representations of ob-

ject-directed activity, these representations are not yet applicable separately and independently to either the self or to others. In effect, even if
infants can follow or direct their mother's attention to a ball, they do not
yet think, "I see the ball" or "Mom sees the ball." Rather, infants' understanding is more akin to recognizing the difference between "We see the
ball" (if attention is shared) or "We don't see the ball" (if attention is not
shared). At this point, psychological relations are still a property of interactions, not yet of people.

7

Social Behavior and Commonsense Psychology in the Second Year of Life: Self–Other Equivalence and Psychological Diversity

During the second year of life infants become transformed into children. There are many profound ways in which this happens. Developments in motor control allow characteristically human forms of movement. For example, infants take their first steps at about 12 months, and are able to run and jump by the time the next year has passed. The development of a flexibly opposable thumb means that objects can be manipulated more efficiently and a variety of tools used more productively. Another distinguishing feature of human beings—language—also sees its florescence during the second year as children start to use words and then sentences to communicate with others around them. In parallel with early language development, toddlers enter the imaginative world of pretend play (McCune, 1995). Finally, and of most interest for us in this chapter, there are significant social and emotional changes occurring in the second year. Having described the changes in social behavior and the corresponding developments in commonsense psychology, we will turn in chapter 8 to language and the imagination.

In chapter 6, we reviewed evidence that infants have solved the challenge of understanding the object directedness of many psychological relations by about 12 months. What, then, of the challenges of understanding self–other equivalence and diversity of relations? It is in the second year of life that infants rise to meet these challenges. We shall see that they are intricately intertwined in the social cognitive development of toddlers. It is often thought that children develop a distinction between self and other during the second year. In fact, this is only one part of the story, because young infants can already distinguish self and others in the sense of discriminating information derived from self and others. What toddlers acquire in the second year of life is the understanding that self and other people are the same kind of thing—psychological agents—and yet are distinct and can have different psychological relations to objects in the world.

SELF–OTHER EQUIVALENCE AND DIVERSITY
IN PSYCHOLOGICAL RELATIONS

As seen chapter 2, understanding self–other equivalence in the context of psychological relations means having a concept of a psychological agent that encompasses both self and other. Psychological agents act in relation to goals and have perceptual and emotional experience in relation to objects and states of affairs in the world. A psychological agent, then, is an entity that has both an objective identity (or that exists as an independent entity in a world of objects) and subjective experience, including intentions, perceptions, and feelings. Our adult conception of psychological agents, particularly in the West, tends to be an individualistic one whereby agents are recognized to have an identity separate from others and to be individual centers of intention and experience in relation to the world.

There are two complementary sides to gaining an understanding of self–other equivalence. First, infants must become aware of themselves as objective agents. This means they are aware that when they are experiencing the first-person or subjective side of a psychological relation, they are also aware of themselves from a third-person point of view, as the agent of that experience. Because little of themselves as an objective agent is given in direct perceptual experience, infants must be able to imagine themselves, as it were, from the outside, acting in the world. Thus, when they turn and see an object, they are aware that they are also moving the head and eyes in the direction of the object, and when they act on a desire for an object within reach, they are also extending the arm and grasping the object. Perhaps more importantly, becoming aware of self as an objective agent involves recognizing the self's identity, just as infants can recognize other individuals by their appearance. Second, infants must be able to recognize that when they observe another person acting in relation to an object, that person also has first-person experience like their own. In other words, for example, the observation of someone smiling, reaching, and grasping an object corresponds to the first-person information of wanting the object. Similarly, the observation of someone turning and looking at an object corresponds to the first-person information of seeing the object. In summary, infants have to understand that they present third-person information like others do and that others experience first-person information like they do. In this way both self and other are understood in terms of integrated first- and third-person perspectives (Barresi & Moore, 1996).

Understanding self–other equivalence is tied up intricately with the idea of diversity of psychological relations. This is (partly) because the clearest way to show that children understand themselves as an objective entity is to show that they recognize themselves as distinct from others. Similarly, the only way to show that children understand others as subjective experiencers is to show that they recognize that others' experience is different from their own. So in this chapter we will review evidence on both aspects of commonsense psychology—self–other equivalence and relational diversity—in parallel.

THE OBJECTIVE SELF

For almost as long as psychology has been a science, it has been recognized that a distinction may be made between first-person and third-person perspectives on the self. William James (1890/1950) distinguished the *I* from the *Me* and more recent authors have adopted a similar distinction (e.g., Lewis & Brooks-Gunn, 1979; Neisser, 1988). The *I* represents the self that acts and has subjective experiences, whereas the *Me* represents the self that can be thought about objectively. For these authors, even infants in the first year can be said to have an *I*, but a *Me* is considered not to be present until sometime during the second year.

So what kinds of evidence can we draw on to identify the presence of the *Me* or objective self? We saw in chapter 3 that even 3-month-old infants are able to detect first-person information arising from their own activity, such as proprioceptive information (e.g., Bahrick & Watson, 1985). In fact, such young infants can also recognize their own faces. Three-month-old infants who are shown prerecorded videos of both themselves and another same-aged infant in a preference paradigm spend more time looking at the other infant than they do at themselves (Bahrick, Moss, & Fadil, 1996). It is likely that regular exposure to mirrors in the first few months of life allows infants to acquire enough experience with their own faces that this stimulus is already familiar within a few months of birth. As a result, infants prefer to look at the relative novelty provided by the face of another child. However, recognizing the facial image of the self as familiar is not the same thing as recognizing that image as the self. The latter form of recognition entails having an objective self that is understood to have third-person properties like others but that is also individual and unique.

One approach to demonstrating when children recognize the self as the self is to show children pictures of themselves and other children and ask,

"Who is that?" When this is done, children as young as 15 months sometimes respond with their names to the picture of self only (e.g., Lewis & Brooks-Gunn, 1979). Use of the personal pronoun *me* typically comes later, but is usually present by the end of the second year (Lewis & Ramsay, 2004). However, whereas this method might appear to demonstrate the development of self-recognition, there are good reasons to harbor reservations. On the one hand, of course, it is a verbal method and as such not useful for children much younger than about 18 months, because it might lead to an underestimate of younger children's recognition of self. On the other hand, it is possible that children are able to use their name to label the picture of self in the same way that they can label any person or object they recognize—simply through having learned an association between the name and the referent. Although such an explanation may not apply to the use of the personal pronoun, which changes its referent depending on who says it, it could well apply to the earliest self-reference using the proper name.

Given these kinds of issues, the preferred method for demonstrating self-recognition in young children is to observe the child's behavior in front of a mirror in particular when the child's face has been secretly marked using makeup or a sticker. This approach was first developed as a nonverbal method to study self-recognition in chimpanzees by Gordon Gallup (e.g., 1970). Gallup anesthetized the chimps and applied red dye to different parts of their bodies. When the animals awoke, they were placed in front of a mirror. Gallup reported that under these conditions, chimpanzees explored the red marks and in particular used the mirror to explore marks on their faces. The procedure was first adapted for use with young children by Beulah Amsterdam (1972), who used rouge to mark the cheeks of children from 3 to 24 months of age and then recorded their behavior in front of a mirror. Amsterdam reported that late in the first year and early in the second, children's most common response was to show a combination of social behavior to the mirror image, searching for the image in or behind the mirror, and observing the effects of their own movement in the mirror. Only after 18 months did children start to show evidence of recognizing the image as the self by touching the mark on their own faces.

This basic finding has now been replicated many times (e.g., Bertenthal & Fischer, 1978; Johnson, 1982; Lewis & Brooks-Gunn, 1979; Nielsen, Dissanayake, & Kashima, 2003; see Fig. 7.1), but although the developmental pattern of behavior is quite generally agreed on, there is still debate over what the behavior means. Some have argued that mirror self-recognition reveals little more than the learning of the reflective properties of mirrors and the use of mirrors to explore the body (e.g., Loveland, 1986, 1992). However, most authors agree that mirror self-recognition does tell us something interesting about the development of the objective self. Two main interpretations of how changes in self-understanding enable mirror self-recognition have been proposed (Mitchell, 1997). The first is that mir-

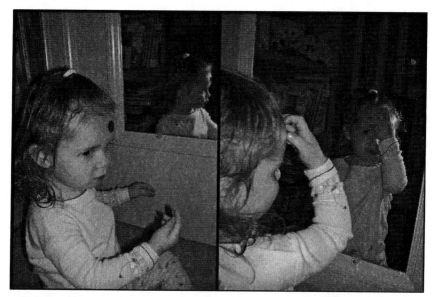

FIG. 7.1. Photo showing mirror self-recognition (courtesy Lisa Dale).

ror self-recognition evidences the child's self-concept. An important component of this self-concept is facial appearance. As seen earlier, younger infants can recognize their facial appearance. What is different about mirror self-recognition is that the facial appearance observed in the mirror is understood by children to be the same as the facial appearance that is part of the children's mental image of themselves. As a result, when children see the mark on the face in the mirror, they immediately know that the mark is on their own face. Therefore mirror self-recognition shows that children can imagine themselves from an objective point of view—as *me*.

The second interpretation is that mirror self-recognition depends not on matching a visual percept in the mirror with a remembered visual image, but on children's ability to match the visual information provided by the mirror and the proprioceptive information provided by the children's movements while in front of the mirror. This matching is not simply a detection of the contingency between the visual and proprioceptive information, which, as seen in chapter 3, even very young infants can do, but rather it is an understanding that the two forms of information are equivalent (Mitchell, 1997; Povinelli, 1995). Given this equivalence, children determine that what is true of the image in the mirror is also true of the self and therefore that the mark exists on their own face.

Although these two interpretations differ in terms of emphasizing visual appearance alone versus contingency relations between vision and proprioception, they share a key feature. In both cases what is fundamental is that 18-month-olds are able to recognize the identity relation between what is seen in the mirror and a mental image of the self. Therefore both interpretations are consistent with the idea that children develop an objective self.

Most research on the objective self has focused on awareness of identity. An alternative approach is to examine children's understanding of self as a physical object. Following an observation made by Jean Piaget (1953) that his daughter Jacqueline was unable to give a blanket on which she was sitting to another person at 18 months but did so a month later, Geppert and Küster (1983) and Bullock and Lütkenhaus (1990) sat toddlers on a small blanket and then asked the children either simply to give the blanket to the experimenter or to retrieve an attractive object hidden underneath the blanket. Most children were able to pass this task by 18 months, although it was uncertain to what extent their success was the result of learning from similar situations that may have occurred regularly in natural circumstances. In a recent study, we (Moore, Mealiea, Garon, & Povinelli, 2005) extended this idea to a new task involving a novel situation in which the children needed to reflect on the self as an object in order to pass the task. We encouraged children to push a toy shopping cart to their mothers who were seated about 2 m away. The shopping cart had been modified by attaching to the back axle a small rug that extended for about 50 cm behind the cart. The placement of the rug was such that if the children attempted to push the cart from behind they would have to step on the rug and their weight would then impede their ability to move the cart. Children of 15 and 21 months were tested on this task and the results showed that the older toddlers quickly realized that they had to get off the rug in order to move the cart forward. In contrast, the younger toddlers continued to try to push the cart as they stood on the rug without success. It seems, then, that being able to think about the self as an object with the physical property of weight develops around the middle of the second year.

This ability to think about the self as an object coincides developmentally with the onset of mirror self-recognition. Indeed, in another study with 18-month-olds, it was shown that children's performance on the shopping cart task was correlated with their performance on the mirror self-recognition task (Moore et al., 2005). This result confirms that children develop a relatively general ability to think of the self from an objective or third-person point of view about halfway through the second year.

A final manifestation of the objective self worth mentioning occurs in the emotional domain. As we have seen, certain emotions are evident in infants' behavior early in the first year, including happiness, sadness, fear, and anger. These emotions are sometimes called basic or primary emotions because they can be experienced directly in relation to objects or events. For example, fear is expressed by infants in relation to strangers from the middle of the first year. In contrast, other emotions depend on the children's awareness of others' attitudes toward them. For example, to experience pride or embarrassment children must be aware of themselves as the object of another person's or persons' attention. Such emotions are therefore sometimes referred to as the social or self-conscious emotions (e.g., Lewis, Sullivan, Stanger, & Weiss, 1989).

Studies examining the development of the social emotions have demonstrated that they appear most obviously during the second year, coincident with other measures of the objective self. Michael Lewis and his colleagues (1989) assessed children at 22 months on mirror self-recognition as well as different situations designed to elicit emotion. In one situation, a stranger approached the child and in another the child was asked to dance for the parent and experimenter. Videotapes of the children's behavior in these two situations were coded for both fear or wariness and embarrassment. The results showed that whereas the expression of fear did not depend on self-recognition status, children who showed mirror self-recognition were much more likely to exhibit embarrassment in the dance situation than children who did not show mirror self-recognition. This finding confirms that emotions, such as embarrassment, that are elicited by being the focus of another's attention develop at about the same time as the ability to think of the self from an objective point of view.

In summary, a number of lines of research converge in showing that the understanding of the self as an objective entity that has a particular appearance and that can be the focus of others' attention emerges around the middle of the second year. This understanding means that at around 18 months, children have integrated their directly perceived first-person experience of their activity with information about themselves from a third-person perspective. This third-person information is not directly perceived but rather has to be imagined.

THE SUBJECTIVITY OF OTHERS

In parallel with developing an understanding of the self as an individual with an objective identity, children acquire an understanding of others as individual agents with first-person perspectives. This change is seen in a variety of circumstances in which children are able to attribute to other people psychological relations that are different from their own. There is evidence for understanding diversity of the full range of types of psychological relations, including epistemic, emotional, and conative kinds, and we shall look at examples of each.

By the end of the first year infants are able to use another person's gaze and point to locate interesting sights, and they are able to direct another person's gaze to something that they are interested in. They can both follow and direct attention to spaces within an increasingly differentiated three-dimensional world that includes locations out of immediate view, such as behind barriers and in closed containers (e.g., Moll & Tomasello,

2004). All of these cases involve infants coordinating their own visual perspective with that of the interactive partner. Thus, for example, pointing implies that infants are trying to share their experience of an interesting sight with their interactive partner. Where infants have problems is in showing something interesting to another person if to do so would thereby remove the interesting sight from their own visual experience. Lempers, Flavell, and Flavell (1977) asked children from 12 to 36 months to show a picture on a card to an adult seated opposite at a table. They found that by 18 months most participants showed the picture but only flat on the table so that they could see it at the same time. This reveals that these young children needed to maintain their own visual connection to the object in order to show it to another person, and that they did not recognize the other person's visual relation to be independent of their own. By 24 months, the majority of participants were content to turn the picture around vertically so that they were deprived of the sight of the picture even as they showed it to the other, thereby indicating that they did now realize that the other person would see the object even when they themselves did not. In another task, a hollow wooden cube with a picture affixed to one of the inside faces was used. The picture was only visible by looking into the cube through the open face opposite the picture. The children were shown the picture in the cube and then asked to show the picture to the other person sitting opposite them. Over the second year, children became more likely to orient the cube appropriately so that the other person could see inside. Indeed, by 24 months all of the children did so. At 18 months about half of the children oriented the cube appropriately. Most of the rest showed an interesting tendency to locate the cube with the open end up between the self and the adult and tilt it back and forth so that both could see into it, indicating that they needed to maintain their first-person view of the picture as they attempted to show it to the other.

Not only do children develop an ability to distinguish their own and others' visual perspectives during the second year, they also start to appreciate what may be novel and interesting to others. Following up on a procedure introduced by Michael Tomasello and Katerina Haberl (2003), Amy MacPherson and I (2004) arranged for 12- and 18-month-olds to play with an experimenter while a series of toys were introduced into the play session. For two of the toys the experimenter left the play table and sat at a different table while she talked on the phone. In one of these cases, the child played with the toy without the adult and in the other case the adult played with the toy without the child. After all the toys had been introduced, they were all presented on a tray to the child. At this point the experimenter looked at the child and held out her hand as she said in an animated voice, "Oh wow! Look at that! Can you give it to me?" The large majority of children in the 12-month-old group gave the toy that they had not yet played with, whereas 18-month-olds were more likely to give the toy that the experimenter had not yet played with. This result indicates that by the middle of the second year, children are starting to recognize what is new to another person even if it is not new to themselves.

Understanding diversity in emotions also shows clear advances in the second year. Throughout the first year, infants respond to others' emotional expressions, both vocal and facial. They engage in emotionally arousing interactions with familiar people and they can use emotional expressions to guide their action toward novel objects or situations. However, the other's emotional orientation is not yet clearly distinguished from the child's own. One important manifestation of this change is seen in the development of empathic behavior (Hoffman, 1975; Thompson, 1998; Zahn-Waxler & Radke-Yarrow, 1990). Even young infants show a natural sensitivity to the expression of negative emotion such as distress by someone else. For example, in newborn babies, the sound of one baby crying often leads another baby within earshot to start crying. In addition, before long infants who observe facial expressions of distress in another person show facial signs of upset. The result of this sensitivity is that the children experience some degree of distress from a first-person perspective when they are exposed to third-person signs of distress in others. During the first year such contagion of distress leads infants to seek comfort for themselves, typically by going to their mothers if available. As the second year passes, the children become less likely to get upset themselves and more likely to show some action directed at alleviating the other's distress, either by directly comforting the other or by recruiting their mother's assistance. This pattern is revealed in experimental contexts where children play with an experimental confederate in a lab setting. In the course of the play session, the play partner feigns distress, either from injury or breaking a toy, and starts to cry. Older 1-year-olds tend to show concern and often attempt to intervene, whereas younger children become upset themselves and retreat to the comfort of their own mothers (e.g., Zahn-Waxler, Radke-Yarrow, Wagner, & Chapman, 1992). This behavioral pattern reveals that older toddlers are able to empathize with the observed distress but at the same time recognize that the expression by the other means that it is the other person that is upset and needs comfort.

A more explicit experimental demonstration of young children's understanding of diversity in emotions was provided by Repacholi and Gopnik (1997). They showed children of 14 and 18 months of age a bowl each of crackers and broccoli. They first asked the children which food they liked and not surprisingly all the children chose the crackers. Once the children had made their choice, another adult tried both foods in turn and very expressively reacted with pleasure to the broccoli and disgust to the crackers. Finally, the children were given the chance to give one of the foods to the same adult. The 18-month-olds gave the adult the broccoli for which she had previously expressed a liking even though they preferred the crackers. In contrast, the 14-month-olds gave the adult the crackers–the food that they themselves liked. These results are also consistent in showing that it is at about 18 months that children recognize that others have psychological orientations to objects that may differ from their own.

Turning to conative psychological relations, developments in imitation and cooperative behavior during the second year provide the best insight into children's growing awareness of others' goals as independent of their own. We have seen that, by the middle of the first year, infants already recognize that simple actions such as reaching and grasping are not just random arm movements but are directed at particular objects. Soon, imitation of actions on objects becomes an important means by which infants learn new ways of achieving desired ends. By 9 months infants imitate novel actions that produce interesting effects on objects (Meltzoff, 1988; Piaget, 1962). The purpose of these early imitative acts is to reproduce the witnessed effect achieved by the observed action, but the effect is still tied to the action used to achieve it so the whole action is reproduced. In chapter 6, I suggested that initially infants understand human actions in terms of object-directed actions rather than goal-directed agents. As infants gain more familiarity with actions on objects, they start to anticipate the effects that actions will have, and by early in the second year, it is the anticipated effects rather than the observed effects that guide the infants' imitative action. At this point, actions have been separated from the effects they are directed toward. Now we can speak of infants imitating goal-directed intentions because actions are imitated even if the anticipated effect does not actually occur.

Research by Meltzoff (1995) illustrates the distinction between imitating actions on objects and imitating goal-directed intentions (although, see Huang, Heyes, & Charman, 2002). Meltzoff (1995) presented 18-month-olds with various objects that could be manipulated in different ways. One was a small dumbbell with removable blocks on the ends. In advance of letting one group of children manipulate the objects, the experimenter demonstrated actions that appeared to be designed toward some goal but failed. For example, the experimenter grasped the block on one end of the dumbbell and pulled but only succeeded in slipping his fingers off the end. Comparison groups of children either saw successful actions (the experimenter succeeded in pulling the block off the dumbbell) or irrelevant actions (the experimenter manipulated the dumbbell without trying to pull the block off). The children were then given the opportunity to manipulate the objects. The children who had observed the adult successfully pull the block off the dumbbell tended to do likewise when given the opportunity, but, interestingly, the children who had seen the adult try and fail to remove the block were just as likely to pull the block of the dumbbell. This finding shows that these children were imitating the adult's action based on their reading of the adult's intention, not on the actual events. In contrast, the pulling action was rarely produced by children who had observed the adult do something else with the object. Follow-up work has shown that 15-month-olds behave much like 18-month-olds in this task (Meltzoff, 2002). In contrast, 12-month-olds imitate successful actions but not unsuccessful intentions (Bellagamba & Tomasello, 1999).

Although this result is good evidence for the imitation of goal-directed intentions rather than just actions on objects, it is not quite yet evidence for recognizing the diversity of intentions of independent psychological agents. In effect, children are able to recognize and use the other's action directed at a goal to set up their own goal and then act toward it. This is similar to being able to use another person's looking behavior toward an unseen object to guide their own search for the object. Children do not have to understand that both participants are engaging in action toward their own independent goals. Nevertheless understanding others' goal-directed action is an important step—with it, children have the potential for differentiating the goals of self and other.

Infants of the same age can also detect when someone is imitating them. Meltzoff (1990) had 14-month-olds interact with two adults across a table. Similar objects were available to each person. One of the adults always copied what the infant did, whereas the other adult also responded contingently but performed another action (typically modeled after infant behavior in a different test session). The children paid more attention to the imitating adult than the nonimitating one and also engaged in testing behavior where they performed different actions and then looked to the imitating adult to check on her response. This result shows that 14-month-old infants can recognize the correspondence between their own action and that of an imitating interactive partner.

Alone, neither of these two manifestations of imitation—imitating goals and the recognition of being imitated—demonstrates the recognition that both self and other are independent psychological agents or the possible diversity of the intentions of self and other. However, when both manifestations occur together, then children will have demonstrated that they can simultaneously take a third-person point of view on self and a first-person point of view on others. This is exactly what happens in the latter half of the second year with the elaboration of an interactive form of imitation in which children coordinate their imitative behavior with others. This manifestation of imitation, sometimes called *synchronic* imitation, blossoms during the second half of the first year and becomes the most significant form of peer play at this time (e.g., Asendorpf & Baudonnière, 1993). When placed in a play context with peers, even unfamiliar peers, toddlers often start to copy each others' actions without any prompting. They continuously monitor the actions of the other and start and stop different activities in close synchrony. In this way, extended sequences of imitative play can occur with participants aware of the other's activity and how it corresponds to their own. Synchronic imitation, therefore, reveals that toddlers recognize the equivalence between their own and others' intentional actions during play as they adjust their behavior to correspond to their play partner's behavior.

In imitation, one person observes and adopts the actions of another. Many interactive situations, however, require the participants to take up separate and complementary roles in relation to joint goals. In this regard, it is interesting that whether children from the middle of the second year can start to take complementary roles when achieving a goal depends on coordinated cooperative action. Brownell and Carriger (1990) tested children from 12 to 30 months in age-matched pairs on various cooperation tasks that required one child to operate a handle or lever that would release a toy from an apparatus for another child to retrieve. The working of the apparatus was initially demonstrated to each pair of children. The authors reported that the greatest improvement in performance on these tasks occurred between 18 and 24 months. By 24 months the children were able to adopt complimentary roles in solving these cooperation problems.

The findings we have reviewed from a wide range of studies on toddlers' responding to others' psychological relations yield a consistent story. From late in the first year and into the second, infants are able to coordinate their own action with the object-directed action and then goal-directed intentions of others. By the middle of the second year, they show an ability to respond to another person's psychological relation even if it contrasts with their own. They can show something to another person even when they cannot see it or are relatively uninterested in it. They can respond appropriately to another's emotional state even if it contrasts with their own. They can recognize the goal-directed nature of another person's action even if their own action is different. Together these findings reveal that during the second year, toddlers can be said to understand the subjectivity of others independently of themselves.

THE COGNITIVE BASIS OF COMMONSENSE PSYCHOLOGY IN THE SECOND YEAR

We have reviewed a number of phenomena from the second year relating to the understanding of the objectivity of self and of the subjectivity of others. Jointly these phenomena evidence children's developing understanding of the self and of others as agents with independent psychological relations. Further support for the notion that developments in understanding self and others are related comes from correlational studies that reveal a developmental correspondence among these different forms of social behavior. The logic of these studies is to examine the different developments of interest in the same children. For example, although we have seen that on average children begin to show both mirror self-recognition and empathic responses to other people's distress at about 18 months, it is important to emphasize that this is the average age of these developments. Some children show mirror self-recognition earlier than 18 months and some later. Similarly, some children show empathy earlier than 18 months and some later. Because of this developmental variation, we can ask whether the children who show self-recognition earlier than average also show empathy earlier than average, and whether the children who show self-recognition relatively late also show empathy relatively late. If there is a good correspondence in the age at which individual children progress in different skills, then a reasonable inference is that the skills are related.

A number of authors have suggested that self-recognition and empathy both reflect a more general understanding of people as individual agents and have tested this suggestion by investigating these two types of social skills in the same children. For example, Doris Bischof-Köhler (1991) gave a group of 16- to 24-month-olds the mirror self-recognition test by observing their reaction in front of a mirror after they had been surreptitiously marked on the cheek with blue makeup. The children were also involved in a play session with a familiar female adult and her teddy bear. During the play session, the adult accidentally broke her teddy bear's arm at which point she dropped the bear between the child and herself and started to sob. Bischof-Köler found that children who helped or comforted the adult all showed evidence of self-recognition in the mirror test. In contrast, those who did not show self-recognition in front of the mirror appeared indifferent or perplexed in the empathy situation. These results and those from similar studies (e.g., D. Johnson, 1982; Zahn-Waxler et al., 1992) show that the sensitivity to others' emotional states evidenced in empathy situations is developmentally linked to the ability to view oneself as an objective agent.

Jens Asendorpf and colleagues (Asendorpf & Baudonnière, 1993; Asendorpf, Warkentin, & Baudonniüre, 1996) suspected that, despite not having anything obviously in common, synchronic imitation depended on the same type of social understanding as mirror self-recognition and they used a similar kind of correlational approach to test this idea. Asendorpf and Baudonnière first assessed a sample of 19-month-olds on mirror self-recognition and then paired the toddlers up with an unfamiliar peer who was either at the same level or a different level of self-recognition. These dyads were provided with pairs of toys and then allowed to play together. The authors found that pairs of self-recognizers engaged in more extended bouts of mutual imitation than either recognizer-nonrecognizer pairs or nonrecognizer pairs. This finding shows that children who are capable of self-recognition tend to spontaneously imitate their peers and that therefore the two abilities develop together.

A common interpretation of these correlations in the developments in social understanding seen at about 18 months is that these developments all depend on general changes in representational ability (Asendorpf, 2002; Asendorpf & Baudonnière, 1993; Bischof-Köhler, 1991; Perner, 1991b; Suddendorf & Whiten, 2001). As seen chapter 3, the second year of life witnesses a significant change in representation whereby children become capable of holding in imagination one representation of an object or event while simultaneously engaged perceptually with the world. As a result, children are able not only to respond to perceptually available information, but also to consider that information in relation to some other information held in imagination. As a result these two elements of information—imagined and perceived—can be combined into a more complex representation. The most clear-cut manifestations of this significant advance in representational ability are the symbolic skills of pretense and language, which we will review in chapter 8. However, the various aspects of social understanding reviewed in this chapter also appear to depend on this advance. For example, in order to show self-recognition, children have to pay attention to the perceptually available image in the mirror and compare it to an image of the self, brought to mind from memory. Similarly, in order to respond empathically to another person in distress, children must be able to consider the other's expression of distress and consider the expression as an outward manifestation of subjective feelings remembered from earlier episodes of experienced distress.

The combination of perceived and imagined social information yields representations of people's psychological acts that include both first-person and third-person information. In making sense of either others or the self, children must be able to compare both directly perceived information and imagined information (see Table 7.1). It is typically the case that to understand others, children perceive the third-person information available from their action and imagine the first-person information corresponding to that action. In contrast, to understand the self, children perceive the current first-person characteristics of their psychological state and must imagine the corresponding third-person characteristics of that state. On this view, it is therefore no simple coincidence that understanding the objective identity of self independently of others and understanding the subjectivity

TABLE 7.1

Information Components Involved in Concepts of Self and Other As Independent Psychological Agents

	Perception Supplies	*Imagination Supplies*
Self	First-person information	Third-person information
Others	Third-person information	First-person information

of others independently of the self develop together. Both forms of understanding depend on having an integrated concept of psychological agents for which first- and third-person forms of information are combined. Because only one component is available in immediate perception—first-person for self and third-person for other—the integrated concept requires the imagination to provide the other component. Thus, as children experience from a first-person point of view the information pertaining to their own currently experienced psychological relation, they are able simultaneously to imagine that psychological relation from a third-person point of view. Similarly, when children observe from a third-person perspective another person exhibit a particular psychological relation, they are able simultaneously to imagine that psychological relation from a first-person point of view. By understanding the psychological relations of both self and others as involving both first- and third-person points of view, children achieve a uniform concept of psychological agency and have solved the challenge of self–other equivalence.

THE IMPLICATIONS OF COMMONSENSE PSYCHOLOGY IN THE SECOND YEAR

To many readers, this analysis of commonsense psychology in the second year may seem rather abstract. However, the implications are very concrete, as any parent will attest. With a firm grasp of the self as an individual agent and of the diversity of psychological orientations to objects and events, toddlers charge into the third year with a new sense of independence and purpose. They begin to assert themselves with a will heretofore unheralded. Much of infants' social activity is motivated by sharing experience with others—the mutual enjoyment evident in dyadic interactions, the bonding with the mother characteristic of attachment, and the joint orientations to objects of the triadic interaction phase. But as children approach and pass 2 years of age, their social interactions, at least with parents, may take on much more of an oppositional tenor, and the period of the so-called terrible twos is born. The 2-year-old regularly insists on doing things "by myself." *No* and *mine* become popular words. Inevitably this newfound independence can lead to conflict with others because children's recognition of their independence is not yet matched by an awareness of their still rather comprehensive dependence on others. For parents this can be a challenging time as they seek to allow their children to grow psychologically without harming themselves or others. It is particularly challenging because the emotional intensity of the children's expressions of independence is not yet tempered by well-developed emotional regulation abilities. For the children, anger is a common emotion as a result of being regularly frustrated from exerting their independence and this anger can sometimes spiral out of control. Parents need to be able to set reasonable limits on their children's independence, and maintain these limits within a context of caring, even as the children severely test their goodwill. Anger needs to be acknowledged rather than suppressed so that children can start to become aware of that anger and bring it under self-control. In the long run, the payoffs will be great. With exposure to consistent and regular patterns of interaction, children will continue to build a model of social interactions in which self and other respond sensitively and appropriately to the actions of the other.

Although this phase of social development is often woven with conflict it is also a time of immense new opportunity for both children and parents. Very generally it allows children to enter into a new phase of social interaction in which they can interact with others on a more equal footing. Parents also enjoy this change as they can start to involve their children in richer interactions over a broader array of topics, including ones that are products of the imagination and memory. As I have indicated, many of these interactions that occur after infancy take place through the medium of language, and it is to that topic that we now turn in chapter 8.

SUMMARY

In this chapter we have reviewed a variety of developments in understanding self and others occurring during the second year. Around 18 months, toddlers show mirror self-recognition and other signs that they can represent the self as an objective entity with a particular identity that is distinct from others. They also show empathic awareness of others' emotional states and sensitivity to the independent perceptions and goals of others. That these various manifestations of commonsense psychology develop closely together suggests strongly that more general developments in information processing are somehow involved. I proposed that the ability to mentally represent one thing while attending perceptually to another is the key change at this age. Toddlers are now able to represent their own activity from an imagined third-person point of view and others' activity from an imagined first-person point of view. Together, this means that children have for the first time an equivalent way of representing self and other. By the time they make the transition from infancy to early childhood, then, children have met the challenge of self–other equivalence. They understand that both self and others are independent psychological agents who have both an objective identity and subjective orientations to objects and events that occur in the world.

During this period, children also start to meet the challenge of representing diversity of psychological relations. They begin to understand that another person may see, feel, or want differently from them. So, for the first time, they are able to engage in perspective taking. Of course, perspective taking occurs at many levels of complexity and these young children are not yet at the stage where they can represent divergent opinions on abstract concepts. Nevertheless, where real objects or events in the world are involved, 2-year-olds do recognize that others may see a different object from the one they are looking at, or may like something that they dislike, or may have a different goal from the one they hold. Even if they are not always willing to tolerate this diversity of perspective in the pursuit of their own goals, they do at least know it exists.

By the age of 2 years, having met the challenges of object directedness and self–other equivalence, and having made inroads into understanding psychological diversity, children have made significant progress in their commonsense psychology. This progress has been achieved by regularly engaging with others in interactions involving real-world objects and events. But they have not yet tackled head on the world of the imagination. Further progress in commonsense psychology, in particular, the understanding of psychological relations to representational or perspectival objects and the understanding of psychological continuity, cannot be made without engaging with others in relation to imagined objects. And for this children need a medium within which interactions involving such objects can occur. That medium is language.

8

Language: Gateway to Childhood

Despite the remarkable achievements in commonsense psychology that we reviewed in chapter 7, there is no question that the most significant developmental advance in the second year of life is the acquisition of language. For most children, it is during the second year that they become adept and sophisticated users of language, and it is language that does the lion's share of the work in transforming the baby into the child. With language, the scope of social engagement expands enormously. Children first learn to use words to refer to objects and then events that are around them. Before long, they are able to share interactions with others about topics that are no longer tied to the concrete objects in their immediate environments. They are able to communicate about absent objects, about the past and the future, and about imaginary things. They are able to communicate about themselves and their beliefs, desires, and feelings. With language children are prepared to take up their role as a fully functioning member of the symbolic species (Deacon, 1997).

Language occurs as the representational developments of late infancy and the social interactional motivations manifested in dyadic and triadic interactions come together. During the second year, the representations that are made possible by the development of the imagination are put to use in the object-centered social interactional contexts established by the end of the first year. Any account of the development of language needs to recognize these two fundamental aspects of language—that it represents and that it is a form of social interaction.

That language is a form of representation is quite obvious to us as adults. We talk quite naturally about the meaning of the words and sentences we use—what these words and sentences stand for. In large part, words stand for concrete and abstract entities, attributes of these entities, events, and so forth. Sentences stand for more complex relations among entities, their attributes, and the events in which they participate. In order

136

to produce and understand language, children must be able to pay attention to the words as well as to imagine the things to which the words refer. Using language therefore requires the kind of cognitive ability that develops during the second year of life. Children must be able to hold in mind a mental representation of the referent at the same time as paying attention to the spoken words.

It is important to add that the relation between linguistic elements and the things to which they refer is an arbitrary one. There is no necessary relation between the representation—the word—and the thing represented. Words do not typically resemble their referents in the way that most pictorial representations do. The representational relation between a particular word and a particular referent is entirely conventional or dependent on the members of a community agreeing, implicitly or explicitly, to abide by that representational relation. The reason that words can survive and indeed prosper as essentially arbitrary constructions is that they are born into and nourished by the social interactions that are so fundamental to early life.

In examining the origins of language use, it becomes clear that the representational function of language grows out of the broader communicative, and hence social, function that language plays. Language is first and foremost a communicative system, a system that allows speakers to interact with each other in sophisticated ways, in order to coordinate and regulate these interactions. As such, it is developmentally continuous with the kinds of social interactions present in the first year of life. Just as the triadic interactions evident from about 9 months of age involve the coordination of social intentions around objects, so language use involves the coordination of social intentions involving words and their referents. Spoken words are initially the actions that are used to coordinate joint attention to objects (see Fig. 8.1). Words serve to regulate interactions in much the same way as gestures and facial expressions do. They are acquired as infants mold their vocalizations through imitation to the sounds they hear others making toward them. In this way, imitation leads infants to adopt the same vocal means as others to regulate their triadic interactions.

There is one highly significant difference between words and other types of joint attentional behaviors. Most conventional communicative gestures such as pointing are broadly applicable to a wide range of objects and events. In contrast, most words are used in a highly constrained way. Particular words are used in the context of joint attentional interactions with particular objects. Thus, mother may point at cookies, books, and Dad, but she only utters *cookie* in relation to cookies. As they imitate vocalizations in context, infants become able to perform particular linguistic actions in relation to specific referents. So, in contrast to most gestures, words quickly acquire communicative functions that are limited in their domains of reference.

These vocally mediated communicative interactions, in which both participants use the same sounds in relation to particular objects, present

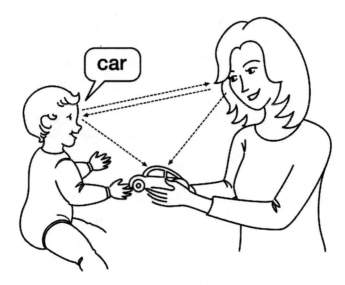

FIG. 8.1. Language use as a form of triadic interaction.

children with patterns of experience that yield conventional referential connections between sounds and objects. A word is an auditory stimulus that is heard from others and used by the self, in the context of joint attentional interactions with a particular visual stimulus. In effect infants can perform cross-modal cross-person pattern detection. Once children are both responding to and producing a particular word in relation to a specific referent, then the word becomes strongly attached to that referent—it now stands for or represents that referent. Not surprisingly, before long the word can evoke in infants the idea of that particular thing in relation to which it has been consistently used. Thus conventional connections between words and referents are established as infants detect the reliable patterns that occur in their vocally mediated object-centered interactions with adults.

In summary, all linguistically mediated communication is premised on the ability to engage in triadic interaction and to share attention with another person in relation to some third object or event. Linguistic interaction goes beyond preexisting triadic interactions through the use of the arbitrary representations—symbols—that have specific reference and are recognized to be shared across self and other. As Tomasello (2003, p. 8) put it, "Linguistic symbols are social conventions by means of which one individual attempts to share attention with another individual by directing the other's attentional or mental state to something in the outside world." So language use is fundamentally a form of joint attention, but it is a form in which the attention of the interactive partners is shared through the use of representations that are recognized to be equivalent for self and other.

THE ORIGINS OF SYMBOL USE IN COMMUNICATION

I now turn to a more detailed examination of the facts of early language acquisition. That language is a form of social interaction is best seen by observing the earliest origins of children's verbal productions. Although they can usually understand a number of words by the end of the first year, most children acquire their first productive words at around 12 months of age. These early words are produced singly and often combined with gestures. They occur within the kinds of joint attentional frameworks that characterize mother-infant interaction in the last third of the first year. Typically, mother and infant share attention to some object, perhaps by playing a ball game, looking at a book, or jointly focusing on some task such as feeding. First words are commonly produced for the two main triadic functions earlier identified with pointing—the imperative and the declarative. Imperatives are essentially requests for the communicative partner to do something for the child, for example, provide a desired object or perform an action. Declaratives are essentially attempts to share attention to some object or event with the communicative partner for the purposes of facilitating an interaction around that object or event.

In summarizing the earliest communicative functions of children in the second year, Tomasello (2003, p. 37) identified the variety of categories listed in Table 8.1. The majority of these functions can be seen to be occurring in a triadic context in which the child communicates with an interactive partner about a third thing. These communicative acts are of two main types. Continuous with protoimperative gestures, there are requests whereby the child attempts to get the partner to provide an object, person, or event involving an object or person. Continuous with protodeclarative gestures, there are indicatives whereby the child points out to the communicative partner an object, person, or event. Although early words may overlap with other communicative forms such as gestures and facial expressions, they soon provide a wealth of communicative opportunity hardly available to prelinguistic forms of communication. For instance, language provides an option not only for pointing out an object, but also for sharing information about that object. Thus, indicatives also include references to attributes or locations. Furthermore, linguistic forms allow the requestive and indicative functions to be combined. Young children ask simple questions that essentially serve as requests for information rather than for objects or events. It is worth pointing out that early verbalizations

TABLE 8.1

Functions of Children's First Words (after Tomasello, 2003)

Function	Examples
Request or indicate the existence of objects	Daddy, baby
Request or indicate the recurrence of objects of events	more, again
Request or indicate dynamic events involving objects	up, down, open, close
Request or indicate the actions of people	eat, kiss
Indicate the location of objects and people	here, outside
Ask basic questions	What's that? Where go?
Attribute a property to an object	pretty, wet
Use performatives to mark specific social events and situations	hi, bye-bye, thank you, no

are not all clearly triadic; young children also acquire a few utterances, performatives, that serve to regulate the social interaction either dyadically, such as marking the beginning and end of interactions (*hi, bye-bye*), or triadically, such as responding to requests (*yes, no*).

Although it is relatively common for a few early words to be used in very narrow communicative contexts and therefore perhaps not as symbols, most words are used symbolically—to stand for objects or events—from the start. Symbolic use is typically inferred when children use a word spontaneously or not directly in response to adult elicitation and in a context different from that of the initial context of use. Using such criteria, Susan Goodwyn and Linda Acredolo (1993) found that for 22 toddlers, the average age of initial symbolic word use was at about 12.5 months. Other studies have shown that in many cases new words that are acquired are immediately generalized beyond the initial referent (e.g., Lucariello, 1987). The early part of the second year is characterized, however, by relatively slow growth in word learning. Goodwyn and Acredolo reported that it took on average 2 months for the children in their sample to reach an average of 5 symbolic words. Nevertheless, through the first half of the second year, children start to use words in a flexible way to achieve their interactive goals.

The subsequent course of language acquisition through the second year of life is characterized by two significant developments (Anisfeld,

Rosenberg, Hoberman, & Gasparini, 1998). First, vocabulary size grows at a positively accelerating rate with a particular acceleration often occurring after about 18 months (and sometimes called the vocabulary spurt or naming explosion). From this point on, the use of linguistic symbols starts to proliferate and before long many new words are learned every day. Second, after the initial early phase of using largely single-word utterances, children start to combine words productively into simple phrases also at about 18 months. Interestingly, these two patterns appear to be related in individual patterns of development during the second year (Anisfeld et al.), so children start to combine words at about the same time as they rapidly increase their vocabulary sizes.

It is possible that both the vocabulary explosion and the onset of word combinations mark a transition from the use of words simply as symbolic devices to serve interactive goals to the recognition that words stand for things. Once children recognize that when they use a word it means the same thing as when someone else uses the same word, then words become independent of users—they have their own meaning. At this point, words become attached to objects and children can then start to focus on determining the referents of different words—hence the proliferation in vocabulary. Children quickly become adept at the naming game, the purpose of which is simply to identify various objects with words. In a nutshell, children move from acting with words to acting on words.

At the same time, once words have become attached to objects, then they too can become the focus of the children's (and others') intentions. Thus, children start to interact with others over words as stand-ins for referents, not just over the referents of words. Now, by the middle of the second year the preferred form of communicative interaction for the child has become symbolic. So, once words become the focus about which children and adults share attention, then children start to use language in relation to these words. One word may be used to regulate the joint attentional interaction with the interactive partner in relation to another word and, thus, word combinations are born. It is important to point out that this process demonstrates how word combinations start out as mechanisms for establishing and manipulating joint attention in relation to words and their referents. Such communicative interactions retain an inherently triadic structure—the two participants are producing social acts while jointly focused on a third thing. But words are now being used in a multipurpose way—both to represent the object of the joint focus and as the communicative action that regulates the interaction (see Fig. 8.2). The use of words as forms of communication about other words is what initially yields a defining feature of language—its hierarchical nature. Simple linguistic structures become the focus of a communicative exchange and thereby, become embedded within a more

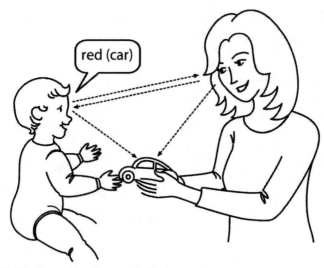

FIG. 8.2. Word combination as triadic interaction.

complex linguistic structure. Ultimately, as we shall shortly see, even complex syntax retains this original triadic structure.

In connection with these changes in language use during the second half of the first year, it is interesting that there is also a change in the appreciation that words have special status in communicative exchanges. We have seen that some gestures, such as pointing, are used communicatively prior to words. By the middle of the second year, many children use gestures symbolically as well (Acredolo & Goodwyn, 1988). For example, a panting action may be used to represent a dog, or an arms-out gesture used to represent an airplane. Interestingly, there seems to be no advantage at this early stage for learning gestures or words as symbols. Laura Namy and Sandra Waxman (1998) presented 18- and 26-month-old children with novel gestures or novel words as they named certain objects. Novel gestures including actions such as dropping the hand as a fist and opening it palm down as it dropped or a side-to-side movement of the hand extended as if to shake hands. Novel words were simple single-syllable nonsense words such as *dax* or *ziv*. Acquisition of the symbols was tested by examining to what extent children provided the originally named objects or related objects (such as objects within a shared category like fruit). They found that 18-month-olds were equally able to learn the novel gestures as the novel words to refer to objects. The 26-month-olds also learned the novel words, however, they did significantly worse than the 18-month-olds in learning gestures as symbols. These results illustrate that soon after 18 months, gestures lose their status as potential symbols for children. By about 2 years of age, the preferred functions of gestures and words have diverged, with gestures being used primarily as devices for directing attention and emphasis, and words being used as the central representational devices.

GENERAL REPRESENTATIONAL DEVELOPMENT AND LANGUAGE

The rapid development in language during the second year coincides with other developments in representational ability. The other arena of activity in which there is clear evidence of the use of representation is play, and many authors have noted the connection between language and play (e.g., Lyytinen, Poikkeus, & Laakso, 1997; McCune-Nicolich, 1981; Piaget, 1962; Werner & Kaplan, 1963). Toddlers start to engage in play in which there is a relatively clear separation of real and pretend actions during the first half of the second year and like language it rapidly increases in frequency and complexity during the second year. The origins of pretense can be seen in the first year when infants perform actions apart from their usual purpose. For example, 10-month-olds may perform a drinking action from an empty cup even though they know it is empty. In such performances infants recognize the object and the action associated with it but there is no evidence of recognition of the difference between a genuine act and a pretend one. Infants do not mark the play action by smiling or otherwise changing their demeanor. Early in the second year children do start to show awareness of the distinction between a real and a pretend action and by indicating pretend actions with an exaggerated gesture or facial expression that shows that the action is not to be taken literally (McCune-Nicolich). During the first half of the second year, children perform pretend actions involving either the self or another agent, even an inanimate one. The pretense lies in the fact that the actions are common ones that are being performed apart from their usual goals, for example, drinking from an empty cup or mock sleeping, and that children mark the pretense. Children are thereby using the pretend action intentionally to stand for the real action. This stage corresponds developmentally with the initial use of language, where children use a word to communicate an intention. These parallel developments in pretense and language also resemble each other structurally in that in both cases there is an action (the pretend act or the utterance) that stands for a real action or object.

As the second year passes, children's play grows more complex. Children may perform a pretend action on multiple recipients, for example, feeding a doll, then feeding a teddy bear. During the second half of the first year, a series of pretend actions may be sequenced (Fenson & Ramsay, 1980), for example, children may first make a doll drink, then make her eat, and finally put her to bed. In addition, object substitution in play occurs often by the end of the second year. In object substitution, one object is used as if it is something else, for example, a piece of paper may be used as a doll blanket (Lezine, 1973, cited in McCune-Nicolich, 1981). Play involving object substitution is more sophisticated because the child performs a pretend action on a pretend object. As such it marks a shift toward a more hierarchical form of play—one play element is embedded within another play action—just as productive word combinations mark a shift toward hierarchical language (McCune-Nicolich).

Studies examining both language and pretend play in the same children have typically shown them to be correlated independently of age (e.g., Lyytinen et al., 1997; McCune, 1995; McCune-Nicolich, 1981). Lorraine McCune arranged to observe children between 8 and 24 months of age playing with a standard set of toys with their mothers in their homes. In order to get a clear picture of the children's spontaneous level of play, she asked the mothers to let their children take the lead in how the play developed. McCune also took measures of the children's spontaneous language, including both individual words and word combinations. She found that the onset of single-word use was strongly linked to the onset of pretense. To examine the correspondence in the use of hierarchical play and the use of word combinations, McCune compared the children's tendency to use more multiword utterances than single-word utterances with their tendency to perform play actions with pretend objects. Again, there was a strong association between these more sophisticated levels of language and play. These findings confirm the notion that both language and play are representational forms of activity that develop from an initial phase beginning at the start of the second year, in which children can use representations in their play and in their interactions with others, to a phase toward the end of the second year in which they can embed representations within other representational acts.

So far I have talked as if language use depends on social interaction and general changes in representational ability. However, it is important to recognize that language plays an important part in the development of children's conceptual systems. From the earliest days of their participation in linguistically based interactions, children use the information provided by language to refine their understanding of the world. We have seen that throughout the first year infants build more complex conceptual representations of their worlds by detecting the patterns that are evident in the information provided to them. Language provides another source of information for this pattern detection because children can use language to help determine similarities that may not be particularly obvious otherwise. When an adult uses the same word in relation to two or more things that may not appear at first glance to be similar, then children have critical information that indeed there is something common to those things.

Research by Sandra Waxman and Dana Markow (1995) illustrates the way language assists in pattern detection and conceptual development from a very early age. They tested infants at about 12 to 13 months who were at the threshold of language use. The study was set up as a simple joint attention situation in which an adult experimenter and the infants interacted over a series of toys. The adult presented in turn four toys that looked fairly different but were part of a superordinate set in that they shared some commonality (e.g., the toys were different animals). The infants were allowed to manipulate the toys freely for 30 seconds each. This familiarization part of the procedure was carried out under different language conditions. In one condition, the adult used the same unfamiliar word twice to refer to each toy, saying, "See the X" and then "Do you like the X?" In a second condition, the adult used neutral nonspecific wording, saying, "See here" and then "Do you like that?" After the four toys had been presented and played with in turn, the experimenter presented two additional test toys together, simply saying, "Look!" One of these toys was a member of the same set as the original four (e.g., another animal) and the other was not (e.g., a tool). Based on the logic of novelty preference, if infants recognize the commonalities among the toys from the familiarization set (e.g., that they are all animals), then they should show more interest in the test toy that was not a member of this set (e.g., the tool) than in the test toy that was also a member of the set (e.g., the new animal). So the amount of interest the infants showed in the two test toys during a 45-second period was measured.

The results showed that infants who heard the unfamiliar word during the familiarization period tended to show more interest during the test in the toy that was not part of the familiarization set. In contrast, infants who had been presented with nonspecific language during the familiarization did not show this preference. It appeared, then, that the addition of the unfamiliar word had in some way focused the infants' attention on the commonality among the toys presented during the familiarization phase. This is an important finding because it shows that the use of the same word in the context of different but related objects highlights the similarities among them. In this way, words can help the natural pattern detection abilities of infants. The use of the same word for distinct objects recognizes the fact that although they are different, they are also similar. As Waxman and Markow (1995) put it, "Words serve as *invitations* to form categories.... Words focus attention on commonalities among objects, highlighting them especially in cases where the perceptual similarity among objects may not be ... apparent" (p. 298, emphasis in original). If words can help children induce similarities across concrete objects, then it is reasonable to expect that they may also serve a similar function for psychological information. We will return to this issue in chapter 9.

SOCIAL INFLUENCES ON EARLY LANGUAGE ACQUISITION

There is now good general evidence that the acquisition of various aspects of productive language is tied to the richness of the communicative interactions occurring between infants and mothers. For example, Tamis-LeMonda, Bornstein, and Baumwell (2001) measured a variety of interactive patterns for mothers and their infants when the latter were both 9 months and 13 months of age. They also measured certain language milestones in the children through the second year, including first words, attainment of 50 words, and attainment of word combinations. They found that the infants' achievement of these milestones was related to the patterns of mother-infant interaction. In particular, the infants who were more advanced in both vocabulary size and complexity enjoyed patterns of interaction in which the infants tended to try to involve the mothers in toy play and the mothers responded appropriately to their infants' interactive and communicative attempts. In other words, infant-mother interactions characterized by triadic communicative play with toys were linked to more advanced infant language skills.

The suggestion that language acquisition grows out of the triadic contexts evident in mother-infant interactions was originally made by Jerome Bruner in the 1970s (Bruner, 1983). At that time, most language acquisition researchers sought answers to how language is acquired in the developing syntactic or cognitive skills of the child. It was Bruner who forcefully made the point that language, first and foremost, is a communicative ability, and that communication initially occurs in interactive contexts in which mother and child share attention to objects and events in their immediate environments. Sometimes, at least in Western cultures, such triadic interactions become routinized into interactive formats such as the naming game, in which mother and child share attention to a series of objects or pictures in turn as the mother (or even the child) asks, "What's that?"

Since Bruner's (1983) insight, many studies have focused on joint attention formats as the most important contexts for language learning. Early research focused on how mothers might manipulate the joint attentional setting when language was used in order to facilitate language learning. Observational studies (e.g., Carpenter et al., 1998; Tomasello & Todd, 1983) of mothers and their 12-month-olds infants demonstrated that the more time infants engaged in joint attention, especially where the mothers followed the children's focus of attention rather than redirecting the children's attention, the larger the children's vocabularies during the 12- to 18-month period. These studies confirm the general point that language is a form of social interactive behavior that is acquired as the triadic forms of social interaction started in the first year of life become further elaborated.

The particular importance of joint attention for language acquisition was also demonstrated in numerous experimental studies. The most compelling demonstrations come from studies in which children are exposed to new words, sometimes real words that they do not know yet but more often made-up or nonsense words (e.g., *toma, modi, gazzer*), under different conditions to see how well the new words are picked up by the children. In an early study, Michael Tomasello and Jeffrey Farrar (1986; see also Dunham, Dunham, & Curwin, 1993), allowed toddlers of about 18 months of age to play with a set of four unfamiliar household objects. While each child was playing, an experimenter introduced the four corresponding novel words using sentence frames such as, "Here's the *clip*." The adult introduced two of the words while the child was holding and looking at the appropriate objects (follow-in condition). In contrast, the other two words were introduced when the child was not focused on any particular object (direct condition). After the play session, the four objects were placed in a row and the adult asked for each in turn using the corresponding word introduced during the play period. Children were significantly more likely to give the corresponding object for the words introduced in the follow-in condition than for the words introduced in the direct condition. This result confirmed in an experimental format the finding that creating joint attention contexts facilitates young children's acquisition of new words. Importantly, it showed that children learned novel words more easily when they were already attending to the target object than when they were not.

These results show that adults can facilitate word learning by introducing new words for things as children are engaged with them. It is likely that this strategy is effective because the attentional demands of the word-learning situation are reduced under follow-in settings. When an adult introduces a novel word for an object that the child is already interested in, the child is already engaged in processing the object. In contrast, when the adult redirects the child's attention to a different object as the new word is introduced, the child has to process both the novel object and the new word, thus placing greater demands on the information-processing system. Nevertheless, infants are sensitive to the adult's focus of attention in word-learning contexts, as we shall now see.

THE ROLE OF COMMONSENSE PSYCHOLOGY IN THE ACQUISITION OF WORDS

Although adults play an important role in structuring the joint attentional interactions in which words are most easily learned, they are not wholly responsible for their children's language acquisition. Children play an active role in determining word meaning by attempting to read the communicative intentions of their conversational partners. In other words, children use their developing commonsense psychology to make inferences about what the speaker intends to refer to when novel words are used. Dare Baldwin (1991) first showed that children monitored and used their conversational partner's gaze direction to determine to which of two possible toys a novel word referred. In this study, 16- to 19-month-old toddlers sat in an infant seat at a table with a novel toy in reach. Also present was a small bucket containing a different novel toy. An experimenter sat with the child and introduced two novel words, one in each of two conditions, when the child was playing with the toy that was in view on the table. In the follow-in condition, the experimenter looked at the toy and used one of the novel words, saying "It's a *toma*." In the discrepant labeling condition, the experimenter used the other novel word in the same way ("It's a *peri*") while looking into the bucket. In all, each word was used by the adult four times in its respective condition (follow-in or discrepant labeling). The children's acquisition of the novel words was subsequently tested by presenting them with both toys and asking them to point to the *toma* or *peri*. The results showed that the children picked the toy with which they had been playing more often than chance only for the word introduced in the follow-in condition. Even though both novel words had been produced by the adult while the children were playing with the same toy, the children only interpreted the word used while the adult was looking at that same toy to refer to it. Therefore the children had used the adult's attentional relation to determine the intended referent of her communicative act.

This general approach has now been used in many studies to show that by 24 months, children respond to quite varied aspects of the speaker's intentional action in order to determine the intended referent of a novel label. Children do not simply use the speaker's gaze to work out whether a particular object is the correct referent. They can use other aspects of the intentional structure of the speaker's communicative action to ignore one object that is looked at immediately after the introduction of a novel word in favor of another one that appears somewhat later in the proceedings. To illustrate this flexibility, consider a study by Michael Tomasello and his colleagues (Tomasello, Strosberg, & Akhtar, 1996), who showed 24-month-old children a row of four toy buckets in each of which was a novel object. The adult then announced her intention by saying, "Let's find the *gazzer*." She proceeded to look in the buckets in turn, remove the toy, and hold it up. As she held up the toy, she either scowled at it, replaced it, and moved on, or held it up with a satisfied smile and terminated the search. Over a series of searches, the smiled-at toy could appear in any of the buckets. In some cases, the "correct" toy appeared right after the introduction of the novel label and in other cases it appeared after another toy had been held up for inspection. In a subsequent test, children were able to choose the correct toy when asked to pick the *gazzer*, whether or not it had been the first toy shown to them, thereby demonstrating that they had used the adult's cues of rejection versus acceptance to work out the correct meaning of the novel word.

These studies on word learning have shown how young children use the speaker's intentional action to determine the meaning of novel labels or nouns. In fact, this general approach is applicable to other types of words also. In a particularly revealing study, Tomasello and Akhtar (1995) introduced 2-year-olds to a new word in the context of a novel action performed on a novel object. Prior to this event, the children were exposed to a discourse context that either highlighted the novelty of the action or highlighted the novelty of the object. For example, in the novel-action condition, a number of different actions were performed by the adult and child on the target object. Then the final target action on the same object was performed using a simple chute apparatus as the adult introduced the nonsense word in a single word utterance, "*Modi!*" In the novel-object condition, the target action using the chute apparatus was performed on a series of objects and then the same action was performed on the final target object as the adult introduced the word as in the novel-action condition. In this way, the children all saw the same final action performed on the same object with the same word used. However the prior events biased interpretation of the nonce word toward interpretation as either a verb or a noun. In the test phase, the children were shown all the objects used in the earlier phase as well as the chute apparatus and were asked, "Can you show me *modi*?" The majority of the children in the novel-action condition proceeded to perform the target action without choosing the target object. In contrast, the majority of the children in the novel-object condition picked the target object but did not perform the target action. These results show quite clearly that children use the interactional context to determine not just to which object a new word might refer, but also whether a new word is a noun referring to an object or a verb referring to an action.

I noted earlier that linguistic symbols are social conventions that come to be understood with meaning independent of particular speakers. Even as toddlers are paying attention to the speaker's intentional behavior to discern the intended referent of novel words, they assume that the meanings of novel words are shared among speakers. This may be called the *conventionality assumption*. To demonstrate the conventionality assumption, Henderson and Graham (in press) adopted the procedure introduced by Tomasello et al. (1996). Working with 24-month-olds, the experimenter announced her intention to find a *mido* and then proceeded to look in various containers, finding a different toy in each one, but responding to only one of the toys with a satisfied smile. After a number of rounds of this finding game, all of the toys were removed and placed in a bucket, at which point the original experimenter left the room. A few seconds later, either the original or a second experimenter, who had not been present during the finding game, came into the room and showed the child the set of toys as she asked the child, "Show me the *mido*." As in Tomasello et al.'s study, children picked the target object at rates significantly greater than chance, and their success did not differ depending on which experimenter asked the test question. These results show clearly that children treat newly acquired words as independent of speakers and tied to their referents rather than as specific to particular speakers.

These and other studies demonstrate that children as young as 18 months make sense of language by entering into a joint attentional frame and attempting to infer what the speaker intends to communicate through language (Tomasello, 2003). It should be noted that it is not always the case that there has to be joint visual attention for word learning to proceed. Although initially children need to be able to see the potential referent of a novel word in order to learn the word, before long children are able to engage in joint conceptual attention, whereby they can imagine the referent of a novel word from other intentional cues that the adult offers. As such, the child's developing commonsense psychology plays a critical role in language acquisition. Without an understanding of others as independent agents with separate psychological relations to objects and events, children would not be able to interpret their communicative behavior as directed at objects or situations in the world.

THE ACQUISITION OF COMPLEX LANGUAGE

It is important to recognize that the approach to language acquisition illustrated in the previous section, sometimes called the "social-pragmatic" approach (Akhtar & Tomasello, 2000), is not limited to explaining the acquisition and use of individual words. On this view, more complex aspects of language, including syntax or grammar, are used and acquired in the same way. Syntax includes the manner in which words are combined into phrases and sentences to represent and express more complex meanings involving various relations between and among agents, objects, actions, and other events. There are various ways in which such relations are expressed, including word order and grammatical marking of words (e.g., case marking). Like individual words, syntax has both a representational function and a communicative function. Where words stand for entities, attributes, and actions, syntactic structures stand for events or states of affairs in which entities take part and play different roles. To take an example, the sentence *John gave Mary the ring* represents an event involving three entities (*John, Mary, the ring*) as well as a particular event (a transfer of possession). The syntactic form in which this event is expressed has a standard ditransitive structure that is also used for many other events involving one person in some sense providing something for someone else (see Table 8.2).

Complex language is also used to allow the speaker to first establish a joint frame of reference with the listener (the given information) before communicating the intention of the utterance (the new information). For example, in English, word order can convey this given–new distinction. The subject of the sentence typically specifies the given information whereas the predicate typically specifies the new information. In this way

TABLE 8.2
Different Forms of the Ditransitive Construction

Subject	Verb	Recipient	Object
John	gave	Mary	the ring
Mary	blew	John	a kiss
Martha	baked	Donald	a cake
Shannon	read	Mackenzie	a book

the same event may be expressed differently depending on what part of the event is already part of the information shared by speaker and listener and what part is not shared (see Table 8.3).

The Origins of Simple Constructions

As with the acquisition of individual words, the acquisition of complex language is a product of the communicative interactions children have with others. This is seen most clearly in the fact that the forms children acquire are tied quite closely to the forms they hear around them. Most children start to combine words together during the second half of the second year. From the start there are some regularities in their word combinations, but the regularities tend to function with respect to particular words, sometimes referred to as *pivot* words (Braine, 1976; Tomasello, 2003). For example, children may learn a pivot schema for combining the word *more* with a variety of other words to express recurrence or repetition. Similarly, children may express their desire for a range of objects using the pivot schema *want-X*. Strictly speaking, these constructions do not have syntax because the order of the elements, although consistent, does not in itself specify anything about the roles of the elements in the construction. Rather, the word

TABLE 8.3
Active and Passive Sentences Parsed
According to Given and New Information

	Given (Sentence Subject)	New (Sentence Predicate)
Active	The cat	licked the dog
Passive	The dog	was licked by the cat

order reflects the word order evident in the language that children hear when interacting with others.

Syntactic marking using word order first appears early during the third year, when children are able to comprehend and produce sentences in which word order alone specifies the meaning. For example, when asked to act out potentially reversible transitive sentences such as *The cat pushes the dog* or *Cory kisses mommy*, young 2-year-olds can usually succeed (e.g., de Villiers & de Villiers, 1973; Roberts, 1983). However, such studies have typically used very familiar verbs and so the generality or abstractness of the syntactic marking is unknown. Detailed studies on verb acquisition (e.g., Tomasello, 1992) have shown that syntactic forms are initially rather limited in scope, used only for one or a very few verbs, and have very little generality across different verbs (what Tomasello called "verb islands"). So, rather than children acquiring syntactic roles such as agent or patient, they initially acquire verb-specific roles such as pusher or person kissed. Again, these patterns reflect the patterns of usage that children encounter in their communicative exchanges with others.

That the acquisition of syntactic structures depends on communicative experience with those structures is demonstrated by studies using nonsense verbs in complex sentences. Akhtar (1999) presented English-speaking children of 2, 3, and 4 years with nonsense verbs in both normal English (subject-verb-object, SVO) and nonnormal English word orders (subject-object-verb, SOV; verb-subject-object, VSO) as they were shown puppets performing novel actions on objects. For example, the children were shown one puppet knocking an object down a chute and at the same time they heard "Elmo *gopping* the car," "Elmo the car *gopping*," or "*Gopping* Elmo the car." After training on a variety of actions with different novel verbs, the children were given an opportunity to perform the actions and both spontaneous and elicited descriptions of the actions were recorded. The results showed a clear developmental change, with the older children regularly producing the novel verbs but almost always using them in sentences with the standard English SVO word order, thereby showing that they would transform the sentences that they heard to fit their acquired syntactic forms. In contrast, the younger children also used the novel verbs but often in nonnormal orders, producing both SOV and VSO orders, albeit not at the rate that they produced SVO orders. These results confirm that younger children acquire syntactic forms in verb-specific ways before later learning more abstract rules.

The performance of the 4-year-olds in Akhtar's (1999) study illustrates the fact that by this age, children do learn more abstract syntactic forms that they then use to organize their language. Such learning probably occurs because children gradually pick up on the similarities in forms that are evident across different verb constructions. In effect, the natural pattern detection mechanisms that operate throughout development find regularities in the forms that children are exposed to (e.g., in the multiple ditransitive cases shown earlier in Table 8.2). Pattern detection here is an example of the structure mapping I introduced briefly in chapter 3 (Gentner & Medina, 1998). It is a relatively abstract variety of structure mapping (similar to analogical thinking) in which what is detected is not so much the particular lexical elements but the way in which they relate to each other. The pattern that is derived incorporates various roles in relation to each other (e.g., agent, patient) but is not tied to any particular elements.

The findings from syntax development confirm the general developmental story I have been telling—pattern detection from multiple social interactional experiences. Children are exposed through language-based interactions with others to instances of events involving agents and other entities. Initially, the children's ability to make sense of these events is tied closely to the particular forms to which they are exposed. As they are exposed to more forms with similar structures, children start to detect the patterns among them and are able to abstract regularities in these forms. In the end, that is what syntactic rules amount to—sets of patterns among linguistic categories that can be used to communicate about and represent events involving various roles into which can be incorporated a wide variety of specific lexical elements.

The Origins of Complex Constructions

There is one final type of construction that we need to consider in preparation for our later study of commonsense psychology during the preschool period. We have seen that as children engage in linguistically mediated communicative interactions over words, they generate word combinations and simple syntactic constructions. This hierarchical process of communicating over linguistic representations continues at further levels of complexity. Once children can communicate using syntactic constructions, they can start to communicate in reference to the propositions expressed by those constructions. For our purposes, the most important manifestation of this level of syntactic complexity is the use of so-called modal verbs to express deontic and epistemic functions (Tomasello, 2003; see Table 8.4). Deontic modality is expressed in the use of verbs such as *must* and *have to* in connection with potential actions (e.g., *You must feed the cat every day*). Epistemic modality involves cognitive verbs, most commonly *think* and *know*, to express an attitude toward some information about an action or state of affairs, itself expressed in propositional form (e.g., *I think Lisa gave Carly the tickets*). As Table 8.4 shows, in both deontic and epistemic cases, the modal verb stands in relation to some other propositional content, which is now the topic of the communicative exchange. The modal verb functions to modulate the communicative interaction by expressing the speaker's attitude toward that content.

TABLE 8.4

Deontic and Epistemic Modal Constructions

Modality	Expression of Speaker's Attitude	Propositional Content (Request or Information)
Deontic	You must	feed the cat every day (request)
Epistemic	I think	Lisa gave Carly the tickets (information)

The use of deontic modality has its developmental origins at about 2 years of age as children start to use the contracted forms *wanna, gonna,* and *hafta* to express their attitude toward desired or intended actions (Gerhardt, 1991). Deontic modality may therefore be seen as the outgrowth of earlier imperative or requestive functions as children express a request or intention to do something. In contrast, epistemic modality is at least in part an outgrowth of earlier indicative functions, and appears in the use of early-appearing cognitive verbs such as *think* and *know,* usually by about 3 years. By 2 to 3 years, then, children are able to use modal constructions in conversations to express attitudes to propositions. This achievement enables them to start to reflect on those attitudes and this, as we shall soon see, is an important condition for the further development of commonsense psychology.

SUMMARY

In this chapter, we have seen how language develops as the representational abilities developing during the second year become used in the joint attentional interactions already in place by the end of the first year. Language is first and foremost a means for establishing and regulating joint attention. Initially, words serve as the devices for regulating joint attention to their referents and they soon become the preferred means for doing so. At the same time, words become organizing anchors for concepts. Similar experiences become grouped together under labels. By the second half of the second year, as children recognize the independence of words from speakers, words and their referents become the objects around which joint attentional interactions are focused. New words are now acquired at a rapid rate as children use their commonsense psychology to help determine to what adults are referring when new words are used.

Once children can attend with others to words and meanings they are in a position to start to use words productively in combinations. Children use their communicative repertoire to regulate joint attention in relation to these words and meanings and because words themselves are the most prominent form of communication, words are used in relation to other words. At the same time, of course, others are doing likewise, so children are exposed to patterns in the way others use their multiword utterances. Paying attention to the regularities in the way others combine their words soon yields an inventory of linguistic constructions in children that is the basis of syntax.

Language is a product of the representational and social interactional developments in early childhood, but in its turn it contributes much more to subsequent representational and social development. Throughout life, language retains its primary function as a means of coordinating joint attention in relation to linguistic representations. However, the representations about which the communicative participants interact become ever more complex and abstract. Linguistic representations can expand the capacity for joint attention beyond simply communicating about perceptually available objects or events. Representations can stand in for objects and events that are not present, such as those that are from other times or are completely imaginary. Thus, child and adult can communicate about the past, the future, or fantasy. In addition, language becomes the means through which children can further elaborate their commonsense psychology. It is not only objects and events that can be represented, but also an agent's psychological relation to those objects and events. Language allows speakers to express their attitudes and intentions and it is through conversations with others that more complex aspects of commonsense psychology, including understanding diversity of psychological relations to perspectival objects and understanding personal identity, become elaborated by children. In summary, language becomes the primary representational medium for children to construct and communicate about nonpresent and imaginary situations and about attitudes toward those situations. It therefore plays an essential role in the subsequent elaboration of commonsense psychology.

9

Commonsense Psychology in the Preschool Years

By 2 years of age, children's model of the psychological world has started to resemble clearly that of adults. They understand that people, including themselves and others, have perceptions, feelings, and desires in relation to objects and events in the world around them. They can even participate in play interactions with others over imaginary objects. As we will soon see, 2-year-olds express this understanding in the conversations they have with others. But there is more to be learned. In the preschool years from age 2 to 5, children elaborate their commonsense psychology further to include a variety of more complex psychological relations, most importantly those that involve perspectives (see chap. 2). They start to construct a model of the world that distinguishes the perspectival from the real. In this chapter, we examine these further developments in commonsense psychology.

As has been the case at every point in development we have so far examined, children's participation in social interactions plays a formative role in the continued progression toward a mature commonsense psychology. Social interactions provide both the emotional and the communicative context in which more sophisticated concepts of commonsense psychology are elaborated (Carpendale & Lewis, 2004; Dunn, 1988). Two changing aspects of these interactions are noteworthy. First, whereas in infancy, interactions with adults play almost an exclusive role, in the preschool period sibling and peer interactions start to take on a greater significance. Of course, interactions with adults are still important. For example, there is evidence that parents who make frequent references to their young children's thoughts, feelings, and intentions, as they talk to them, have children who develop commonsense psychology earlier on average (Meins et al., 2002). So, children who have parents that openly

156

treat them as if they are psychological agents understand these concepts sooner. In addition, parents who encourage their children to take the perspective of others in conflict situations, for example, by encouraging them to think about how their actions might affect other people's feelings, have children with more advanced commonsense psychology (e.g., Ruffman, Perner, & Parkin, 1999). In this chapter and the next, we shall look at some examples of how the extent to which parents communicate with their children about psychological matters is important to their children's developing commonsense psychology. However, it is more often in interactions with other children, commonly during pretend play, that children are regularly forced to confront and coordinate a range of points of view that may often conflict with their own. Indeed, some studies have shown that the number of siblings that preschool children have is related to the development of their commonsense psychology (Jenkins & Astington, 1996; Perner, Ruffman, & Leekam, 1994; Peterson, 2000). Children with more than one sibling tend to perform better on measures of commonsense psychology than children with only one or no siblings.

Second, unlike in the first 2 years, the development of commonsense psychology is now crucially dependent on the newly acquired linguistic medium. We saw in chapter 8 that language allows children to achieve certain communicative goals by sharing attention with others to lexical representations of objects and events. Complex linguistic constructions are born from the use of language to coordinate joint attention to lexical representations. Utterances involving constructions do not just represent objects and events, they make some comment on the object or event and thus also express a particular perspective in the form of a proposition. For example, to say "book" is simply to indicate that object. But to say "John gave Mary the book" is to pick out a particular perspective on the book that the speaker deems worthy of communicating. Thus, once children have moved beyond the use of single words, language becomes inherently perspectival.

As seen at the end of chapter 8, the hierarchical use of language allows another important function of complex language and that is to express and comprehend an attitude toward the information that is to be conveyed. By "attitude" I essentially mean speakers' psychological relation to the content of the utterance. Thus, speakers can express various psychological orientations to the content of their expression, including desires, feelings, and opinions. Attitudes are commonly conveyed lexically through the use of psychological terms, such as *like*, *want*, and *think*. Some of these terms, such as *want*, can be used to express attitudes both to actual objects and events expressed as words (*I want a drink*) and to perspectives expressed as propositions (*I want the kitchen painted yellow*). Other psychological terms are particular to the expression of propositional attitudes, such as *think* (*I think that Casablanca is playing at the Arts theater*). By using psychological terms, speakers attempts to elicit joint attention (through the use of language) not only to the content of their utterance but also to their attitude toward that content. So in the example just mentioned, the speaker guides the joint attention not only to the information that *Casablanca* is playing at the Arts theater but also to the speaker's lack of certainty about the truth of this information. In this way, commonsense psychology is made explicit in the conversation and may become a topic of the conversation. In the first half of this chapter, we describe in more detail how children start to express their commonsense psychology linguistically.

As with all words and the concepts they encode, the linguistic communicative process facilitates the development of psychological concepts (Astington & Baird, 2005). We saw in chapter 8 how the use of new words in communicative exchanges can help young children recognize commonalities across disparate objects and potentially form more abstract categories of objects (Waxman & Markow, 1995). Through language, children and adults can also share attention to the expression of attitudes, such as opinions and desires, and in so doing these attitudes become more easily conceptualized (Baldwin & Saylor, 2005). Once children have acquired such concepts they can be incorporated into their own reasoning and into more complex discourse with others. In the second half of the chapter we examine one popular approach to the study of children's reasoning with more complex psychological concepts—an approach commonly known as children's theory of mind. This approach has examined children's psychological concepts by examining when and how children attribute different psychological states to themselves and others.

THE LANGUAGE OF COMMONSENSE PSYCHOLOGY

The language of commonsense psychology begins almost as soon as language itself. Inge Bretherton, and her colleagues (Bretherton, McNew, & Beeghly-Smith, 1981) found that 30% of a sample of 20-month-old children were already using some words referring to internal states, most commonly words referring to physiological states such as tiredness and pain, but also words referring to emotional states such as distress, disgust, and affection. Bretherton and Beeghly (1982) asked the mothers of these children at 28 months to report on their children's use of a variety of words referring to internal states using the six categories shown in Table 9.1. The mothers were provided with inventories that listed some 78 different words and were asked to identify those words that they had heard their children use. The findings revealed an impressive level of use of psychological terms in these children not yet 2.5 years old. Most children had already acquired some terms for each of the major psychological relations— epistemic (including perceptual and cognitive categories), emotional, and conative. The perceptual term *see* was used by all but one of the children and the conative or desire term *want* was used by all but two. A large major-

TABLE 9.1

**Percentage of Children Using Internal State Terms at 28 Months
(from Bretherton & Beeghly, 1982)**

Internal State Category	Common Examples	Percentage
Perceptual	See	97
	Hear	50
	Taste	67
Physiological	Hungry	77
	Thirsty	80
	Tired	83
Emotional	Like	80
	Mad	73
	Scared	73
Conative	Want	93
	Can	73
Cognitive	Know	66
	Think	33
	Remember	30
Moral	Good	93
	Bad	87
	Have to	57

ity of children had also acquired one or more emotion terms, most commonly *like, mad,* and *scared.* The category that was least represented in the children's language was cognitive terms, which, apart from *know,* appeared in fewer than one third of the children's vocabularies. Uses of *know,* though quite common, were often limited to the formulaic phrase *I don't know,* which likely meant that the children were not using the word with much if any understanding of its meaning.

The Function of Psychological Terms in Young Children's Talk

Simply recording the presence of psychological terms in children's productive vocabularies tells us when these terms appear but not how children use these words in their communicative interactions. For that it is necessary either to interview mothers to gain contextualized examples of their children's psychological talk, or to observe children directly talking to others. In this way, we can examine in what kinds of utterance these words occur and for what kinds of communicative function the utterances are used. Subsequent research has used such approaches to delve more deeply into how children communicate with adults about psychological relations and also how adults communicate with their children about psychological relations. This research has focused primarily on three groups of terms—those referring to emotions, desires (a group of conative terms), and cognition (a group of epistemic terms).

As we have seen, emotion terms such as *happy, sad,* and *mad,* often enter children's vocabularies by the end of the second year. The initial uses tend to be expressions of an emotional orientation, for example, *yucky* used while rejecting a food. But almost as soon as children are able to incorporate emotional terms into multiword utterances, they are commenting on a wide variety of aspects of emotional events, including what the emotions are about, what caused the emotions, and what resulted from the emotions (see Table 9.2; Bretherton, Fritz, Zahn-Waxler, & Ridgeway, 1986). Consistent with the evidence discussed in chapter 7, that children have by this age a clear sense of self–other equivalence, references are common to both the emotions of self and the emotions of others (Bretherton & Beeghly, 1982; Dunn, Bretherton, & Munn, 1987). Emotion talk is not just about presently occurring emotional events. The world of emotion is detachable from immediate reality. Children talk about past emotional experiences and they anticipate possible future emotions (see Table 9.2). By the middle of the third year, then, children already evidence through their language a quite coherent sense of how emotions are involved in daily social life.

TABLE 9.2
Sample Emotion Utterances
From Bretherton, Fritz, Zahn-Waxler, and Ridgeway (1986)

Aspect of Emotional Event	Example (Age Produced)
Aboutness of emotion	It's dark. I'm scared. (28 months)
Cause of emotion	Grandma mad, I wrote on wall. (28 months)
Result of emotion	I'm mad at you Daddy. I'm going away, goodbye. (29 months)
Past emotion	Mommy you went away. I was sad. (25 months)
Future emotion	He's sad. He'll be happy when his daddy comes home. (27 months)

Emotional states typically have salient manifestations from both first- and third-person perspectives, so it is perhaps not surprising that they are talked about early. Other psychological relations are not so obvious, and the developmental pattern of their linguistic expressions varies. Like emotions, desires may be very salient for young children and the desire term *want* is often acquired by 2 years of age. Initially it tends to have a rather limited function: *Want* is used primarily by young children to express their desires rather than to talk about the desires of self or others. Indeed, as seen in chapter 8, the pivot schema *want-X* is commonly used by young children in the earliest stages of word combinations. Even as *want* becomes incorporated into more complex sentences such as those involving complement phrases, it still is most commonly used by children to express their immediate goals (e.g., *I wanna go in the garden*; Bartsch & Wellman, 1995; Tomasello, 2003). Nevertheless, by the middle of the third year, children do extend their references to desires to encompass other people's desires and to talk about desires rather than just express them. In an attempt to determine when young children start to use desire terms beyond simply expressing their immediate desires, Karen Bartsch and Henry Wellman conducted an exhaustive analysis of some of the language samples stored on the CHILDES database, a repository of language data (MacWhinney & Snow, 1990). This database contains a number of detailed transcription records of the spontaneous use of language in the everyday lives of various children who had been studied by different researchers. Bartsch and Wellman selected the records of 10 children for whom language samples were available from 18 months to 5 years, and they recorded all utterances involving various desire terms, including *want, hope,* and *wish.* In fact, well over 90% of the desire utterances involved *want.* They found that some 30% of desire utterances before 3 years of age had a second- (*you*) or third-person (*he, she,* etc.) subject. Commenting on their own desires is evidenced by utterances in which children remark on the outcome of a previous desire or on the prospect for a future desire. Such talk occurs commonly in the fourth year as illustrated by the following examples (from Bartsch & Wellman, 90):

Adult: Do you remember [what you got as a present]?
Abe (3;3): A net [a basketball hoop].
Adult: Uh huh.
Abe: 'Cept I didn't want it. I wanted a bat and a baseball.

Ross (3;6): Are you going to die?
Adult: Not until you get to be an old man.
Ross: If you die, I want mommy to get another you.

Desire terms can be used both as the main verb of an utterance (1) or to express an attitude to a proposition denoted by another verb (2). Because of the more complex syntax, the use of desire terms to express an attitude to a proposition generally occurs later in development, from around the middle of the third year, than the use of desire terms to express an attitude toward a real object. Similarly, cognitive term utterances such as *know* and *think* usually appear as so-called matrix verbs to express attitudes to propositions (3).

(1) John wants a cookie.

(2) John wants his team to win the World Cup.

(3) John thinks his team won the World Cup.

It is no surprise, then, that, as noted earlier, cognitive terms, most commonly *know* and *think*, generally are acquired a bit later than emotion and desire terms. Nevertheless, they are in the productive vocabularies of most children by the middle of the third year (Bretherton & Beeghly, 1982). In an early study examining how children use these words, Marilyn Shatz and her colleagues (Shatz, Wellman, & Silber, 1983) examined the cognitive term utterances of one child from the CHILDES database, Abe, from 2 years 4 months to 4 years. Although a wide variety of cognitive terms were included in the corpus of utterances, the two words, *know* and *think* accounted for over 70% of all cognitive term utterances. Shatz et al. designed several codes to reflect the different functions these cognitive term utterances could serve. As in Bretherton and Beeghly's study, the most common cognitive term utterance before age 3 was the formulaic *I don't know*. Two other functions appeared noteworthy in the transcripts before 3 years. First, Abe used a cognitive term utterance to direct attention or introduce a topic (e.g., *Know what?* or *I guess I'll go for a ride*). Second, cognitive terms (again notably *know* and *think*) were used to mark the degree of certainty with which a statement was made (e.g., *I think this is a lamb* said to convey uncertainty or *I know this fits too* said to mark conviction). These functions may collectively be called *conversational* functions, and they occurred at similar levels throughout the age range studied. The use of cognitive term utterances to refer to psychological events first appeared infrequently at the end of the third year and then increased through the next year so that by the age of 4, this was the most common use of cognitive terms.

The developmental pattern reported by Shatz et al. (1983) was confirmed by Bartsch and Wellman (1995), who examined cognitive terms as well as desire terms in the language samples they analyzed. They found that all 10 of the children in their study, including Abe, showed a marked increase in the use of cognitive terms to make reference to thoughts and beliefs during the fourth year. The following example nicely illustrates the difference between the conversational use of a cognitive term utterance to introduce a topic and the psychological use to make reference to someone's thoughts (Bartsch & Wellman, p. 46):

Mark (3;8): Do you know what? When we were going on our walk I thought we were lost. I thinked we were lost. When we were going on our walk and it was dark.

Genuine references to thoughts are best revealed in utterances in which children explicitly contrast one person's thought or knowledge with a contrasting state of the world or with someone else's thought. Such contrastives can occur within a single utterance, as in the following example from Bartsch and Wellman (1995, pp. 52–53):

Abe (3;6): The people thought Dracula was mean. But he was nice.

They can also occur across discourse turns as in the following example from my daughter, Mackenzie, the week before her fourth birthday, which occurred in a conversation with her friend who attended a different school.

Mackenzie: We had cupcakes at school today.
Aislinn: I know.
Mackenzie: Well no, you don't know. You can't know.

As a rule these uses of cognitive terms that clearly distinguish the different perspectives of the speaker, listener, or some third person appear in children's language as the fourth birthday approaches.

So far we have reviewed how psychological terms are used in young children's speech. Clearly children's psychological talk, whether used to express their feelings or attitudes or to comment on the psychological activity of self and others, occurs in communicative interaction with others. In order to understand how preschool children start to incorporate psychological references into their communicative exchanges it is important to examine how others use psychological references as they participate in interactions with the children. Although parents retain their position as the most influential people in the early lives of children, through the preschool period, interactions with siblings and peers start to play a more prominent role. Inevitably these interactions also serve to hone the development of commonsense psychology.

Studies of mothers and children together have generally shown very interesting associations between mothers' and their children's patterns of use of psychological terms. The first relevant study was carried out by Marjorie Beeghly and her colleagues (Beeghly, Bretherton, & Mervis, 1986), who examined the various categories of internal state terms identified by Bretherton and Beeghly (1982) in a sample of 30 mothers when their children were 13, 20, and then 28 months of age. They found different patterns of change for the different types of terms. Volition (or what I call conative) terms, which included the very common *want*, were used very frequently at all ages. Emotion terms also showed no change with age. However, cognitive terms increased significantly over the period of the study at the same time as perceptual terms were reduced significantly. Clearly, mothers made frequent reference to emotions and desires at all ages but turned to talking less about perceptually available objects and events and more about thoughts as their children developed through this period. At each point of observation, mothers' overall use of internal state terms was correlated with their children's use; this suggests that young children's psychological language is influenced by their linguistic interactions with their parents. However, given that the children were very young at the time of the observations, and thus used some types of internal state terms very infrequently, Beeghly and her colleagues did not examine whether particular types of internal state terms were associated between mothers and their children.

In a study of 14 mothers and their children observed at 2, 3, and 4 years of age, we (Moore, Furrow, Chiasson, & Patriquin, 1994) found, as Beeghly and colleagues (1986) had at a younger age, that mothers' use of desire terms was high at all ages but that their use of cognitive terms increased significantly from when their children were 2 to when they were 3 years old. From 3 to 4 years, mothers' use of cognitive terms remained stable. In comparison, children's uses of desire terms increased significantly from age 2 to age 3 and then were stable, whereas their use of cognitive terms increased throughout the period of study. There were also significant correlations between the mothers' and children's use of cognitive terms at all the ages studied. These results, along with those from other studies (Beeghly et al.; Brown & Dunn, 1991), show that mothers' pattern of use of desire and cognitive terms corresponds to their children's pattern, but is 6 months to a year ahead. Because the children's use follows their mothers' use, it appears that mothers provide a context for psychological talk that allows their children to acquire and use psychological terms. Children tend to adopt the psychological language that their mothers have been using for a little while, but as they do, their mothers are already moving on to incorporate more advanced psychological language into their conversation.

To further explore the potential role of mothers' use of psychological terms in the development of their children's use, in their study of the use of cognitive terms by young children and their mothers, Furrow and colleagues (Furrow, Moore, Davidge, & Chiasson, 1992) used a functional coding scheme that was modeled on the one Shatz et al. (1983) developed for children. Furrow and colleagues examined the use of cognitive terms in the everyday conversations of 19 mothers and their children in various home contexts when the children were 2 years old, and again when they were 3 years old. Like the other studies on maternal use, they found that mothers increased their use of cognitive terms enormously from when their children were 2 years to when they were 3 years old. Despite this overall increase, use of cognitive terms for different functions did not change proportionally across age. The most common use of cognitive terms by mothers at both time points was for directing action or attention in some way. Some attention-directing utterances were relatively constraining in that the mother used a cognitive term to propose an action or interpretation ("Do you think that's a garage?"), whereas others appeared more to direct the children to think about what they were doing ("Do you know where that goes?"). Mothers also used cognitive terms to talk about psychological states ("Think about it in your head"). Importantly, the study found that mothers who used more cognitive terms to talk about psychological events or to direct their 2-year-olds' thinking had children who at 3 years were using more cognitive terms themselves. These results confirm the importance of maternal input to the acquisition of cognitive terms. But it was not merely the appearance of these terms in the mothers' conversation that was important, it was the mothers' use of these terms to refer to, or encourage, their children's thinking that appeared to be of particular value. Importantly, because mothers' use of cognitive terms in this way when their children were only 2 years old was linked to children's use of cognitive terms at 3 years, the results imply that the mothers' language influences their children's use rather than the other way around.

By the late preschool period, there is evidence that more psychological talk occurs in conversations that children have with siblings or peers than in conversations with parents. Jane Brown and her colleagues (Brown, Donelan-McCall, & Dunn, 1996) studied a sample of children at 47 months of age interacting in one home session with their older siblings and mothers and in another home session with their best friends. They recorded all utterances involving a cognitive term and coded them according to Shatz et al.'s (1983) scheme. The overall rate of cognitive term talk was approximately twice as high when the children talked to their siblings or to their friends compared to when they talked to their mothers, although the mother-child conversations were more often about psychological events than the conversations among children. Nevertheless close to 50% of cognitive term utterances in conversations among children made reference to a psychological state. Also noteworthy was the finding that much of the cognitive talk occurring between friends occurred within the context of pretend play. Clearly, then, there is considerable opportunity for young children to explore their understanding of psychology within their interactions with siblings and peers.

A study by Jennifer Jenkins and her colleagues (Jenkins, Turrell, Kogushi, Lollis, & Ross, 2003) shows more directly the kind of impact that conversations about psychological states among siblings may have on development. They observed 40 families with two parents and two children who were about 2 years apart in age. The first observation took place when the younger children were on average 2 years and 4 months old and the second observation about 2 years later. This design meant that they had observations of both siblings in each pair at approximately the same age of 4 years and 4 months. At each observation point the families were observed for six 90-minute home sessions. These sessions were naturalistic except that major distractions such as TV or video games were not allowed. Overall, and consistent with Brown et al.'s (1996) finding, the children spent more time interacting with each other than they did with their parents. From transcripts of these sessions, the authors recorded all instances of emotion, desire, and cognitive terms, although they did not code them for function. Focusing on the younger children showed that, consistent with other studies, use of cognitive terms increased significantly over the period from 2 to 4 years whereas use of desire terms declined somewhat. Emotion talk remained constant over this age range. The pattern of change over time in mothers' psychological utterances mirrored the younger children's. Indeed mothers used more cognitive terms than desire or feeling terms by the time their younger children were 4 years old. In some ways the most interesting comparison was between the psychological talk of the younger and older siblings when they were the same age. The older siblings who had reached the age of 4 with a younger and therefore less verbal sibling in tow used far fewer cognitive terms at this age than the younger children who had had a more sophisticated older sibling through these preschool years. This direct comparison of children at the same age within the same families attests to the importance of child-child interactions in the development of social competence.

The developmental story that may be told from the various studies of children's production of different psychological terms is quite consistent and relatively simple. Children first acquire psychological terms to express the range of psychological relations that they experience and to regulate their interactions with others. Emotion and desire terms are acquired very early because they typically express psychological relations to real objects or states of affairs—liking, fearing, or wanting things. Cognitive terms appear later because they primarily serve to direct attention to, or express varying degrees of subjective certainty about, more complex information that is expressed propositionally. In all cases, however, these expressions are fundamentally communicative devices to achieve interactive goals—to alleviate an emotion, to satisfy a desire, to direct someone's attention to novel information. At the same time, children's interactive partners are also expressing similar kinds of psychological relations and children need to respond appropriately. Once the terms have been acquired in this way, the expressions themselves become potential topics of discourse so children can start to talk about psychological relations even when they are not currently being expressed. In this way, it is evident that the elaboration of commonsense psychology occurs first in the discursive contexts in which the psychological relations of the child and significant others are topics.

But this is not the end of the story. Although young children use a wide variety of psychological terms to refer to psychological relations of self and other by 4 years of age, they have not yet acquired a systematic conceptual understanding of the psychological relations they are talking about. Rather, the appropriate uses of psychological terms to represent particular psychological events occur in particular contexts to express particular functions. Children understand individual words and their referents without understanding how they fit into a systematic conception of commonsense psychology (Astington & Peskin, 2004; Nelson & Kessler Shaw, 2002). There are two broad types of testing situations in which this limitation is evident. First, studies on children's comprehension of the distinctions among various psychological terms show that children perform quite poorly when required to differentiate the appropriate use of contrasting psychological terms. Second, studies designed to test children's understanding of the psychological referents of these terms also reveal a lag between appropriate conversation about psychological relations and conceptual grasp of the referents.

Comprehension of Psychological Terms

As adults, we have a relatively coherent semantic and pragmatic system for psychological terms that differentiates the meanings and uses of these terms. The commonly studied distinction between *know* and *think* suffices to make the point.

(4) John knows that *Casablanca* is playing at the Arts theater.

(5) John thinks that *Casablanca* is playing at the Arts theater.

We understand that sentences (4) and (5) differ in their semantic presuppositions, such that the complement clause of (4) is true of the world whereas the complement clause of (5) may or may not be true of the world. The agent (*John*) may have arrived at his epistemic state in a variety of ways. He may know the truth because he had direct perceptual evidence or he inferred it in some way. Alternatively, he may not know the truth because his evidence was incomplete or his sources unreliable.

Semantic analyses of language attempt to treat meaning independently of use, but in the lives of young children, language is all about use, so we may rephrase the semantic distinction in more pragmatic terms in the following way. We recognize that sentence (4) is an appropriate utterance for a speaker if the speaker and conversational partner are both sure about the truth of the complement. In this case, the speaker, listener, and agent of the sentence (*John*) all share knowledge. In contrast, sentence (5) is an appropriate utterance for a speaker under a variety of conditions in which the listener and John do not share the same opinion. Speaker and listener may share knowledge that differs from John's (perhaps they both know that *Citizen Kane* is actually playing at the Arts theater and the speaker uses the utterance to share with the listener the fact of John's false belief). Speaker and listener may have different opinions (perhaps the speaker is trying to invoke John's opinion in support of the speaker's attempt to convince the listener of her opinion). Finally, speaker and listener may both be unsure of the truth of the complement (and the speaker may be invoking John's belief to guide their joint opinion). In this way the use of *know* versus *think* in otherwise equivalent sentences marks the correspondence or lack thereof between the speaker's, listener's, and sentence agent's psychological relation.

(6) I know that *Casablanca* is playing at the Arts theater.

(7) I think that *Casablanca* is playing at the Arts theater.

Imagine now that rather than referring to another agent's opinion, the speaker refers to her own opinion, as in (6) and (7). Here the opinion of the speaker and the agent of the sentence necessarily coincide so there is no possibility for the opinion of the agent and the listener to vary independently of the speaker. Under this condition, *know* is used when a speaker is sure of the truth of the complement, either to affirm an opinion shared between speaker and listener, or to convey the certainty of the speaker's opinion to an uncertain listener. In contrast, *think* is used when the speaker is uncertain whether the listener has a firm opinion.

Regardless of whether the sentence is produced with a first- or third-person subject, the key point about the *know* versus *think* distinction is that it involves the coordination of multiple perspectives on the proposition that follows in the sentence. In order to make the distinction reliably and appropriately, children must be able to coordinate these multiple perspectives. In short, they must be able to appreciate that the opinions of self and others about propositions relating to the world may or may not be shared, and they must be able to distinguish these circumstances.

A variety of studies have been carried out with young children to determine when they are able to distinguish psychological terms according to these semantic and pragmatic criteria (e.g., C. Johnson, 1982). For example, Abbeduto and Rosenberg (1985) investigated when young children recognize the different presuppositions for various cognitive terms. They presented children from 3 to 4 years old with a series of sentences that first set up a context, then introduced a test sentence containing one of the cognitive terms, and finally asked a test question (see Table 9.3). Notice that there was no way to answer the question from the information presented in the

TABLE 9.3

Sample Items From Abbeduto and Rosenberg (1985)

	Does Not Presuppose Truth of the Complement	*Presupposes Truth of the Complement*
Context	I have a friend named Mary. Mary has a cat	I have a friend named Mary. Mary has a cat
Test sentence	Mary thinks that the cat is slow.	Mary knows that the cat is slow.
Test question	Is the cat slow? (correct answer = don't know)	Is the cat slow? (correct answer = yes)

context questions. The only way to answer correctly was to pay attention to the cognitive term employed in the test sentence. Children could answer "yes," "no," or "don't know." In this study, 4-year-olds but not 3-year-olds reliably answered both *know* and *think* cases correctly, showing that they could distinguish these verbs based on the truth status they conferred on their complements.

Children's understanding of the relative certainty expressed by utterances including *know, think,* and related terms has also been studied (Hirst & Weil, 1982; Moore, Bryant, & Furrow, 1989). My colleagues and I (Moore, et al., 1989) presented children with a game in which they had to find a candy reward hidden in one of two boxes over a series of trials. The only clues they had were pairs of utterances made by two hand puppets, manipulated by the experimenter, that were introduced to the children as helpers. On each trial the two puppets made one statement each and these statements varied only in the critical cognitive term that was used. For example, one puppet said, "I know it's in the red box" and the other puppet said, "I think it's in the blue box." The children were then allowed to choose one of the boxes. In order to guard against learning during the session, the chosen boxes were all set aside until the trials were over, at which time the children were allowed to look in each box. At first glance, this game appears particularly easy; nevertheless the performance of children younger than 4 years was at chance. They could not use the statements to guide their search. In contrast, 4-year-olds and older children were reliably able to pick the box that had been indicated by *know*, the term expressing greater certainty.

In contrast to the considerable literature on young children's developing comprehension of cognitive terms such as *know* and *think*, their understanding of desire terms has attracted rather less interest. We do know, however, that although children use desire terms very early, their understanding of desire term distinctions is no better than their understanding of cognitive term distinctions. The two most commonly used terms, *need* and *want*, differ in a variety of ways. For example, *need* often expresses an instrumental desire, whereas *want* expresses an intrinsic desire. We (Moore, Gilbert, & Sapp, 1995) examined this distinction in 3- to 5-year-old children who were told stories with toy props in which two characters expressed a desire for an attractive yet functional object. The circumstances of the two characters differed such that one required the object for a purpose whereas the other did not. The children were then asked whether each character "wanted" or "needed" the object (see Table 9.4). Even though they could remember the facts of the story in answer to the memory control question, the 3-year-olds performed at chance—they did not see a difference between *want* and *need*. In contrast, by 4 years, children correctly said that the character with the instrumental desire "needed" the object whereas the character with the intrinsic desire "wanted" it.

These and a variety of other studies using experimental approaches to the comprehension of psychological terms show that from about 4 years of age children have a good grasp of the distinctions between the most common psychological terms, *know* and *think, want* and *need*. They are therefore able to coordinate the multiple perspectives of speaker, listener, and sentence agent and recognize when these perspectives coincide or diverge. Importantly, the results from these comprehension tasks fit well with the results from observational studies that show the most sophisticated uses of cognitive terms to represent differing perspectives appearing toward the end of the fourth year (Bartsch & Wellman, 1995). In summary, by 4 years of

TABLE 9.4

**Sample Story and Questions From the Comprehension Study
of Desire Terms *Want* and *Need* (Moore, Gilbert, & Sapp, 1995)**

Sample story
    This is a story about two little boys named John and Bill. One day John and Bill are outside playing on the slide. Then Daddy tells them it is time to go home: "Come on boys it's time to go home." John slides down the slide, falls down but is okay and walks over to Daddy. Bill slides down the slide, falls down, cuts his knee, and starts to cry, "Daddy my knee hurts!" They all walk home and Mummy has just come home from the store, and she has brought home this bandaid [the child is shown a Band-Art bandaid with colourful pictures on it]. John is okay, but Bill's knee is still bleeding. When the two boys see the bandaid, they both say, "Gimme the bandaid please mummy."
Test questions
    Does John want the bandaid or does he need the bandaid?
    Does Bill want the bandaid or does he need the bandaid?
Memory control question
    Who fell off the slide and cut his knee?

---

age, children's language shows that they understand that different people may have different psychological relations to representational or perspectival information.

The developmental sequence observed with the production and comprehension of psychological terms reflects the pattern of hierarchical language development that we have seen before. Children first participate with others in structured interactions involving psychological terms. These terms are initially used in utterances designed to regulate those interactions—to express emotions and desires, to direct action in relation to ongoing events, or to modulate certainty about information. So psychological terms arise first as a means to regulate joint attentional interactions around objects, events, or information. However, once in place, these utterances involving psychological terms may themselves become the focus of further interactions. Children and parents can begin to talk about the emotions and desires expressed or about the epistemic attitudes to information. In so doing, these psychological perspectives and their potential diversity across different people can start to be understood.

UNDERSTANDING PSYCHOLOGICAL RELATIONS TO PERSPECTIVES

The studies on cognitive terms show that both the production and comprehension of the linguistic distinctions reflecting the coordination of perspectives is seen from about 4 years of age. Understanding perspectival psychological relations may also be studied by investigating experimentally whether children can adopt a perspective that differs from their own. The developmental study of perspective taking has a long history that was initially focused on children's ability to adopt the visual perspective of someone else (e.g., Cox, 1980; Piaget & Inhelder, 1956). In their classic work, Piaget and Inhelder presented children with a model of a landscape with three mountains. Children were asked to identify, from a series of pictures representing different perspectives on the model, which picture captured their own point of view and which captured the point of view of another person seated in a different location around the model. Piaget reported that it was not until 6 or 7 years that children were able to work out what would be seen of this complex three-dimensional display from a location other than their current one. Subsequent work showed that this result was in large part due to the complexity of the model. Studies in which the display was very simple showed that younger children could indeed adopt the perspective appropriate to a different viewing location (Borke, 1975). Flavell and his colleagues reported that even 2-year-olds understand that someone else will see something different from the self if the two viewers are looking at opposite sides of a card on which different pictures are printed back to back (Flavell, Everett, Croft, & Flavell, 1981;

Masangkay et al., 1974). However, when the task is to determine how something appears from another point of view, for example, upside down or right side up, then children do not succeed until about 4 years. Flavell and colleagues dubbed this difference Level I versus Level II perspective taking. The difference is really between recognizing that someone else may see a different object from oneself and recognizing that the appearance of even the same object may differ between self and other from different points of view. Using the terminology introduced in chapter 2, we can say that Level I perspective taking corresponds to understanding diversity of psychological relations to real objects, whereas Level II perspective taking corresponds to understanding diversity of psychological relations to representational or perspectival objects.

Tied in with the recognition that people may have different visual perspectives on something is the understanding of the difference between the appearance of something and its real nature (Flavell, Flavell, & Green, 1983). The standard demonstration involves the use of deceptive objects such as a sponge that looks like a rock. Children are first shown the sponge and asked what it is. The naive answer comes back: "a rock." Children are then given the object to hold and manipulate and they discover that in fact it is not hard but is made out of sponge and can be squashed. The rock-sponge is then placed on the table again and the children are asked two questions: the reality question, "What is this really, really—a sponge or a rock?" and the appearance question, "What does this look like—a sponge or a rock?" Three-year-olds typically answer both questions in the same way, usually in terms of the identity of the object. Thus, they say it really is a sponge and it looks like a sponge. What is happening here is that younger children do not adequately differentiate perspective and reality. Four-year-olds commonly do make this differentiation, and so they happily say that the object looks like a rock but is really a sponge.

Another way of construing younger children's failure with the appearance–reality distinction is to say that in effect, they do not appreciate that their visual perspective (their apprehension of the appearance) does not match their mental perspective (their take on reality). In recent years, it has been mental rather than visual perspective taking that has dominated research under the rubric of "children's theory of mind" (Astington, Harris, & Olson, 1988; Frye & Moore, 1991; Wellman, 1990). The core concept that has been most studied in this area is that of false belief. The central role of false belief in research on preschoolers' social understanding originates in the idea, introduced in chapter 2, that to predict others' action it is important to understand what they think is true rather than what is actually the case. When people's beliefs accurately reflect the state of reality, then using one's own knowledge of the world to predict the others' action serves just fine. But if others believe something that is untrue, then accurate prediction of their action is only possible if one can set aside one's own knowledge of the world and consider the others' misrepresentation of the state of the world. Indeed some would argue that it is only reasonable to say that individuals understand beliefs at all if they can demonstrate an understanding of false beliefs (e.g., Dennett, 1978).

In any event, the generation of tests for false belief understanding in the 1980s led to a huge amount of research on the topic. The first test was developed by Heinz Wimmer and Josef Perner (1983). In their task, the children are told a story about a boy named Maxi as the story is acted out with props. Maxi's mother brings home some chocolate and asks Maxi to place it in one location. Maxi then leaves the scene and while he is away his mother removes the chocolate from the original location, uses some of it, and replaces the remainder in a different location. Maxi returns and the child participants are asked where Maxi will look for the chocolate. Various control questions are also asked to ensure that the children remember the key facts of the story. This task requires the children to set aside their own knowledge of the actual chocolate location and consider the situation from Maxi's uninformed perspective. In their original work, Wimmer and Perner found that it was not until about 5 years that children pass this task by saying that Maxi will look in the location in which he originally placed the chocolate. However, subsequent research found that modified versions of this changed location task that stay true to the logic of the task while simplifying and clarifying the task demands yield quite good performance in young 4-year-olds (Wellman, Cross, & Watson, 2001).

A different type of false belief task requiring little in the way of narrative comprehension also yields evidence of developmental change at about 4 years of age (Perner, Leekam, & Wimmer, 1987). In the "misleading contents" task the children are first shown a container that is easily recognizable, such as a Smarties or M&Ms box. The children may be asked what is in the box and the answer is reliably what the box looks to contain. The children are then shown that in fact the box contains something else, perhaps pebbles. Finally, the box is closed up again as it was at the start of the task, and the children are asked what another child who has not yet seen the box will think is in it when he or she first sees it. Younger preschoolers typically answer, "pebbles," showing again that they have difficulty setting aside their current epistemic relation to the contents in order to work out someone else's epistemic relation. By about 4 years, children start to recognize that the other's knowledge differs from their own and they can pass the task.

These false belief tasks are valuable methods for assessing the understanding of diversity of epistemic relations across self and other. The misleading contents task is also adaptable to assessing the understanding of perspectival diversity within the self across time. In this case, the task is presented in the same way but rather than the children being asked about another person's belief about the contents of the box, the children are asked what they thought was in the box before it was first opened (Gopnik & Astington, 1988; Perner et al., 1987). This version of the task shows very similar results to the version where the children have to judge another person's thoughts. There is, therefore, strong evidence that understanding perspectival diversity in self and others develops in parallel (see also Gopnik, 1993).

Since the development of these tasks, the topic of false belief understanding has become one of the most heavily studied in all of developmental psychology, with many studies directed at showing that rather young children can perform well on the task and a few showing that even older children perform poorly. Henry Wellman and his colleagues (2001) at the University of Michigan recently carried out a meta-analytic review of some 178 separate studies of false belief understanding in preschoolers. They concluded that indeed understanding false belief shows clear developmental change: "At younger ages—essentially 41 months (3 years 5 months) and younger—children performed below chance, making the classic false belief error. At older ages—essentially 48 months (4 years) and older—they performed above chance, significantly correct" (p. 663).

So why do 3-year-olds fail false belief tasks? Remember that such young children answer the test question with reference to their own knowledge. They know where the chocolate is or what is really in the box and so others must too. What 3-year-olds have trouble doing is recognizing that their own current knowledge is not relevant because the other person has a different perspective on the situation. Interestingly this failure extends to their thinking about their own previous perspective. They also overgeneralize their current knowledge to prior thoughts. In a very general way, then, the children's current knowledge intrudes on the assessment of anyone's beliefs about the situation.

What is required for people to take a perspective that is at odds with their own current perspective? Let us look at the classic changed location false belief task. First, of course, it is necessary to represent Maxi's epistemic psychological relation and this means recognizing that because Maxi did not witness the change in location, he will think the object is still where he first put it. But alone, that is not enough because the children have witnessed the change in location and so know the object is in the other location. This knowledge is much more salient because of its immediacy and as a result it tends to dominate in determining the children's response. So, second, in addition to representing the other person's epistemic relation, the children have to be able to represent their own current epistemic relation. In this way the children's current knowledge can be unhitched from the response and the children can determine which perspective is relevant to the problem. In short, understanding false belief requires children to be simultaneously aware of both their own current psychological relation ("I know X") and the other person's psychological relation ("He thinks Y"). Only when children can represent both together can they be said to appreciate the perspectival nature of the situation. From this analysis, it can be seen that the representational demands of perspectival problems are more taxing than those that only involve the kind of diversity of psychological relations that may characterize current actions in relation to real objects (Frye et al., 1995, Perner, 1991b).

The focus on epistemic psychological relations, such as visual perspective and belief, in this section so far reflects the bulk of the research on children's understanding of perspectival psychological relations. However, some research has been carried out on the understanding of the perspectival nature of desires. In collaboration with Chris Jarrold and James Russell at the University of Cambridge, we (Moore et al., 1995) devised a task that was modeled on the structure of the typical false belief task. Recall that in the Maxi and the chocolate task, the children are first exposed to one situation that sets up an initial belief (that the chocolate is in one place). Next they are exposed to additional information that changes their initial belief to a second belief that is incompatible with or conflicts with their first belief (the chocolate is moved to the second place). At the same time, the other character, Maxi, is not exposed to the additional information and so does not share the second belief with the child participants. The children are then asked to report the other person's belief. Our conflicting desire task starts with the child and a play partner (in this case a puppet called "Fat Cat") playing a game in which they have to find pieces to complete a puzzle of a frog. Initially both play partners each have a body piece and they each have to get a head piece before they can get the eyes piece. The game proceeds with each player in turn drawing a card from a deck containing cards marked white, red, or blue. In order to make further progress on the puzzle, each player must draw a red card, which represents the head piece. Because the experimenter has fixed the order of the cards in the deck, the children draw a red card first and claim a head piece for their puzzle. As a result, the children's initial desire to draw a red card has now changed to a desire to draw a blue card (which represents the eyes piece), whereas Fat Cat's desire to draw a red card has not changed. At this point, the children are asked about Fat Cat's desire and about their own previous desire (before drawing the red card). In order to succeed on this task, the children have to be able to distinguish their own current desire from both their own previous desire and from Fat Cat's desire. Interestingly, 3.5-year-olds performed as poorly on this task as they did on the standard Maxi false belief task, showing that when the task demands are similar, children have similar difficulty with understanding desires that differ across people as they do with understanding diverse beliefs.

In summary, results from a wide range of experimental tasks (including visual perspective tasks, appearance–reality tasks, and false belief tasks) suggest that young preschoolers have great difficulty recognizing that there can simultaneously be more than one psychological perspective on an object, event, or state of affairs. In many cases this amounts to not understanding that their own current perspective is not the only one. To do this requires being able to represent and reflect on both their own immediate perspective and that of another person, or of themselves at an earlier time, simultaneously.

THE ROLE OF LANGUAGE AND MULTIPLE REPRESENTATIONS IN UNDERSTANDING PERSPECTIVAL DIVERSITY

We have explored children's understanding of the diversity of perspectives in two types of situation. First, we looked at how children's acquisition of psychological terms comes to reflect an understanding of perspectives. Then we reviewed children's developing ability to think about different perspectives in situations where there are two or more representations of the same object or state of affairs. In principle, these two manifestations of the understanding of perspectival diversity might occur relatively independently. Perhaps children gain a facility with psychological terms by engaging with others in conversations using those types of words. Within these conversations, they learn how these words are involved in the modal constructions used for expressing perspectives. In parallel, children may gain an understanding that the world can be represented in more than one way through experience with contrasting representations of that world. For example, they may remember situations in which they first thought a misleading object was one thing and then discovered it was something else, or situations in which a sibling told them that their mother was out, but they had seen her return a few minutes earlier.

In contrast, it is possible that these two manifestations of understanding perspectival diversity occur together and support each other. In this scenario, children have experiences with contrasting representations of objects or states of affairs, but these contrasting representations are highlighted for them by the conversations that accompany these experiences. In fact, research using training experiments substantiates this story. Training studies are a particularly valuable method for investigating the conditions supporting development. In this method, different groups of children are first pretested to determine that they are not yet at a target level of understanding. The different groups are then exposed to different types of experiences that might be effective in improving their performance in the chosen area of competence (the experimental treatments). Sometimes, one group of children serves as a control group in that they do not receive any experiences that might be helpful but instead receive an experience that is presumed to be innocent in effect. Finally, after the training exposure, the children are all tested on a set of posttests that gauge their abilities in the area of interest. If the children who receive the experimental treatments perform better in the posttests than those in the control group, we can infer that the experimental experiences may well play a role in promoting development.

A number of training studies have now been carried out to examine what kinds of experiences might help children develop an understanding of perspectival diversity, particularly as manifested by false belief understanding (e.g., Appleton & Reddy, 1996; Clements, Rustin, & McCallum, 2000; Lohmann & Tomasello, 2003; Slaughter & Gopnik, 1996). For our purposes, the most informative of these studies is that of Heidemarie Lohmann and Michael Tomasello. They were interested in the role of different kinds of language experience as well as of experience with objects that could be represented in more than one way. To explore these issues they devised four main types of training experience (see Table 9.5). Children of about 3.5 years of age were presented with a variety of misleading objects that initially appeared to be one thing and then on further inspection would be discovered to be something else. Those children in the full training group were shown the objects in turn as the experimenter asked them what they first thought the objects were and then, after discovering their real nature, what they now thought they were. The children were also asked to predict what another character, a hand puppet, would think the object was. In this way, the children received experience both with psychological language and with objects that could be represented in two ways. The other training groups presented children with only some components of the full training. For discourse only training, the children had the same experience with the objects as did the children in the full training group and the experimenter highlighted in conversation the misleading nature of them but no psychological language was used by the experimenter. For complements only, the children saw the same objects and the experimenter talked about them with

TABLE 9.5

Training Conditions in the Study by Lohmann and Tomasello (2003)

Training Condition	Components of the Training		
	Experience With Misleading Objects	Psychological Terms	Discourse About the Objects
Full training	Ö	Ö	Ö
Discourse only	Ö	C	Ö
Complements only	C	Ö	Ö
No language	Ö	C	C

the children using psychological verbs such as *know* and *think* that occur with complements, but the deceptive nature of the objects was not demonstrated or highlighted by the experimenter. Finally, a fourth no language group got to see the misleading nature of the objects but the experimenter did not talk to the children about them or use any language that would highlight the contrasting representations of the same objects.

All of the children were pretested on a misleading contents task assessing the understanding of false belief in self and others (Gopnik & Astington, 1988) whereby the children were first shown an egg box and asked what they thought was in it. They were then shown that it contained a toy car before the box was closed again. Finally, they were asked what they thought was in it at first and what another child would say was inside on first seeing it. As seen earlier, 3-year-olds tend to perform poorly on this kind of task and most of the children in Lohmann and Tomasello's (2003) study gave the incorrect answer, saying both that they thought, and that the other child would think, that the egg box contained the car. Importantly, the children were equally likely to perform poorly on this pretest task across all training groups. After training, the children were all tested on the same misleading contents task again, as well as on a change of location false belief task and an appearance–reality task. These latter two tasks were included in the posttest to determine to what extent the children had learned something more general about perspectival diversity rather than something specific about misleading objects.

The effects of these different training conditions were seen both in performance improvement on the misleading contents task from pretest to posttest and in performance on the other tasks of the posttest. All of the training conditions led to improvement in performance on the misleading contents task but improvement in the full training group was about twice as good as that in the other groups. This result was paralleled by condition differences in performance on the change of location false belief and appearance–reality tasks, where again the children who had received the full training did better than the children who had received the other kinds of training. When performance results in all of the posttests were considered together, it was found that full training led to significantly greater performance in the posttest than all of the other training conditions, and that these other training conditions did not differ from each other in terms of their effects on performance in understanding perspectival diversity.

Because children in the discourse only, complements only, and no language conditions did show some improvement in their understanding of false belief from pretest to posttest, the study by Lohmann and Tomasello (2003) provides evidence that both conversation involving psychological terms and experience with objects or situations that can be represented in two ways are important for the development of the understanding of diversity in psychological perspectives. However, the fact that the full training condition led to much better performance than the other conditions demonstrates effectively that experience with representational diversity that is then highlighted in conversation through the use of psychological terms is particularly valuable to children in the construction of this level of commonsense psychology.

COORDINATING PERSPECTIVES IN SOCIAL INTERACTION

In some ways, the attainment of a level of commonsense psychology in which differing perspectives on the world are recognized represents a crowning achievement in the psychological development of the preschool child. In particular, the ability to consider independent perspectives in social situations enables a more sophisticated array of interactive skills in both competitive and cooperative contexts (Astington, 2003). Perhaps the most studied context is deception. Deception can occur in varying levels of complexity, and if we include all manifestations it is a ubiquitous phenomenon in the natural world (Mitchell & Thompson, 1986), with instances appearing in plants as well animals ranging from insects to mammals. However, most forms of deception among animals do not require any commonsense psychology. For example, a bird may be deterred by the eye spots on a butterfly's wings without the butterfly having to understand anything about the bird responding as if those spots were eyes. Only certain forms of active behavioral deception exhibited by humans and perhaps our closest primate relatives (Whiten & Byrne, 1988) are attempts to manipulate the beliefs of a competitor. The key criterion is that the deceptive tactic is directed at creating a false belief in the target individual.

Simple forms of behavioral deception are evident in children as young as 2 to 3 years. For example, Michael Lewis and his colleagues (Lewis, Stanger, & Sullivan, 1989) had an experimenter set up a toy zoo individually with children from 33 to 37 months old in a laboratory playroom. The experimenter told the children that she was going to bring out a surprise toy and they had to close their eyes and not peek until they were told to. After bringing out the surprise toy, the experimenter left the room while the children waited. The children were observed from behind a one-way mirror until they had peeked or for 5 minutes, whichever was sooner. At this point, the experimenter returned and asked the children if they had peeked. Only 4 of 33 children did not peek for the 5 minutes, showing that this is a difficult situation for children to handle. When then asked whether they had peeked, only 11 of the children who had peeked admitted to doing so. The rest either denied peeking or did not answer. It therefore seems that children not quite 3 years old are quite capable of using verbal deception in a simple situation. However, such deception does not mean that the children were attempting to make the adult believe something false. As we have seen, children of this age do not typically understand that others may have false beliefs. Denial

in such a context may be a simple learned strategy to avoid the consequences of prohibited behavior. Nevertheless, gaining an understanding of
false belief may lead children to be more likely to deny similar transgres-
sions. Polak and Harris (1999) followed up Lewis and colleagues' research
and found that 3-year-olds with little or no understanding of false belief
were almost as likely to admit to a transgression as to deny it. However,
those children who performed better on false belief tasks were almost
uniformly likely to deny their transgression.

A more complex deception situation than the one just considered involves providing false information rather than simply denying something.
In a study by Beate Sodian (1991), children were presented with a game in
which they had to either prevent or assist a puppet in finding a reward. At
the beginning of the task, the children were introduced to two puppets: a
helpful king who would give prizes to the child and a nasty robber who
would keep prizes for himself. Over a series of trials, the children hid the reward, a gold star, in one of two boxes. During the hiding, the puppets were
absent so they could not see where the star was hidden. The king or the robber was then brought back and asked the children where the star was. The
children had to indicate by pointing or identifying one of the boxes. The
puppet always looked in the indicated box. On trials with the king the children received the star, whereas on trials involving the robber the robber
kept the star. Therefore, in order to keep the stars the children had to indicate the baited box when the king asked and the empty box when the robber
asked. All children virtually always indicated the baited box on the king trials. However, on the robber trials, a clear age effect was found. Younger
3-year-olds almost always pointed to the baited box and thereby lost the
star. However, by 4.5 years, the large majority of children were able to point
to the empty box and thereby keep the star for themselves. This finding has
been replicated in other studies and interestingly good performance on this
task is related to the ability to pass standard false belief tasks (Russell,
Mauthner, Sharpe, & Tidswell, 1991).

Deception need not always have a nefarious purpose. Peskin and
Ardino (2003) studied two deceptive situations that are prosocial and commonplace in the lives of young children—playing hide-and-seek and keeping a secret. Both require the ability to keep information from another
person, but now for a purpose that is ultimately cooperative. As any parents of preschoolers will attest, young children are very bad at keeping others ignorant when required. Games of hide-and-seek with 3-year-olds may
involve them "hiding" in full view of the seeker. In similar fashion, although young children know that they should not reveal secrets, even
when they succeed in not blurting out the truth, they do not appreciate how
their behavior may be informative. To illustrate, consider this example:
The day before Father's Day in June of 2003, when she was just 4 years old,
my daughter greeted my return from work with, "I had a great time at

school today. All the other kids made presents for Father's Day, but I didn't." Peskin and Ardino arranged for 3- to 5-year-old children to know about a surprise birthday cake for someone and examined how well they could not point out the hidden cake when that person asked for something to eat. They also involved the children in games of hide-and-seek with the children playing both hider and seeker roles. Here they looked at whether the children made errors such as telling the seeker where they were going to hide or looking at the hider as she tried to hide. Children were also tested on typical false belief tasks. The results showed that only the 3-year-olds did particularly badly on both the keeping-a-secret and hide-and-seek games. Furthermore, as with the work on deceptive informing, performance on keeping a secret and hide-and-seek was strongly related to how well the children did on false belief tasks.

We have seen that deception involves an intentional attempt to keep someone from knowing something. The opposite of deception may be conceived as an intentional attempt to move a person from not knowing something to knowing it (Frye & Ziv, 2005). Such intentional acts we know more commonly as teaching. When we consider that teaching depends on the awareness that someone else does not know something or thinks something is false, it is evident that teaching depends on recognizing that others may hold different perspectives from our own (Frye & Ziv, 2005; Kruger & Tomasello, 1996; Olson & Bruner, 1996).

Very little research has been carried out on young children's ability to teach less knowledgeable individuals. However, it too points to developments at about 4 years of age. Using an extremely simplified teaching situation, Ashley and Tomasello (1998) recruited pairs of children to participate in a cooperative task involving an experimental apparatus where each had to adopt a complementary role to achieve a shared goal, which was to retrieve a toy from the apparatus. One child had to push a lever down on one side of the apparatus while the second had to raise a handle on the other side. After the children had learned their respective roles, the children were switched in position so that they had to take up the opposite role. In this way, the children learned both parts of the task. Finally, each child was paired with a same-aged novice to see how the experienced child would react to being with a partner who was ignorant. Pairs of children at 24, 30, 36, and 42 months were tested. Teaching was measured by active attempts by the experienced children to direct their naive partner to the appropriate location and inform them of what they had to do. Although the ability to cooperate on this task and in particular to play both roles equally improved over the age range studied, it was only the oldest children who showed any clear tendency to teach novice partners, verbally or by demonstration, how to work the apparatus. Thus, it was only the oldest children who appeared to appreciate that their novice partners did not know what to do and that they could provide them with the necessary knowledge. With more complex teaching tasks, such as board games, that require more verbal explanation, teaching is seen a bit later but normally by 4 to 5 years (e.g., Strauss, Ziv, & Stein, 2002).

So far in this section we have focused on the relations between children's developing understanding of epistemic psychological relations and their social interactive behavior in particular experimental situations, such as deception and teaching. Deception and teaching quite clearly require the understanding of diverse epistemic perspectives because the children have to recognize that the interactive partner may not share their own perspective on some matter. Adopting a wider angle of focus, it is also possible to look at the development of preschool children's broader social competence with peers on the grounds that superior social understanding should be associated with better social skills. Social competence can be measured in a number of different ways and different researchers have adopted different approaches.

Perhaps the most direct approach to examining the social correlates of theory of mind has been to derive measures of social behavior from naturalistic observations. Janet Astington and Jennifer Jenkins (1995) examined 3- to 5-year-old children's theory of mind in relation to their behavior in naturalistic play settings with familiar peers. The understanding of false belief was assessed using standard change of location and misleading contents tasks, as well as an unexpected picture task, similar in structure to the misleading contents task. Naturalistic social behavior was assessed by videotaping the children playing in groups of three or four in their day-care settings. Measures included the amount of pretend play, the proportion of joint proposals for which children involved both self and other in some play activity, and the proportion of role assignments for which children explicitly assigned a pretend role to self or another child. Children's general language ability was also measured. The results showed that even after controlling for the effects of age and language ability, false belief performance was significantly associated with the proportion of joint proposals in play and the proportion of role assignments. These results were the first to document the relationship of theory of mind to social behavior in a naturalistic setting.

In a follow-up study, Jenkins and Astington (2000) examined similar measures longitudinally in a sample of 20 preschoolers. Children were first assessed between 34 and 45 months of age and then twice more at approximately 3.5-month intervals. At each age, children were tested on typical theory of mind tasks. They were also assessed for language ability and observed in pairs during a 10-minute play session. From the play sessions, joint proposals and role assignments during pretend play were again measured. Jenkins and Astington examined the correlations among the various measures both within each age and across ages. Interestingly, they found that theory of mind scores at younger ages predicted the social play variables at older ages, whereas social behaviors at the younger ages did not predict theory of mind performance at older ages. These results imply that being more advanced on theory of mind facilitates role play in peer play situations.

Because naturalistic observations of real-life social behavior can be difficult to collect, some researchers have relied on reports of children's social competence from those that know them well. For example, in two studies, Watson, Nixon, and Wilson (1999) tested 3- to 6-year-old children on standard false belief tasks. They also assessed the children's general language skills and collected teacher ratings of the children's social skills, using standard rating scales. Results showed significant relations between false belief performance and social skills ratings, even after taking into account the effects of age and language ability.

If social understanding in the form of theory of mind is related to more sophisticated social competence, then a further interesting issue is whether peers respond appropriately. This question can be answered by using assessments of peer popularity. The best way to do this with young children is to show them individual photos of the children in their peer group, say their day-care or kindergarten class, and ask the children to rate their peers by sorting the photos into three piles: those that they like a lot, those that they are more neutral toward, and those that they do not like. When all the children have rated all the other children in the group, we can generate a measure of popularity for each child by assigning a numerical score to the three categories, multiplying these scores by the number of ratings the child gets in each category, and dividing by the number of children in the group. Virginia Slaughter and her colleagues (Slaughter, Dennis, & Pritchard, 2002) reported two studies using this technique with children from 4 to 6 years old. In both studies they found that theory of mind was the best predictor of popularity in children older than about 5 years. Maria Angelopoulos (1997) also reported significant positive correlations between peer popularity measured in this way and theory of mind in a sample of 4.5-year-olds.

The various studies we have reviewed in this section provide a coherent body of evidence that the changes in commonsense psychology occurring at about 4 years are related to changes in social behavior. There appears, therefore, to be a reliable link between the understanding of different perspectives as assessed by experimental tasks and children's functioning in their social worlds.

SUMMARY

Children make significant strides in commonsense psychology during the preschool years. The acquisition of psychological terms is a key component of this development. Children initially express their psychological attitudes in language and then become able to participate in conversations about their own and others' psychology. Such conversations start with a focus on relatively simple and overt emotions before moving on to more complex and covert epistemic relations. Consistent with the primary functions of all language, language about psychological relations serves both to represent those psychological relations and to share attention with others to those psychological relations. Early acquired terms, such as those of emotion and desire, highlight psychological relations to real objects. By 4 years, the acquisition of syntactically more complex psychological terms such as *think* and *know* allows the representation of the diversity of perspectives across self and other.

In line with the research on children's understanding of psychological terms, research that more directly assesses children's understanding of perspectival diversity shows that at about 4 years of age, children are clearly able to understand that under different circumstances, they and others may have different beliefs and desires about the world. This level of commonsense psychology reflects children's ability to think about the connection between their own and another person's perspective on the world. It depends on additional changes in representational thinking allowing children to consider simultaneously two conflicting representations of psychological relations to a situation.

These developments in commonsense psychology are reflected in social behavior. By about 4 years, children show various forms of social behavior that depend on an understanding of perspectival diversity. They become able to promote false beliefs or ignorance in others in the service of both nefarious and playful goals. They start to recognize that teaching is possible and try to assist others who know less than they do. They become more adept at adopting different roles in joint play with peers. These social behaviors evidence a new level of social skills, a level that appears to be recognized by both peers and adults.

We have come a long way in the development of commonsense psychology, but one challenge remains to be addressed. By 4 years of age children understand that psychological relations can be diverse across people and even within themselves over time. The latter development indicates that children have a sense of the continuity of self across time, but we have said very little about this final aspect of commonsense psychology. In the next chapter we tackle it head-on.

10

The Self in Time

In this chapter we turn again to the place of the self in commonsense psychology. When last we discussed the self in chapter 7, we documented the fact that by the end of the second year, young children have acquired an ability to reflect on the self from a third-person point of view. Among other phenomena, they show mirror self-recognition and self-conscious emotions such as embarrassment, which indicate an appreciation of an objective sense of self. This objective sense of self accompanies their first-person experience and allows them to understand self and others in the same terms as agents of psychological activity. However, as seen in chapter 2, understanding self–other equivalence represents only one step along the way to a mature notion of agents. Adult commonsense psychology recognizes agents as having a temporally continuous identity—an identity that spans the past, present, and future. Thus, the person who performed certain activities and had certain experiences at particular moments in the past is understood to be, in an essential way, identical with the person who is now acting or experiencing. Furthermore, this person will continue to be essentially identical to a person who will act and experience things in the future.

In developmental psychology, this difference between having an objective sense of self and understanding the temporal continuity of the self is nicely illustrated by an extension of the mirror self-recognition task introduced by Daniel Povinelli and colleagues (Povinelli, Landau, & Perilloux, 1996). They devised a modification of the well-studied mirror self-recognition procedure that we reviewed in chapter 7. In their procedure, children were told that they were going to be videotaped while engaged in some play activities and they first posed for the camera with a particular stuffed toy. They then participated in the play activities in view of the video camera. During this period of play, the experimenter surreptitiously marked the children's heads with a very visible sticker. After the play period had ended, the tape was rewound and the children sat down to watch what had just happened. As the children watched, the marking event appeared and the children could be seen in the picture with the sticker on their head. The children's spontaneous reactions were noted and the children were asked who was in the picture and what was on their heads. Instances of the children reaching for the sticker on their own heads were noted. Unlike a mirror or even live video, the delayed video image does not provide immediate feedback about the self. Rather it provides information about the self at an earlier point in time. Under this condition, younger 3-year-olds typically failed to reach for the sticker, whereas by 4 years most children did. The 3-year-olds' failure occurred despite the fact that they could name themselves in the video and that when subsequently presented with a mirror, they all reached for the sticker on their heads.

The failure of 3-year-olds on the delayed video self-recognition task shows that although children have acquired a sense of the objective self by 24 months, it is not yet a sense of the self as a temporally continuous entity. The younger children in the delayed video self-recognition task did not appreciate the connection between the image of the self from the past and the self in the present—they did not have a temporally extended self. Let us look in more detail at what it means to have a temporally extended self. First, a key idea here is that of identity. The temporally extended self entails recognition of the identity between self-representations from different moments in time. In a sense, the self provides a common semantic thread for the interpretation of memory information. Thus the person who participated in events at one moment in the past is the same person as the one participating in events at another moment in time. However, recognizing an identity between the agent acting at any two moments in time is not enough because that agent would not necessarily be recognized to be identical with the current self. So, second, the identity must also be between one or more noncurrent self-representations and a current self-representation. For example, in my own case, I recognize the identity between the person that went to the university each day this week and the person that is right now staying home on Sunday and writing. Merely recognizing an identity between two noncurrent self-representations—for example, memories of the particular person that went to work on Monday of this week and Friday of this week—would not constitute a temporally extended self if those representations were not also recognized to be identical with the current self.

Third, a temporally extended self entails more than just a simple identity relation involving the current self and one or more noncurrent self states. Certainly, we are able to say that the *I* that went to work on Friday is the same as the *I* that stayed home on Sunday. However, we are able to connect these self-representations in richer ways. We understand that there is a contingent ordering of these self states such that one event involving the self preceded another event involving the self. Most obviously, remembered self-related events precede the current situation. In addition, the existence of a system of temporal units—seconds, minutes, hours, days, weeks, and so on—provides a standardized method for providing such a link between the contingent self states and the series of events occurring in the world independently of the self. Furthermore, events can be causally ordered in the sense that certain earlier self-related events are understood not just to precede other self-related events but also to be necessary for certain of these later self-related events (Povinelli, 2001).

In the research literature, this richer sense of self is often referred to as "autobiographical memory" (e.g., Nelson & Fivush, 2004). This term essentially denotes the story that each of us constructs regarding our own lives. Autobiographical memory consists of the events in which we can remember participating recalled from a personal perspective and woven together into a narrative. Thus, when we recall a particular event from our pasts, we do not remember it in isolation: rather, it has a place in the narrative of our lives.

So far we have discussed the temporally extended self as a series of self states existing from the past through to the present. It is important to recognize that the extrapolation of the self into the future is also a fundamental part of the temporally extended self. We are able to imagine future points in time and the activities in which we may engage. Just as with the past, we recognize the identity between the agent acting in those future events and the current self. We also recognize that future activities will have a particular ordering in which some events will precede others in a necessary way. All impending events extend out into the future from the current point in time, so in a sense the present self is the key causal agent in determining the future of the self. A significant difference between imagining the future and remembering the past, of course, is that the future is not fixed, whereas the past largely is. It is true that our representation of the past can change, even to the extent that our memories may reorder episodes we experienced. Nevertheless, our memory is strongly anchored in the real events of the past, whereas our imagination of the future is much less constrained.

A further characteristic of the temporally extended self that is important to emphasize is that it has a subjective, or first-person, dimension. For example, when we recall personally related events from our past, we can feel again the pride of a hard-gained achievement or the sorrow of a loss. Similarly, when we imagine the future, we can also feel pleasure or sorrow depending on the imagined success or failure of our's actions. It is not just the emotional concomitants of past and future events that we experience. We can also reinstate to some extent the perceptual qualities of prior experiences and imagine how something might look from a future perspective. The general ability to reexperience specific events from ours past is known as episodic memory (Tulving, 1985, 2002). Episodic memory is a particular form of memory in which the self is explicitly represented as an agent in the event and the time of the event is explicitly represented as being in the past.

The corresponding ability to imagine our personal future has recently been dubbed episodic future thinking (Atance & O'Neill, 2001).

We saw in chapter 7 that the ability to understand others as subjective agents requires imagination and empathy—we must feel into our feelings and yet attribute them to the other. What is less obvious is that the same is true for being able to represent the self at another time. At any moment, we have direct or immediate first-person experience of our current psychological activity—what we can see, how we are feeling, and so on. In order to think about psychological relations from our past or potential psychological relations in our futures, we must engage in an act of imagination and empathize with our noncurrent selves. This typically means first bringing to mind the self's involvement in the to-be-remembered situation from a third-person point of view. The corresponding subjective or first-person components of that situation can then be experienced. In the case of memory of the past, this means remembering our part in some event and reexperiencing the first-person components of our action. In the case of the future it means imagining some future scenario involving the self and pre-experiencing a first-person perspective on that scenario. In short, the representation of noncurrent self states occurs both from a third-person perspective and from a first-person perspective. Events from our past are remembered as experiences, involving the full range of first-person experience available to us in the present, even if the intensity of that experience is attenuated. Similarly, imagined future events involving the self are correspondingly represented at least in part from a subjective point of view. This first-person connection to noncurrent states of self is fundamental to the nature of the temporally extended self. Just as empathizing with others reinforces our connection with them, so our tendency to share feelings with noncurrent states of self cements our identity over time. In a nutshell, then, the temporally extended self involves an integrated first- and third-person representation of the self that is understood to be noncurrent and yet connected in a causal way to the current self.

This consideration of the nature of the temporally extended self has pointed to two fundamental characteristics that need to be developed. First, children must be able to bring to mind past and future episodes involving the self in such a way that both objective and subjective information relevant to the self's involvement can be represented. Second, these self states must be bound together into an autobiography that is understood to involve contingent and necessary connections. In the remainder of this chapter, we consider the evidence of the development of these two characteristics of the temporally extended self, starting with the earlier development—representing noncurrent episodes.

BRINGING TO MIND NONCURRENT EVENTS INVOLVING THE SELF: THE DEVELOPMENT OF EPISODIC THINKING

Given that all forms of learning involve present action being affected by past events, we can say that in some sense memory is functioning from almost the beginning of life. However, in many cases of learning, attention is not oriented to the past, it is oriented to the present or immediate future. Infants can clearly learn from experience but there is no evidence that they remember past events independently of their effects on current action. Action is simply affected in part by past experience. Similarly, by the end of infancy, experience with regularly occurring structured events has allowed children to build up representations of familiar events or general event memories (Nelson, 1986; Nelson & Fivush, 2004). For example, children may have general event memories for bedtime routine, going to day care, or going to the park. These general event memories are based on the detection of the recurring patterns of activity experienced during these events and, as such, they resemble scripts that guide young children's participation in common activities. Although general event memories are relatively abstract representations of past experience, they are still not memories for particular personally experienced episodes. For past events to be remembered, they must at least be represented as distinct from present experience and this requires the onset of mental representation. The acquisition of a representational system—in particular, language—is critical for the explicit remembering of previous events. In line with the definition of episodic thinking offered earlier, two features of remembered or anticipated events must be explicitly represented. First, the episode must be understood to be distinct from the present so some kind of temporal marker must be included. Second, the events must be self-related so the self must be represented as an agent in the episode.

When referring to time, it is important to distinguish three parameters (Weist, 1989). One is speech time, which refers to the time when the speaker is actually talking. A second is event time, which refers to the time of the episode being talked about. A third is reference time, which situates the event time in temporal relation to some other time. Reference time can correspond to either the event time or speech time, but it can also vary independently. For example, if I say, "Yesterday, I went to a movie," then the event time is in the past and the reference time corresponds to the event time. However, if I then say, "Before going to the movie, I had a coffee with Michael," then the time of the coffee-drinking event is set with reference to a different time (going to the movie), which itself precedes speech time. The linguistic representation of events in time occurs in a variety of ways.

Tense markers on verbs, temporal terms such as *yesterday* and *today*, and clausal connectives such as *when* all can be used to specify the temporal parameters of events.

Although children's earliest utterances refer to present objects and events (Weist, 1989), it does not take long for children to start talking about past and future events. Children acquire all of the linguistic devices for marking temporal parameters from about 2 to 5 years. Even before the acquisition of these explicit temporal markers, noncurrent events can be represented simply by juxtaposing events in order, as the following example from Clark (2003, p. 259) illustrates:

C: (26 months, sitting in car seat) I get out!
M: Not yet!
C: Get home, get out.
M: Yes. Then you'll get out.

This example also illustrates that children refer to noncurrent events that have personal relevance. We know that children acquire an objective sense of self during the second year. This sense of self is also manifested in language acquisition. By 2 years of age children have typically acquired proper names for both themselves and others and also have mastered the system of indexical words—pronouns such as *me*—that stand for the various participants in events. Pronouns are especially revealing for the understanding of self and its agentive equivalence with others because the same word is used under different circumstances to refer to different people (Bates, 1990). When I say "I" or "me" those words stand for me, but when you say "I" or "me," the same words stand for you. Because others refer to the child as "you," in the early stages of pronoun acquisition, children do sometimes make pronoun reversal errors, referring to themselves as "you" (Bates, Bretherton, & Snyder, 1989), but these errors are rarely seen in the productive language of normally developing 2-year-olds. By then they regularly refer to themselves using the first-person pronouns that they have heard others use to refer to themselves. The fact that young children can recognize that the same words can be used to refer to both self and other shows compellingly that they understand self and other to be equivalent in the roles they can play in events.

So the evidence from children's spontaneous language reveals that by about 2 years, children are already able to think about their own activity in noncurrent episodes. But thinking and talking about noncurrent events is not yet the same thing as representing the events as occurring at a time distinct from speech time. At first, talk about past or future events does not mark reference time. For this to be the case the events have to be marked as occurring at a separate time. By about 2.5 to 3 years, children start to set their talk about noncurrent events in relation to a reference time. The early use of linguistic markers for noncurrent times indicates that children are initially rather confused about the ordering of events in time. Words like *yesterday* and *tomorrow* often make global reference to past and future events (e.g., Harner, 1975). Sometimes, it is not even clear that the past and the future are distinguished. My daughter at 3 years made the following utterance in the context of trying to persuade me of the inconsequence of her spilling a drink on her dress: "Someday, a long time ago, it will dry off." Furthermore, at this stage, the reference time does not vary freely in relation to event time and speech time—it is set at either one or the other. Only later during the fourth year do children clearly start to relate event time and reference time independently of speech time as they start to use words like *before* and *after* to order events in time (Weist, 1989).

The evidence from children's language shows then that children are able to think about noncurrent episodes involving the self and locate them in the past or future sometime during the third year of life. The precision with which these episodes can be located in time is initially poor but it develops significantly over the preschool period. Inevitably this precision is enhanced by the ability to link events together into a narrative sequence or autobiography. However, before we turn to a full consideration of how personally related events are bound into an autobiography, we examine how children first become able to represent noncurrent episodes of personal relevance.

To answer this question, we turn again to consider the communicative interactions that children experience with others. As seen in chapter 9, parents and children talk about psychological relations. Here we examine how they start to talk about noncurrent events in which the children either played a role or will participate in the future. In the research literature the most common approach to this topic is to observe conversations between parents and their young children. These conversations reveal how the temporal continuity of the self is at least in part constructed.

Parents talk to their children about noncurrent events as early as the first half of the second year and as soon as the children are capable of understanding. At this time parents provide the focus and all of the content, but children show their interest by using placeholders, such as acknowledgments, and thereby taking conversational turns. Before long it is clear that children are sharing attention to the noncurrent events by making appropriate responses and holding their place in the discourse. The following conversation between a mother and her 19-month-old illustrates these early joint reminiscences (Reese & Farrant, 2003, p. 37):

M: Where did we go and see Grandad the other day?
C: I don't ti (sic).
M: Where was Grandad?
C: Upital.

M: Hospital. And what was he have, what was he getting fixed?
C: Ahh. somefing.
M: Did he have a sore back? He did? And what did he have at the hospital that you liked? What were you eating at the hospital?
C: I nand.
M: Bananas?
C: Nah.
M: And some grapes. Did you have some grapes? And a lolly.
C: Mmmm.

What is important about these conversations is that information about the child's activity in past events is represented by the parent for the child to think about. Notice that the focus of attention is entirely on the past. There is no immediate purpose for these joint attentional interactions other than to consider together—to share attention to—the past episode. Soon children can not only share attention in conversation to past events in which they participated, they also start to contribute to this reminiscing by elaborating on information that their mothers supply. This demonstrates unequivocally that the children are indeed remembering the past events and drawing on their stored representation to supplement the information provided by their parents. Sometimes children contribute information that the mother forgot and such conversations present an important opportunity for learning about the subjectivity of remembering. In the following example between a mother and her 40-month-old (Fivush, 2001, pp. 44–45), the mother initially probes the child's memory but then the child recalls something that the mother was not expecting. The mother affirms the memory but then also notes that she had not remembered it, before moving on to explore the new information in more detail.

M: What did Mommy find for you that you brought home?
C: Rocks.
M: Yeah, and we got some rocks, didn't we?
C: And fire hats.
M: And fire hats? Yeah, that's right. Those little tiny fire hats. I forgot about those. Where did you get those?
C: Grandma and Grandpa.
M: Grandma and Grandpa gave you those.

Joint reminiscing presents opportunities not just for recording the diversity of recall for the facts of past experiences, but also importantly for exploring the subjective experience of past events. Another example from Robyn Fivush (2001, p. 46) illustrates how emotional orientations may be raised in memory conversations so that children become able to consider noncurrent events in terms of their emotional significance and thereby gain a perspective on themselves. In this case the mother and her 35-month-old daughter were remembering a carnival in which they saw bears:

> M: They were big bears. Did they scare you?
> C: Um-umm. (no)
> M: A little bit? Just a little bit?
> C: Oh, I'm not scared of bears.
> M: You're not scared of bears. Well, that's good.
>   …
> C: Bears scare me.
> M: They scare you. I thought they didn't scare you.
> C: I'm scary (i.e., "I'm scared").

Research on conversations about future events is much rarer than that on joint reminiscing despite the fact that parents talk a good deal to their young children about upcoming events (e.g., Lucariello & Nelson, 1987). Research by Judith Hudson (2001, 2002) reveals that mothers typically help their children to construct more elaborate imaginative scenarios in anticipation of upcoming events by asking questions about what is "gonna" happen. Because the future is necessarily unknown and therefore to some extent hypothetical, mothers may draw on experience of similar past events as well as general knowledge of such events to help structure the anticipation. In the following example from Hudson (2001, p. 68), a mother and her 2.5-year-old are discussing Easter as it approaches. Notice how the mother attempts to invoke general knowledge ("Who comes at Easter?"), episodic memory ("Remember we bought the [egg coloring] kit?"), and future-oriented thinking ("Yeah, you're gonna help me color the eggs?") to structure the experience for the child:

> M: Who comes at Easter?
> C: Easter Bunny.
> M: That's right. And what does he bring?
> C: Candy.
> M: And what else?
> C: Umm.
> M: What does he bring that we're going to color on Friday?
> C: Umm.
> M: Eggs? Yeah, you're gonna help me color the eggs?
> C: Yeah.
> M: Yeah, it's gonna be the first time you get to color the eggs, huh? Remember we bought the kit?
> C: Hmm?
> M: You and me, and Drew, we bought the kit? And we're gonna make pretty colors on the eggs.

C: Yeah.

M: And then on Easter Sunday we're going to Grandma's house.

The 2.5-year-old in this conversation contributes little more than placeholders to the discourse, but by doing so still demonstrates her interest in sharing attention to the future event. By 4 years, children are able to imagine their future involvement in the upcoming event and contribute this information to the conversation. In the following example (Hudson, 2001, p. 69), a mother and her 4-year-old are discussing their summer vacation. The mother still provides structure for the future-oriented thinking. However, now the child offers a plan for the vacation activities based in part on previous episodes and prompted by the mother in only a very general sense:

M: Where are we going?

...

C: Aunt Jean's.

M: Yeah, and what do we do at Aunt Jean's house? Did we go once before?

C: Yeah.

...

M: And what did we do there?

C: We find seashells.

M: Yeah, that's something you and Daddy did together.

C: Yeah, we painted seashells.

M: So are we going to go again this year? What do you want to do this year when we go down there?

C: I want to get more seashells and paint them.

M: You want to get more seashells and paint them. And then how about, what else would you like to do? Would you like to go to the amusement park?

C: Yeah.

M: And what do you like to do there?

C: Go down the slide.

These studies examining mother-child discourses about noncurrent events show that these conversations provide a clear context for joint focus on the past and future. As such they allow children to attend to and think about noncurrent events in a way that both enhances the memory of actual past events and structures the potential courses of action in upcoming events. The fact that joint reminiscing is important for children's developing personal memories was shown in a number of studies that compared different degrees of richness in mother-child reminiscing. Research has pointed to variability in the degree to which mothers encourage elaborative reminiscing of past events. Some mothers are relatively highly elaborative, encouraging shared exploration of the memory, providing information themselves, and following the children's lead in this joint enterprise where possible. Others are more focused and repetitive. When they engage in conversations about past events, they tend to try to get their children to recall a piece of information that they, the mothers, have in mind rather than explore together their memories of the events. It is now a well-established finding that maternal reminiscing style is related to how well children remember events (Fivush & Fromhoff, 1988; McCabe & Peterson, 1991; Nelson & Fivush, 2004; Reese, Haden, & Fivush, 1993). Mothers who tend to be highly elaborative in their memory conversations have children who are able to remember past events with greater fidelity than do mothers who tend to engage in a more focused and repetitive manner.

Elaine Reese and her colleagues (Harley & Reese, 1999; Reese, et al., 1993) have conducted a number of longitudinal studies examining the relation between mothers' elaborative style and their children's recall of information in memory conversations. For example, Harley and Reese observed mother-child reminiscing about two or three specific one-time events when the children were 19, 25, and 32 months of age. Examples of events were feeding ducks and an airplane flight. Mothers' elaborative style was coded at each age point as was children's provision of new information to the conversations. In addition, the children were tested on mirror self-recognition at 19 months and coded for self-directed behavior. The results showed significant relations over time, with children who had highly elaborative mothers producing more information in memory conversations at each time point. In addition, the children who had passed the mirror self-recognition task at 19 months produced more new information in the memory conversations when they were 32 months old than those who had failed the mirror self-recognition task. Indeed the children who passed the mirror self-recognition task at 19 months and had mothers who used an elaborative style in joint reminiscing easily produced the most new information in the memory conversations. These results point to the importance of the objective self as well a structured informative conversational context for the development of rich personal memories.

In a follow-up study, Farrant and Reese (2000) reported on the same sample that Harley and Reese (1999) had observed, when the children were 40 months old. In addition to the assessments of mothers' and children's memory elaborations, they also assessed children's independent remembering when in conversation with an experimenter. They correlated the children's contribution to joint reminiscing and the mothers' elaborative style both concurrently at each age and longitudinally across age points. Consistent with other studies, maternal elaborative style was related to children's provision of new memory information both within and across age, with the strongest effects occurring between the 25- and 32-month age points. In addition, there was some evidence that children's interest in joint reminiscing as measured by their placeholders in the memory conversations was related to their mothers' elaborative style. In other words, by showing their interest in sharing attention to remembered events, children may encourage their mothers to be more elaborative. Finally, the results involving the children's independent memory elaborations with the experimenter showed that maternal elaborative style when the children were 32-months old predicted the children's later independent elaborations. This finding suggests that, through joint reminiscing with their mothers, children acquire a general way of sharing memories that extends beyond their conversations with mothers.

BINDING THE SELF IN TIME: THE DEVELOPMENT OF AN AUTOBIOGRAPHY

Discourse about noncurrent episodes is important for the consolidation of personal events in memory and future thinking. But the development of an autobiography requires the ability to connect these events with the current self into a narrative with a causal structure. Once the child can represent noncurrent events involving the self, there is then the potential for the simultaneous representation of both past and present self that is necessary for the temporally extended self. This next step requires the additional representational complexity available at 4 years. A number of diverse lines of evidence are consistent in supporting the idea that it is at about this age that children are able to connect both current and noncurrent representations of self into a temporally continuous sense of self.

It has been recognized for many years that events from the earliest part of life are not recoverable as memories in adulthood. Retrospective studies of adult personal memories indicate that although isolated events may sometimes be remembered from as young as 2 years, the typical age from which memories can be recovered is about 4 years (e.g., Bruce, Dolan, & Phillips-Grant, 2000; Dudycha & Dudycha, 1941). A variety of explanations have been proposed for this "infantile amnesia," including Freud's (1940/1964) famous idea of unconscious repression. These days the preferred explanation is that the earliest memories are not integrated into an autobiographical memory that extends up to the present time (Nelson, 1993; Nelson & Fivush, 2004; Pillemer & White, 1989, Reese, 2002). Early memories can be recalled for a short time afterward but until these memories are bound together into a temporally and causally connected sequence understood to involve the immediate self, they quickly fade over time.

A second line of relevant research was mentioned earlier in the chapter. Povinelli and his colleagues (1996) conducted a number of studies showing that delayed self-recognition develops rather later than mirror self-recognition. In addition to the finding that 4-years-olds but not younger children pass the delayed self-recognition task, they also showed that the amount of time that has passed between the marking and test events is an important determinant of whether older children search for the mark (Povinelli & Simon, 1998). To demonstrate this they tested children at 3 and 5 years. The children were marked surreptitiously with a sticker on the head while being videotaped with the knowledge that they would watch the video at a later point in time. The children watched the videotape either a few minutes later or after an interval of a week. The older children searched for the sticker when they watched the videotape after the brief delay but not after the long delay. In contrast, the younger children tended not to search for the sticker but when they did it was just as likely to happen after the long delay as after the brief delay. It was only the older children, therefore, who appreciated the different implications of the long and short delays for the likelihood of finding the sticker.

Can it be mere coincidence that children develop an autobiographical or temporally extended self at about the same time they acquire a perspectival form of commonsense psychology? The probable answer is "no." Like the perspectival form of commonsense psychology reviewed in the latter half of chapter 9, the temporally extended self depends on developments in representational ability. In particular, the self must be represented from two separate temporal perspectives, one of which must be that of the present. Therefore, consistent with the development of the understanding of others reviewed in chapter 9, the ability of the child to represent combinations of perspectives likely contributes to the extended self. In order to connect separate perspectives of the self it is necessary to represent simultaneously the self's perspective at the present time and the self's perspective at some noncurrent time, either past or future.

If autobiographical memory requires the ability to represent two self-related perspectives, then it also requires that a causal relation between these two perspectives be understood. The latter form of understanding has been linked to another aspect of theory of mind—understanding the sources of knowledge. In addition to requiring the ability to represent more than one perspective, autobiographical memory may also be related to the understanding that the acquisition of knowledge depends on experience. Other research has found that, unlike older children, preschoolers who have just acquired new knowledge tend to think they always had it and do not recognize how they acquired it. For example, Daniela O'Neill and Alison Gopnik (1991) presented children with a styrofoam tunnel in which various objects could be placed. On different trials, the children learned the contents by looking in the tunnel, by reaching in and feeling the object, or by being told by the experimenter. Having discovered the contents, the children were asked by the experimenter how they knew what was inside the tunnel ("Did you see it, did you feel it, or did I tell you?"). Compared to 4- and 5-year-olds, 3-year-olds were very poor at recalling the source of their knowledge.

So are these aspects of theory of mind related to autobiographical memory? Melissa Welch-Ross (1997) studied 40 children between 3.5 and 4.5 years of age in conversation about specific past events with their mothers. The children were also tested on two kinds of theory of mind tasks. The first kind included false belief tasks, of the sort reviewed in chapter 9, that assess the understanding of diversity of perspectives. The second kind included origins of knowledge tasks, such as the one devised by O'Neill and Gopnik (1991). Welch-Ross focused on two types of response that the children gave to their mothers' elaborative questions and statements during the memory conversations. Some child responses contributed additional memory information, whereas others were placeholders that maintained the conversational structure but added no new information. When the measures of autobiographical memory and theory of mind were correlated, it was found that the more new memory information the children provided, the better they performed on both the perspectival and origins of knowledge tasks. In contrast, the tendency to respond with placeholders was negatively related to performance on these theory of mind tasks. These findings held even though the children's performance on the theory of mind tasks was not related to their mothers' tendency to be elaborative in their memory talk. It appears, then, that better memory for personally experienced events is related to the understanding of both perspectival diversity and how experience leads to knowledge.

TEMPORAL CONTINUITY AND FUTURE-ORIENTED SOCIAL BEHAVIOR

We saw in chapter 9 how the perspectival nature of social understanding achieved by about 4 years of age has profound implications for social behavior. Similarly, the concurrent developments in understanding the temporal-causal connection between temporally distinct events deeply affect children's ability to control their behavior in relation to their own futures. In fact, it is what allows children for the first time to become independently motivated to act in relation to future events. As adults, we make decisions about immediate action based on our future circumstances even if that means incurring some cost in the present. We pass on an appetizing dessert because we worry about future weight gain or other health concerns. We refrain from frittering money on indulgences because we want to save for a spring vacation.

How do we manage to control our action in this way? Such future-oriented prudence is made possible by the imagination of future circumstances and the recognition of the temporal-causal connection between our present action and those future circumstances. Although 3-year-olds can engage in episodic future thinking in the sense that they can imagine future events involving the self, those imagined future events do not lead to future-oriented behavior unless children can understand the connection between their current actions and the future events. Thus, being able to appreciate the link between present action and future consequences is a necessary cognitive skill. In addition to understanding the causal consequences of current action on our future selves, we also have to care about those future selves. So, I will only delay gratification if I am relatively concerned about benefiting my future self. Although such concern may seem natural, it does not always obtain, and there are differences among people in terms of how future oriented they are.

Evidence of the development of the understanding of temporal-causal connections between present and future events and the control of behavior by imagined future events is provided by research on delay of gratification. If children are presented with a choice between a smaller or less attractive reward that they can have immediately and a larger or more attractive reward for which they must wait a short while, 3-year-olds typically opt for the immediately available reward, whereas older preschoolers choose the larger, delayed reward at least some of the time (Mischel, 1974; Mischel, Shoda, & Rodriguez, 1989; Thompson, Barresi, & Moore, 1997). Along with Carol Thompson and John Barresi, I (Thompson et al., 1997) studied children at 3, 4, and 5 years of age on a task in which the children were rewarded with stickers that could be placed in a sticker book. Over a series of trials the children could choose between one sticker immediately or wait until the end of the session to receive two stickers. In order to delay gratification in such a choice task, children must be able to imagine their future circumstances and connect their action in the present to that imagined future. Three-year-olds opted to take the single sticker immediately on most trials. In contrast, both 4- and 5-year-olds opted to delay for the greater reward significantly more often.

This result is consistent with the idea that 3-year-olds are not able to imagine their future interests in contrast to their immediate interests, and therefore they are not able to make decisions in favor of the interests of their future selves. It is, however, possible that younger children are able to imagine their future circumstances and the link between their present action and the future but that they are less future oriented than older children and simply prefer to reward themselves immediately. To test this possibility, we (Lemmon and Moore, 2004) presented 3- and 4-year-olds with choices in which they could gain one sticker immediately or two, three, four, or five stickers later. We reasoned that if younger children simply weighted the value of immediate and future rewards differently from older children, then the younger children should start to increase their future orientation as the differential between immediate and future rewards increased. In fact, we found that for 3-year-olds it did not matter whether they were to receive two stickers in the future or five stickers in the future, they still opted to take one immediately. In contrast, older 4-year-olds opted to delay on trials where five stickers were at stake much more often than on trials where only two stickers were available. This result showed that only the older children adapted their decisions according to the relative value of the future reward and thus appeared to be considering the future in a manner quite different from the 3-year-olds. Together these results on future-oriented decision making show that younger children tend to be fixed in their immediate perspective—they want the reward now—whereas older children are able to take a more objective stance on the decision and consider the interests of their future selves as well as their current selves.

Although there are clear developmental differences in children's ability to make future-oriented decisions, it is worth noting that there are also individual differences in future orientation that are evident in children as young as 4 years of age (Moore & Macgillivray, 2004). When offered delay of gratification choices, some children opt to delay most or all of the time whereas others opt to delay less frequently. Individual differences in delay of gratification have been shown to be quite stable over childhood and indeed how well children are able to cope with delays at 4 to 5 years is a strong predictor of how well children function in both social and academic contexts in adolescence (e.g., Shoda, Mischel, & Peake, 1990). So it would appear that future orientation is a beneficial skill to encourage in young children. Nevertheless, there has been very little work on why such individual differences exist. The few studies that have been carried out point to the role of social relationships in promoting future orientation (Jacobsen, Huss, Fendrich, Kruesi, & Zeigenhain, 1997; Moore & Symons, 2005; Sethi, Mischel, Aber, Shoda, & Rodriguez, 2000). For example, Moore and Symons found a positive correlation between future orientation and attachment security in 4-year-olds. In particular, children who scored well on a measure of secure base behavior showed a greater tendency to delay gratification for superior future rewards. This finding may mean that a secure attachment relationship promotes a sense of trust in the future as well as trust in others.

Earlier I characterized the autobiographical self as extending from the past through the present into the future. The implication is that as children become able to consider nonpresent states of the self in relation to the present self, they are able to do so both for the past and for the future. So it is of interest to consider whether children's ability to connect past and present states of the self develops in line with their ability to consider their present and future self states together. To this end, Lemmon and Moore (2001) tested 3- to 4-year-old children on both delayed self-recognition, as a measure of the connection between the past and the present, and delay of gratification, as a measure of the connection between the present and the future. We found performance on these two tasks to be significantly correlated. Children who showed self-directed behavior in the delayed self-recognition task also tended to opt for the greater future reward when presented with a choice between rewards now or later. This finding supports the idea that, at about 4 years of age, children do indeed develop a temporally extended self that spans past, present, and future.

FUTURE-ORIENTED DECISIONS INVOLVING OTHERS

The development of future-oriented decision making reveals that children can think of themselves in the future from an integrated subjective and objective perspective. They can imagine not just what their future situation might be but also how they might feel about it. There is also evidence that such an integrated perspective is used to think about others in the future. Research using extensions of the delay of gratification task demonstrates that as children are able to think about their own future circumstances, they are also able to do the same for others. One such demonstration comes from studies conducted using a modification of the delay of gratification task. Alongside choices in which children had to decide between taking a single sticker now and opting to delay to receive two stickers, there were also choices in which children had to decide between taking one sticker now and delaying to receive two stickers, which would be divided between them and a play partner, who was an adult experimental confederate (Moore & Macgillivray, 2004; Thompson et al., 1997). Notice that in the latter choice type the child gets no benefit from delaying but the play partner does. On these sharing choices, 3-year-old children tended not to delay in order to share. This result is certainly not due to an unwillingness to share. When no delay was imposed, 3-year-old children were quite keen to share, even sacrificing some of their own rewards to do so. In contrast, as with the traditional delay of gratification choice, 4- to 5-year-olds did opt to delay the reward even though it was only the other who benefited. Furthermore, performance on delay of gratification for self alone was correlated with performance on the delayed sharing task (Moore & Macgillivray), showing that these two types of future-oriented decisions depend at least in part on similar cognitive mechanisms.

An even more striking result comes from a recent study by Angela Prencipe and Philip Zelazo (2005), who compared performance on delay of gratification when the children had to make the choice either for themselves or for another person. The *self* version was the same as seen earlier. Children made a series of choices were they could get one reward immediately or wait to get more rewards later. As other studies found, 3-year-olds chose the immediate reward on most trials, whereas 4-year-olds chose the later reward on about half of the trials. In the *other* version of the task, the children had to make the choice for the experimenter. So, on each trial the choice between a small immediate reward and a larger delayed reward was laid out and the children had to choose which of the alternatives the experimenter should pick. In this version, the children received no rewards themselves so there was no strong pull for them to opt for the immediate reward. Interestingly, in this version the 3-year-olds recommended choosing the larger delayed reward on most trials. However, the 4-year-olds recommended that the experimenter choose the delayed reward on only about half of the trials and choose the immediate reward on about half of the trials. This pattern of response by the 4-year-olds choosing for the experimenter was very similar to that displayed by the children playing the *self* version, choosing immediate or future rewards for themselves. The similarity in performance across the two versions of the task supports the idea that older children use a uniform approach to decision making for both self and other. In both cases, they imagine the future situation from both a subjective and objective perspective and compare it to the current situation, also imagined from both subjective and objective perspective. In contrast, 3-year-olds base their decisions for themselves on their immediate subjective desires ("I want it now") and their decisions for others on entirely objective circumstances ("Two is better than one"). As a result the younger children make different decisions depending on whether they are choosing for themselves or choosing for another person. Together these results from versions of delay of gratification involving decisions for others support the idea that by about 4 years, children make future-oriented decisions for both self and other by using representations of temporally extended persons that combine both subjective and objective perspectives.

SUMMARY

In this chapter we have seen that children become able to think about noncurrent personally relevant events as they move beyond the infancy period. They can remember events in which they participated and they can imagine such events in the future. This temporally displaced thinking is encouraged during conversations with their mothers and from an early age children willingly share attention to linguistic representations of noncurrent events. Conversations about past events serve to reinstate in consciousness events from the personal past. They also provide for a range of interpretations on these events. Joint reminiscing is not a matter of "just the facts." Mother and child may recall different aspects of the past event and so these conversations highlight that people may have different representations of the past. Furthermore, joint reminiscing allows an exploration of the child's psychological relations to the events, thereby helping to reinstate the experience that characterized the event. Joint anticipations necessarily amount to an exploration of possible futures and both child and mother draw on both general knowledge and past experiences to structure these explorations.

Although memories for personally experienced episodes may be available for consideration in conversation, they do not constitute evidence of a temporally extended self until they are understood to be connected in a temporal-causal way to the present self. Different sources of evidence point to a transition at about 4 years of age, as which point children are able to consider simultaneously personally relevant events from both the present and some nonpresent time, either past or future. Once these events become bound into an autobiography they are available to guide personally relevant action decisions in which a choice must be made between courses of action adapted to different points in time. Future-oriented prudence—accepting a less favorable current situation in order to achieve more favorable future circumstances—becomes a part of young children's repertoires as they graduate into the rational world of decision making in time. At the same time, they are able to apply similar rational decision making to others' circumstances.

With the achievement of the temporally extended self, children have met the final challenge listed in chapter 2—that of personal identity. The self is now understood to be a psychological entity that persists in time with both subjective and objective characteristics. Others are also understood to be similar psychological entities with temporal continuity. So children now truly have a uniform conception of persons that spans self and others, past, present, and future.

11

The Construction of Commonsense Psychology

Commonsense psychology is just as much a central part of social life for young children as it is for adults. By the time they are 5 years old, children enthusiastically engage with others in conversations about their own and others' psychological activity. They clearly understand that they and others are equivalent in their status as agents who have psychological relations to objects. They understand that, despite this equivalence, people have different perspectives on those objects, and that one or more of those perspectives may be inconsistent with reality. They understand the continuity of people through time and they identify with their future selves.

By now it should be clear that commonsense psychology plays a series of important roles in the lives of young children. Indeed, it allows children to participate in the rich social lives that human beings enjoy. Early in development, infants are able to engage with others in emotionally intense interactions and relationships that set the groundwork for a lifelong commitment to the social world. Within the first dyadic interactional dances and the early relationships that are established, commonsense psychology starts to grow. Infants begin to understand that others can be invaluable sources of information about the nonsocial world, and so another lifelong commitment, this time to cultural learning, is established. The representational system of language is a central component of cultural learning and with its help children become able to move beyond the confines of the concrete real world of the here and now. It is language that ultimately allows children to consider past and future scenarios in which self and other participate. Perhaps of most importance, children can start to make plans and decisions for the future. They can work toward benefiting themselves and others in the future, even if it may mean a cost in the present.

I started this book by arguing that despite it apparent commonsense nature, understanding people in terms of commonsense psychology would present a number of challenges to a naive learner (see Table 11.1). Common to all of these challenges is the concern that the information available from direct experience of our ongoing psychological activity is quite different from the information that is available from the observation of others' similar psychological activity. In addition, direct experience of our own ongoing psychological activity is of necessity quite different from remembered or imagined information about our own past or future psychological activity. Somehow young learners have to be able to treat these different forms of information equivalently. This entails recognizing both the subjective and objective nature of people and their continuous nature through time. By 5 years of age, children have met these challenges. But it was not always this way—infants start life with essentially no psychological understanding. How does this remarkable conceptual transformation proceed so rapidly and so smoothly?

In order for children to make headway in the construction of commonsense psychology, two conditions need to be met. First, there must be regular occasions when children can experience together expressions of their own psychological activities and of the corresponding psychological activities of others. These occasions occur in the habitual interactive episodes that young children participate in with parents and others. Interactive episodes occur first in the face-to-face dyadic and then object-centered triadic interactive structures typical of the first year. From the second year on, interactions start to take place by means of the represented world of language. Interactions provide children with the appropriate combinations of information about the activities of self and of others. They therefore provide the informational conditions on which commonsense psychology can be built. Experience of the interactive psychological activities of self and others is essential because commonsense psychology involves representations of psychological activity that have both subjective and objective characteristics. Only by experiencing in close connection the activity of self and other is the generation of such representations possible (see also Barresi & Moore, 1996; Carpendale & Lewis, 2004).

Second, for representations of psychological activity to be formed, there must be information-processing mechanisms that can take the information available within the interactive episodes and generate representations that do indeed code both subjective and objective characteristics of action and that therefore are uniformly applicable to both self and others. I have pointed to two main types of information-processing mechanisms—fundamental processes of pattern detection and representation. In this final chapter, we review what we have learned about how commonsense psychology grows out of the function of these information-processing mechanisms operating on social interactive structures (see Table 11.2).

TABLE 11.1
Solving the Challenges of Developing a Commonsense Psychology

Self-other equivalence
How do we come to understand that self and others are the same kind of psychological entity?

Infants engage in dyadic and then triadic interactions with others in which the interactive partners share psychological orientations. Within these interactions infants learn that their first-person experience of their own psychological states is linked to corresponding third-person information of other people in similar psychological states. They construct representations of psychological activity that integrate first- and third-person information. With the onset of mental representation at about 18 months, children become able to apply these integrated representations to both self and others independently.

Object directedness
How do we come to understand that psychological acts are directed at or about things?

During triadic interactions, infants attend to both objects and people. As a result they construct representations of people's actions in relation to objects. Subsequent forms of interaction using linguistic and other kinds of symbolic representations allow an understanding that people have psychological orientations to abstract representations as well as to real objects.

Diversity in psychological relations
How are we able to understand that our own immediate psychological
relation to an object of state of affairs is not the only possible one?

Participation in triadic and linguistic interactions confronts children with situations in which the psychological orientations of the self and other are not shared. The growing capacity to represent others' psychological relations independently of the self's leads to an appreciation of multiple perspectives on the same object of situation.

Personal identity
How are we able to bind memories of the experiences of our past and imagination of our futures into a self that is deemed not only to persist in time but, in some cases, to warrant preferential treatment compared to our present self?

With the onset of mental representation, children become able to think about the self from an objective point of view. Remembered past events involving the self as well as imagined future events involving the self can be thought about. Thinking about such noncurrent self states along with the current self state allows children both to recognize the continuity of the self through time and to identify with the noncurrent self.

TABLE 11.2
The Course of Development of Commonsense Psychology

Age	Birth...........1 year...........2 years...........3 years...........4 years...........5 years			
Interactive structures	Dyadic--------->Triadic---->Communicative---->Linguistic------>Syntactic----->Modal------->			
What kind of psychological information is available to the child?	First- and third-person information not directed at objects	First- and third-person information available through perception about object-directed and later goal-directed activity	First- and third-person information available through perception and through memory or imagination	Representations of psychological relations of both self and other to increasingly complex and abstract objects
What kind of integration of information is occurring through pattern detection?	Integration of first- and third-person information, primarily emotional	Integration of first- and third-person perceptual information pertaining to object-directed activity	Integration of first- and third-person information across perception and memory or imagination	Integration of individual psychological relations across self and other or across time
What kind of commonsense psychology results?	Integrated first- and third-person representations guiding face-to-face interactions	Integrated first- and third-person representations guiding object-directed and then goal-directed interactions	Self and other and their psychological activity represented independently in terms of integrated first- and third-person information	Psychological activity of self and other represented in terms of perspectives; self and other are temporally extended agents

INTERACTIVE STRUCTURES

We have seen that infants become enmeshed in social interactive structures soon after birth. Infants first attend to social stimulation. Human voices attract attention, perhaps because they are already familiar from prenatal experience. Faces also are powerfully attractive stimuli, and given that faces and voices commonly occur together, infants orient more toward their mothers' faces than to other available stimuli. Not only do infants orient toward social stimulation, they soon start to smile in response to it. Smiling is arguably of singular importance in the generation of the first social interactive structures. When infants smile, adults feel tremendously rewarded and try hard to reproduce the expression. Because infants smile to contingent patterns of stimulation, whereby they receive feedback after acting themselves, mothers quickly learn to produce contingent patterns of stimulation—touch, facial expression, vocalization. Over time, infants and mothers tune into the quality of each others' stimulation so that their interactions become finely coordinated. These contingent patterns of stimulation form the nucleus of the dyadic interactions in which infants first experiences together in a reliable way both the first- and third-person components of psychological acts. They are therefore of critical importance to the generation of commonsense psychology.

Smooth dyadic interactions are critical in another way. Because they are highly charged with positive emotion, they serve as the wellspring for the formation of a healthy relationship to the mother—the attachment bond. The attachment relationship fulfills perhaps its most important function in preparing children for healthy relationships in later life. However, this relationship also plays an important role in the development of commonsense psychology. In the first place, it keeps infants close to the mother and therefore available for continued interactions and the concomitant combined experience of first- and third-person information pertaining to psychological activity. Second, the nature of the attachment relationship as a moderator of exploration from a secure base provides some of the first contexts in which infants simultaneously attend to novel objects or situations and their mothers' expressions. As a result, the infants experience in close association first- and third-person information in relation to objects or situations in the world.

In the second half of the first year, infants become adept at acting on objects and objects become incorporated into their interactive structures with others. Infants start to be able to coordinate attention across their interactive partners and the foci of their mutual attention. In this way, dyadic interactions become transformed into triadic interactions. These new triadic interactions present infants with different combinations of first- and third-person information. Alongside the emotional combinations present in dyadic interactions, there is now the possibility for infants to experience in combination first- and third-person information pertaining to epistemic and conative psychological relations. They and others can both look at objects or both reach for, give, and take objects. Infants also learn more about the objects that they are interacting over by imitating the actions they observe their partners perform. The development of triadic interactions is of profound significance for the construction of commonsense psychology. These interactions provide infants with repeated experiences in which their own psychological relations to objects are coordinated with others' psychological relations to the same objects. As a result, infants can construct representations of objected-directed actions that incorporate both the first-person and third-person characteristics of such actions.

Within triadic interactions infants learn to manipulate their partners' action in relation to the objects about which they are interacting. Through indicative acts they can manipulate their partners' attention to objects and responsiveness to them, and through imperative acts they can manipulate their partners in the service of their own desires. The purpose of triadic interactions soon becomes primarily communicative as infants seek to affect their partners' action in relation to objects. Whereas initially infants achieve these communicative goals with gestures and nonreferential vocalizations, by about 12 months infants start to use vocalizations that resemble those they constantly hear from adults. By attending to the correspondence of their own rudimentary vocalizations to those of others, they become better able to imitate the conventional sounds of the language in which they are immersed. They also start to appreciate that particular sounds accompany various interactions with particular objects and thereby become able to use those sounds as stand-ins for those objects. As this referential use of words starts to take hold during the second year, toddlers start to conduct more and more of their interactions with others using words in combination with objects and events. Interactions are now not just communicative, but also linguistic in that the primary mode of communication is language.

The use of language to conduct interactions with others enables three critically important developments in commonsense psychology. First, as children become capable of mentally and linguistically representing things in their absence, interactions can occur over verbal representations of objects and events without those objects and events having to be present. At the same time, pretend play allows children to interact with objects as if they are something different. As a result, the focus of interactive structures becomes unhinged from the perceptible world of the here and now. By the end of the second year, children start to understand that people can have psychological relations to imaginary objects and events or to objects and events that are displaced in time. In other words, they can now recognize that psychological activity can be directed at representations of things as well as real things.

The second contribution that language makes is to represent not just objects and events but also psychological orientations to those objects and events. For this to occur, children have to progress beyond communication using simple words to syntactic and then modal forms of language as they express and respond to the expression of psychological attitudes. Attitudes toward objects, both real and imagined, can be communicated using relatively simple verb constructions. However, attitudes that recognize the potential perspectival diversity of psychological relations require more complex syntax involving modal verbs and embedded clauses. As children progress through more complex syntactic forms of linguistic communication, psychological orientations can become the focus of interactions—children and adults can communicate about their shared and diverse psychological relations. Interactions in which psychological relations are explicitly compared and contrasted present children with an opportunity to construct an understanding of the potential range of perspectives on a joint focus of attention.

Finally, discourse over noncurrent events creates a context whereby children start to be able to consider personal events that are displaced in time. Children and adults talk about events they have jointly experienced in the past and future events in which they may participate. Within these discourses, children are presented by others with an objective perspective on their noncurrent activities, and they can combine this objective perspective with the subjective perspective on those same events available in memory or through the imagination of the future. Consideration of noncurrent events involving the self, along with an awareness of the self in the present, creates a self that is recognized to be continuous in time and allows an understanding both of how the past affects the present self and of how present acts may affect the future.

We can see, therefore, that almost from birth children are engaged in interactive episodes with others. The interactions change in form and complexity and yet they maintain certain core features. Most importantly, they are typically structured in such a way that children are presented with information from their own psychological relations to objects and information from other psychological relations in close association. The contiguous patterning of these two forms of information is essential for the construction of commonsense psychology. However, merely having available relevant information pertaining to commonsense psychology is not enough—children have to be able to process and use that information.

CONSTRUCTING REPRESENTATIONS
OF PSYCHOLOGICAL RELATIONS

Newborn infants are equipped with a propensity to pay attention to certain forms of stimulation that other people offer. From their orienting patterns, we know that very young infants like to look at faces and that they like to listen to voices. What this means is that even from birth, infants preferentially orient to social stimulation. Once their interest has been captured by people, infants are primed to pick up on the regularities and patterns in the stimulation that emanates from people. So, orienting is an important mechanism because it keeps infants focused on the most important sources of stimulation. Of course, infants do not just passively observe, they give back in the form of social acts such as smiling and vocalizing. As we have seen, this responsivity sets the stage for a history of interactive exchanges between infants and others.

Evidence from a variety of sources reveals that infants are extremely good at picking up on regularities and patterns in the perceptual information to which they attend. Detection of patterns is aided by the natural tendency of infants to orient preferentially toward stimulation that is relatively novel. In experimental situations, this preferential orienting is best shown using the habituation-novelty preference procedure whereby infants are first exposed to one pattern and then, after they have lost interest, it is replaced with novel patterns that differ in critical ways from the original. At this point the infants' novelty preferences allow inferences to be drawn about what the infants extracted from the original display.

We now know from many studies that infants can detect patterns within perceptual modalities, such as when they recognize regular sequential patterns of speech sounds, and they can detect patterns across perceptual modalities, such as when they extract amodal temporal or spatial properties common to visual and proprioceptive information about their own movements. Infants detect patterns in temporal information such as contingency, in spatial information such as movement in space or location, and in form such as appearance. They also detect patterns in the combination of these dimensions. They can then use these patterns to anticipate upcoming stimulation.

The particular patterns that are detected in novel stimulation depend on prior experience. Pattern detection begins by discovering regularities at relatively low levels of complexity. Detection of these regularities results in the construction of higher order units that then guide subsequent perception, so that pattern detection becomes the recognition of regularities in the relations among these units. Information processing is a continual process of the discovery of ever more complex arrangements of patterns among patterns.

What this all means for social information processing is that during the first year infants can take advantage of the patterns of information available in streams of information coming from others and from the self and start to recognize patterns of movements, vocalizations, and so on. They can also discover patterns within the contingent interactive episodes in which they are regularly engaged. In the dyadic period, they can pick up on the co-occurrences of first- and third-person emotional information present in their face-to-face interactions with their mothers. As objects become part of their interactions with others, infants can pick up on the regularities in the ways that they and others act on objects and on the regularities in the ways that both participants in triadic interactions act toward each other in relation to the same objects. Out of pattern detection on triadic interactive structures are generated the first representations of psychological activity directed at objects. These representations may be initially tied relatively closely to particular actions, such as reaches, points, and looks. However, object-directed actions tend to occur in combination, as for example when a person looks at an object, smiles, and then reaches for it. The correlations among different object-directed actions allow the recognition of patterns of psychological activity representative of people and their intentions.

Typically, by the end of the first year, infants are able to use and recognize simple words. It is instructive to consider the variety of forms of pattern detection that go into this achievement. Using a word essentially means that infants have extracted a regular sound combination from segmentation of the speech heard from others. Infants may have detected that the same sound combination is produced by different users. They will have detected the commonalities in the situations in which this particular sound pattern occurs, most often the presence of a particular object or type of object. Infants will have matched their own vocalizations to the heard models through refinement of their own initially rudimentary utterances. The result of all of this pattern detection is a conventional and meaningful linguistic element.

Having themselves been born out of pattern detection, words go on to act as powerful aids to further pattern detection. Because the same element—the word—is used for multiple instances of objects or events, words serve, to use Waxman and Markow's (1995) elegant phrase, as "invitations to form categories." In the case of psychological information, words may play a particularly important role in this regard. The same word is used by others to refer both to events where the child only has first-person information about a psychological state and to events where the child only has third-person information about a psychological state. In this way words can help to bridge the gap between first- and third-person information and pull first- and third-person information together into a representation that codes for both.

The transition during the second year into the period of mental representation enables a whole new order of pattern recognition. Because young children can hold in mind a mental representation at the same time as paying perceptual attention to something in the environment, they can start to detect relations between perceptual and mental inputs. Such relations start to free children's commonsense psychology from the constraints of perception. Children can start to recognize that people can have psychological relations to absent or imaginary objects. In addition, children can now fully appreciate that self and other are equivalent in that both have subjective and objective sides.

With the onset of language-based interaction, pattern detection continues in the arena of representational thought. As we have seen, the conversations children have with others present them with opportunities for comparing and contrasting psychological relations across people and across time. Discourse provides the medium through which the detection of patterns across people and across time can occur. Once self and other can be conceptualized in the same terms, the similarities and differences in the ways self and others relate to the world at different points in time can be detected through more advanced pattern detection processes such as analogical reasoning. Analogical reasoning allows children to make inferences about others based on their own knowledge of self and also about themselves based on their knowledge of others.

Pattern detection and capacity for representational thought are the information-processing mechanisms that allow children to use the information available to them in their interactions with others to construct representations of psychological relations. These mechanisms build progressively more complex psychological concepts as they use progressively more abstract forms of information. However, the key to building a commonsense psychology at all levels of complexity is the integration of information derived from the self and information derived from others. It is the patterns evident in these two sources of information together that yield the variety of commonsense psychology characteristic of human social understanding.

THE DEVELOPMENT OF COMMONSENSE PSYCHOLOGY: A DANCE BETWEEN SELF AND OTHER

So the development of commonsense psychology depends on the operation of pattern detection information-processing mechanisms working with information about the psychological relations of self and others available during interactive episodes. Interactions are by definition events in which the activity of one partner depends on the activity of the other. As such they resemble dances in which both partners are continually responding to the actions of the other. Children's experience of interactions necessarily involves information from both self and other that is presented in tightly coordinated patterns of activity. It is these patterns that form the basis for the development of commonsense psychology.

As we have seen, pattern detection is a hierarchical process whereby simpler patterns of information become organized into increasingly more complex patterns. The complexity of the patterns changes as children are able to enter into interactions that occur around ever more abstract foci of attention. As a result, commonsense psychology proceeds through a number of forms but all are at heart representations of the interactive relations between self and other. Although patterns detected in information pertaining to psychological relations derived solely from self—as in visual-proprioceptive correlations of one's own movements—or from others—as in associations between different actions—may be available, they do not alone allow the generation of representations of psychological relations that are uniformly applicable to both self and others. For that, information from self and from others has to be simultaneously available. In closing, I briefly summarize this progression.

During the first 6 months of life, infants show a variety of social behaviors and they become quite skilled at social interaction. They enter into the dance of social relations with their first partner—the mother. However, they cannot yet be said to have any understanding of psychological relations to objects because their awareness of either their own or others' psychological states is not yet coordinated with an awareness of objects. Nevertheless, this first phase of infancy is important for the integration of certain forms of first- and third-person information, in particular, emotional information. Infants' awareness of others becomes tied in with their awareness of self and vice versa. They have started on a long journey during which self-awareness will be intertwined with the understanding others.

The incorporation of objects into social interactions is of profound significance for commonsense psychology. For the first time, infants can start to recognize the object-directed nature of psychological activity. This occurs first for actions that directly contact objects. Once infants start to participate in interactions focused on objects at a distance, they begin to understand that some actions that do not directly contact objects are nevertheless directed at objects. The representations of psychological activity that grow within triadic interactions are initially about object-directed actions. Gradually, as the connections among different object-directed actions start to be forged, these representations come to code more general aspects of intentional, or goal-directed, activity. Because this understanding is developed in the context of social interaction, within which both first- and third-person forms of information are present, these representations are potentially applicable to both self and others. As with the earlier dyadic interactions, self and other are tightly intertwined in commonsense psychology.

During the second year, self and other start to be clearly pulled apart. Children are able to imagine the self from a third-person point of view—how the self appears to others—and others from a first-person point of view—what others are experiencing. This makes an individualistic commonsense psychology possible for the first time. Self and other are understood to be agents with separable psychological perspectives while still being similar in the sense of having both a subjective and an objective side. Others' subjective states can be appreciated by analogy with the self and the self's objective side can be imagined by analogy with the others. By the end of the second year, psychological relations to absent and imaginary objects become part of commonsense psychology as linguistic and other forms of representations can stand in for real objects. Although children now have a clear sense of self and others as individual and separable psychological agents, it is still the case that the representation of any one individual's psychological relations only has meaning in its contradistinction to that of someone else.

Over the next 2 years, young children develop an explicit commonsense psychology in the sense that they become able to talk with others about a variety of psychological relations. In these conversations, they confront situations in which comparisons are explicitly made between the psychological relations of self and other and between psychological relations across time. Conversation focuses attention on the diversity of perspectives and, in the process, children develop a more sophisticated commonsense psychology that recognizes the potential for variability in perspectives on the same situations across people and across time. Now commonsense psychology incorporates a consideration of how psychological relations compare across self and others and across time. As children become capable of recalling events from the past and imagining possible future events, conversation also focuses attention on the continuities and discontinuities across time. This leads to a more sophisticated form of self-awareness that transcends the present. The self becomes a temporally extended person—someone who had experiences in the past that to some extent determine the present and who can do things now to affect what the self will become. Understanding the self as a temporally extended person enables decision making in the interests of the future. This ability to predict and plan toward the future yields lavish payoffs in the organization of social behavior.

FINAL WORDS

Commonsense psychology may be common sense, but that does not mean it is simple or self-evident. There are some significant challenges to its achievement. Children are fortunate to have strong social motivations working both within them and within their caregivers. These motivations set up children and their parents to pay special attention to each other, and to respond appropriately and sensitively to each others' actions. Children are also equipped with powerful information-processing mechanisms that allow them to make sense of the information they receive within the contexts of their interactions with others. Together these social interactive motivations and information-processing mechanisms generate a series of layers of social understanding in which people—self and other—are understood to be psychological agents who relate to real and imaginary objects in a variety of ways. Along the way, they also generate a representational system—language—that plays a key role in transforming further the commonsense psychology constructed through infancy. As interactions extend beyond the immediate family to include a broader range of partners, language acts both as a medium for more complex interactive structures within which relevant social information is provided and as a medium for representation of social concepts. With its support, children can move beyond the here and now and consider the range of possible psychological orientations that they and others experience in relation to objects and situations. Self and others come to be understood as persons who exist across time in psychological connection to each other and to the world. All the while these concepts of self and other fundamentally reflect the history of children's interactive experiences with others.

References

Abbeduto, L., & Rosenberg, S. (1985). Children's knowledge of the presuppositions of *know* and other cognitive verbs. *Journal of Child Language, 12*, 621–641.

Acredolo, L., & Goodwyn, S. (1988). Symbolic gesturing in normal infants. *Child Development, 59*, 450–466.

Adamson, L. B., & Frick, J. E. (2003). The still face: A history of a shared experimental paradigm. *Infancy, 4*, 451–473.

Ainsworth, M., Blehar, M., Waters, E., & Wall, S. (1978). *Patterns of attachment*. Hillsdale, NJ: Lawrence Erlbaum Associates.

Akhtar, N. (1999). Acquiring basic word order: Evidence for data-driven learning of syntactic structure. *Journal of Child Language, 26*, 339–356.

Akhtar, N., & Tomasello, M. (2000). The social nature of word learning. In R. M. Golinkoff et al. (Eds.), *Becoming a word learner: A debate on language acquisition* (pp. 115–135). New York: Oxford University Press.

Amsterdam, B. (1972). Mirror self-image reactions before age two. *Developmental Psychobiology, 5*, 297–305.

Angelopoulos, M. (1997). *Social behavior during the preschool years in relation to theory of mind, future-oriented thinking and language*. Unpublished doctoral dissertation, Dalhousie University, Halifax, Nova Scotia, Canada.

Anisfeld, M. (1991). Neonatal imitation. *Developmental Review, 11*, 60–97.

Anisfeld, M. (1996). Only tongue protrusion modeling is matched by neonates. *Developmental Review, 16*, 149–161.

Anisfeld, M., Rosenberg, E., Hoberman, M., & Gasparini, D. (1998). Lexical acceleration coincides with the onset of combinatorial speech. *First Language, 18*, 165–184.

Appleton, M., & Reddy, V. (1996). Teaching three-year-olds to pass false belief tests: A conversational approach. *Social Development, 5*, 275–291.

Asendorpf, J. B. (2002). Self-awareness, other-awareness, and secondary representation. In A. Meltzoff & W. Prinz (Eds.), *The imitative mind: Development, evolution, and brain bases* (pp. 63–73). New York: Cambridge University Press.

Asendorpf, J. B., & Baudonnière, P. (1993). Self-awareness and other-awareness: Mirror self-recognition and synchronic imitation among unfamiliar peers. *Developmental Psychology, 29*, 88–95.

Asendorpf, J. B., Warkentin, V., & Baudonnière, P. (1996). Self-awareness and other-awareness II: Mirror self-recognition, social contingency awareness, and synchronic imitation. *Developmental Psychology, 32*, 313–321.

Ashley, J., & Tomasello, M. (1998). Cooperative problem-solving and teaching in preschoolers. *Social Development, 7*, 143–163.

Aslin, R. N., Saffran, J. R., & Newport, E. L. (1999). Statistical learning in linguistic and nonlinguistic domains. In B. MacWhinney (Ed.), *The emergence of language* (pp. 359–380). Mahwah, NJ: Lawrence Erlbaum Associates.

Astington, J. W. (1993). *The child's discovery of the mind.* Cambridge, MA: Harvard University Press.

Astington, J. W. (2003). Sometime necessary, never sufficient: False belief understanding and social competence. In B. Repacholi & V. Slaughter (Eds.), *Individual differences in theory of mind: Implications for typical and atypical development* (pp. 13–38). New York: Psychology Press.

Astington, J. W., & Baird, J. A. (2005). *Why language matters for theory of mind.* New York: Oxford University Press.

Astington, J. W., Harris, P. L., & Olson, D. R. (1988). *Developing theories of mind.* New York: Cambridge University Press.

Astington, J. W., & Jenkins, J. M. (1995). Theory of mind development and social understanding. *Cognition and Emotion, 9,* 151–165.

Astington, J. W., & Peskin, J. (2004). Meaning and use: Children's acquisition of the mental lexicon. In J. Lucariello, J. Hudson, R. Fivush, & P. Bauer (Eds.), *The development of the mediated mind: Sociocultural context and cognitive development* (pp. 59–78). Mahwah, NJ: Lawrence Erlbaum Associates.

Atance, C., & O'Neill, D. (2001). Episodic future thinking. *Trends in Cognitive Sciences, 5,* 533–539.

Bahrick, L., Moss, L., & Fadil, C. (1996). Development of visual self-recognition in infancy. *Ecological Psychology, 8,* 189–208.

Bahrick, L. E., & Watson, J. S. (1985). Detection of intermodal proprioceptive visual contingency as a potential basis of self-perception in infancy. *Developmental Psychology, 21,* 963–973.

Bakeman, R., & Adamson, L. (1984). Coordinating attention to people and objects in mother-infant and peer-infant interactions. *Child Development, 5,* 1278–1289.

Baldwin, D. A. (1991). Infants' contribution to the achievement of joint reference. *Child Development, 62,* 875–890.

Baldwin, D. A., & Baird, J. A. (2001). Discerning intentions in dynamic human action. *Trends in Cognitive Science, 5,* 171–178.

Baldwin, D. A., Baird, J., Saylor, M., & Clark, M. A. (2001). Infants parse dynamic action. *Child Development, 72,* 708–717.

Baldwin, D. A., & Moses, L. J. (1996). The ontogeny of social information gathering. *Child Development, 67,* 1915–1939.

Baldwin, D. A., & Saylor, M. (2005). Language promotes structural alignment in the acquisition of mentalistic concepts. In J. W. Astington & J. Baird (Eds.), *Why language matters for theory of mind* (pp. 123–143). New York: Oxford University Press.

Baldwin, J. M. (1894). Imitation: A chapter in the natural history of consciousness. *Mind, 3,* 26–55.

Baldwin, J. M. (1906). *Mental development in the child and the race: Methods and processes* (3rd ed.). New York: Macmillan.

Baron-Cohen, S., Tager-Flusberg, H., & Cohen, D. J. (2000). *Understanding other minds: Perspectives from developmental cognitive neuroscience.* Oxford, England: Oxford University Press.

Barrera, M., & Maurer, D. (1981). Discrimination of strangers by the three-month-old. *Child Development, 52,* 558–563.

Barresi, J., & Moore, C. (1996). Intentional relations and social understanding. *Behavioral and Brain Sciences, 19,* 107–122.

Bartsch, K., & Wellman, H. (1995). *Children talk about the mind.* New York: Oxford University Press.

Bates, E. (1990). Language about me and you: Pronominal reference and the emerging concept of self. In D. Cicchetti & M. Beeghly (Eds.), *The self in transition: Infancy to childhood* (pp. 165–182). Chicago: University of Chicago Press.

Bates, E., Bretherton, I., & Snyder, L. (1989). *From first words to grammar: Individual differences and dissociable mechanisms.* New York: Cambridge University Press.

Bates, E., Camaioni, L., & Volterra, V. (1975). The acquisition of performatives prior to speech. *Merrill-Palmer Quarterly, 21,* 205–226.

Bates, E., O'Connell, B., & Shore, C. (1987). Language and communication in infancy. In J. Osofsky (Ed.), *Handbook of infant development* (pp. 149–203). New York: Wiley.

Bateson, M. (1975). Mother-infant exchanges: The epigenesis of conversation interaction. *Annals of the New York Academy of Sciences, 263,* 101–113.

Beeghly, M., Bretherton, I., & Mervis, C. (1986). Mothers' internal state language to toddlers. *British Journal of Developmental Psychology, 4,* 247–261.

Bell, S., & Ainsworth, M. (1972). Infant crying and maternal responsiveness. *Child Development, 43,* 1171–1190.

Bellagamba, F., & Tomasello, M. (1999). Re-enacting intended acts: Comparing 12- and 18-month-olds. *Infant Behavior and Development, 22,* 277–282.

Belsky, J., Rovine, M., & Taylor, R. (1984). The Pennsylvania infant and family project: III. The origins of individual differences in infant-mother attachment: Maternal and infant contributions. *Child Development, 55,* 718–728.

Bertenthal, B., & Fischer, K. (1978). Development of self-recognition in the infant. *Developmental Psychology, 14,* 44–50.

Bigelow, A. E. (1998). Infants' sensitivity to familiar imperfect contingencies in social interaction. *Infant Behavior and Development, 21,* 149–162.

Bigelow, A. E., & Birch, S. (1999). The effects of contingency in previous interactions on infants' preference for social partners. *Infant Behavior and Development, 22,* 367–382.

Bigelow, A. E., MacLean, B. K., & MacDonald, D. (1996). Infants' responses to live and replay interactions with self and mother. *Merrill-Palmer Quarterly, 42,* 596–611.

Bischof-Köhler, D. (1991). The development of empathy in infants. In M. Lamb & H. Keller (Eds.), *Infant development: Perspectives from German-speaking countries* (pp. 1–33). Hillsdale, NJ: Lawrence Erlbaum Associates.

Block, N. (1994). Qualia. In S. Guttenplan (Ed.), *A companion to the philosophy of mind* (pp. 514–520). Oxford, England: Blackwell.

Borke, H. (1975). Piaget's mountains revisited: Changes in the egocentric landscape. *Developmental Psychology, 11,* 240–243.

Bornstein, M., & Arterberry, M. (2003). Recognition, discrimination and categorization of smiling by 5-month-old infants. *Developmental Science, 6,* 585–599.

Bowlby, J. (1969). *Attachment and loss: Vol. 1. Attachment.* New York: Basic Books.

Boysen, S. T., Berntson, G. G., Hannan, M. B., & Cacioppo, J. T. (1996). Quantity-based interference and symbolic representations in chimpanzees (Pan troglodytes). *Journal of Experimental Psychology: Animal Behavior Processes, 22,* 76–86.

Braine, M. (1976). Children's first word combinations. *Monographs of the Society for Research in Child Development, 41*(1), (Serial No. 164).

Brand, R. J., Baldwin, D. A., & Ashburn, L. A. (2002). Evidence for "motionese": Modifications in mothers' infant-directed action. *Developmental Science, 5,* 72–83.

Brazelton, T. B., Koslowski, B., & Main, M. (1974). The origins of reciprocity: The early infant-mother interaction. In M. Lewis & L. A. Rosenblum (Eds.), *The effect of the infant on its caregiver* (pp. 49–76). New York: Wiley.

Bremner, J. G. (1994). *Infancy.* Oxford, England: Blackwell.

Bretherton, I. (1991). Intentional communication and the development of an understanding of mind. In D. Frye & C. Moore (Eds.), *Children's theories of mind: Mental states and social understanding* (pp. 49–75). Hillsdale, NJ: Lawrence Erlbaum Associates.

Bretherton, I., & Beeghly, M. (1982). Talking about internal states: The acquisition of an explicit theory of mind. *Developmental Psychology, 18,* 906–921.

Bretherton, I., Fritz, J., Zahn-Waxler, C., & Ridgeway, D. (1986). Learning to talk about emotions: A functionalist perspective. *Child Development, 57,* 529–548.

Bretherton, I., McNew, S., & Beeghly-Smith, M. (1981). Early person knowledge as expressed in gestural and verbal communication: When do infants acquire a "theory of mind?" In M. Lamb & L. Sherrod (Eds.), *Infant social cognition* (pp. 333–373). Hillsdale, NJ: Lawrence Erlbaum Associates.

Bronson, G. (1974). The postnatal growth of visual capacity. *Child Development, 45,* 873–890.

Brooks, R., & Meltzoff, A. N. (2002). The importance of eyes: How infants interpret adult looking behavior. *Developmental Psychology, 38*, 958–966.

Brown, J., Donelan-McCall, N., & Dunn, J. (1996). Why talk about mental states? The significance of children's conversations with friends, siblings, and mothers. *Child Development, 67*, 836–849.

Brown, J., & Dunn, J. (1991). "You can cry, mum": The social and developmental implications of talk about internal states. *British Journal of Developmental Psychology, 9*, 237–256.

Brownell, C. A., & Carriger, M. S. (1990). Changes in cooperation and self-other differentiation during the second year. *Child Development, 61*, 1164–1174.

Bruce, D., Dolan, A., & Phillips-Grant, K. (2000). On the transition from childhood amnesia to the recall of personal memories. *Psychological Science, 11*, 360–364.

Bruner, J. S. (1983). *Child's talk: Learning to use language.* New York: Norton.

Bullock, M., & Lütkenhaus, P. (1990). Who am I? Self-understanding in toddlers. *Merrill-Palmer Quarterly, 36*, 217–238.

Bushnell, I. W. R. (2001). Mother's face recognition in newborn infants: Learning and memory. *Infant and Child Development, 10*, 67–74.

Bushnell, I. W. R., Sai, F., & Mullin, J. T. (1989). Neonatal recognition of the mother's face. *British Journal of Developmental Psychology, 7*, 3–15.

Butterworth, G., & Cochran, E. (1980). Towards a mechanism of joint visual attention in human infancy. *International Journal of Behavioral Development, 3*, 253–272.

Butterworth, G., & Jarrett, N. (1991). What minds have in common is space: Spatial mechanisms serving joint visual attention in infancy. *British Journal of Developmental Psychology, 9*, 55–72.

Callaghan, T., Rochat, P., Lillard, A., Claux, M. L., Odden, H., Itakura, S., et al. (2005). Synchrony in the onset of mental state reasoning: Evidence from 5 cultures. *Psychological Science, 6*, 378–384.

Campos, J., Anderson, D., Barbu-Roth, M., Hubbard, E., Hertenstein, M., & Witherington, D. (2000). Travel broadens the mind. *Infancy, 1*, 149–220.

Carey, S., & Diamond, R. (1977). From piecemeal to configurational representation of faces. *Science, 195*, 312–324.

Carlson, S. M., Davis, A. C., & Gum, J. G. (2005). Less is more: Executive function and symbolic representation in preschool children. *Psychological Science, 16*, 609–616.

Caron, A., Butler, S., & Brooks, R. (2002). Gaze following at 12 and 14 months: Do the eyes matter? *British Journal of Developmental Psychology, 20*, 225–239.

Carpendale, J., & Lewis, C. (2004). Constructing an understanding of mind: The development of children's social understanding within social interaction. *Behavioral and Brain Sciences, 27*, 79–96.

Carpenter, M., Nagell, K., & Tomasello, M. (1998). Social cognition, joint attention, and communicative competence from 9 to 15 months of age. *Monographs of the Society for Research in Child Development, 63*(4), (Serial No. 255).

Cassia, V., Simion, F., & Umiltà, C. (2001). Face preference at birth: The role of an orienting mechanism. *Developmental Science, 4*, 101–108.

Chomsky, N. (1965). *Aspects of a theory of syntax.* Cambridge, MA: MIT Press.

Clark, E. (2003). *First language acquisition.* New York: Cambridge University Press.

Clements, W., Rustin, C., & McCallum, S. (2000). Promoting the transition from implicit to explicit understanding: A training study of false belief. *Developmental Science, 3*, 88–92.

Cohen, L. B. (1998). An information-processing approach to infant perception and cognition. In F. Simion & G. Butterworth (Eds.), *The development of sensory, motor and cognitive capacities in early infancy: From perception to cognition* (pp. 277–300). Hove, England: Psychology Press.

Cohen, L. B., & Cashon, C. H. (2001). Do 7-month-old infants process independent features or facial configurations? *Infant and Child Development, 10*, 83–92.

Cohen, L. B., Chaput, H. H., & Cashon, C. H. (2002). A constructivist model of infant cognition. *Cognitive Development, 17*, 1323–1343.

Cohn, J., & Tronick, E. (1987). Mother-infant face-to-face interaction: The sequence of dyadic states at 3, 6, and 9 months. *Developmental Psychology, 23*, 68–77.

Cohn, J., & Tronick, E. (1988). Mother-infant face-to-face interaction: Influence is bidirectional and unrelated to periodic cycles in either partner's behavior. *Developmental Psychology, 24*, 386–392.

Corkum, V., & Moore, C. (1995). Development of joint visual attention in infants. In C. Moore & P. J. Dunham (Eds.), *Joint attention: Its origins and role in development* (pp. 61–83). Hillsdale, NJ: Lawrence Erlbaum Associates.

Corkum, V., & Moore, C. (1998). Origins of joint visual attention in infants. *Developmental Psychology, 34,* 28–38.

Cox, M. (1980). Visual perspective-taking in children. In M. Cox (Ed.), *Are young children egocentric?* (pp. 61–79). London: Batsford.

Darwin, C. (1989). *Voyage of the Beagle.* New York: Penguin Books.

Deacon, T. W. (1997). *The symbolic species: The co-evolution of language and the brain.* New York: Norton.

DeCasper, A. J., & Fifer, W. (1980). Of human bonding: Newborns prefer their mothers' voices. *Science, 208,* 1174–1176.

DeCasper, A. J., Lecanuet, J. -P., Busnel, M. -C., Granier-Deferre, C., & Maugeais, R. (1994). Fetal reactions to recurrent maternal speech. *Infant Behavior and Development, 17,* 159–164.

DeCasper, A. J., & Prescott, P. A. (1984). Human newborns' perception of male voices: Preference, discrimination and reinforcing value. *Developmental Psychobiology, 17,* 481–491.

DeCasper, A. J., & Spence, M. (1986). Prenatal maternal speech influences newborns' perception of speech sounds. *Infant Behavior and Development, 9,* 133–150.

Del Carmen, R., Pederson, F., Huffman, L., & Bryan, Y. (1993). Dyadic distress management predicts subsequent security of attachment. *Infant Behavior and Development, 16,* 131–147.

DeLoache, J. (2004). Becoming symbol-minded. *Trends in Cognitive Sciences, 8,* 66–70.

Dennett, D. (1978). Beliefs about beliefs. *Behavioral and Brain Sciences, 1,* 568–570.

Dennett, D. (1987). *The intentional stance.* Cambridge, MA: MIT Press.

D'Entremont, B. (2000). A perceptual-attentional explanation of gaze following in 3- and 6-month-olds. *Developmental Science, 3,* 302–311.

D'Entremont, B., Hains, S. M. J., & Muir, D. W. (1997). A demonstration of gaze following in 3- to 6-month-olds. *Infant Behavior and Development, 20,* 569–572.

D'Entremont, B., & Muir, D. W. (1997). Five-month-olds' attention and affective responses to still-faced emotional expressions. *Infant Behavior and Development, 20,* 563–568.

de Villiers, J., & de Villiers, P. (1973). Development of the use of word order in comprehension. *Journal of Psycholinguistic Research, 2,* 331–341.

DeWolff, M., & Van IJzendoorn, M. (1997). Sensitivity and attachment: A meta-analysis on parental antecedents of infant attachment. *Child Development, 68,* 571–591.

Dudycha, G., & Dudycha, M. (1941). Childhood memories: A review of the literature. *Psychological Review, 38,* 668–682.

Dunham, P., & Dunham, F. (1995). Optimal social structures and adaptive infant development. In C. Moore & P. Dunham (Eds.), *Joint attention: Its origins and role in development* (pp. 159–188). Hillsdale, NJ: Lawrence Erlbaum Associates.

Dunham, P., Dunham, F., & Curwin, A. (1993). Joint attentional states and lexical acquisition at 18 months. *Developmental Psychology, 29,* 827–831.

Dunham, P., Dunham, F., Hurshman, A., & Alexander, T. (1989). Social contingency effects on subsequent perceptual-cognitive tasks in young infants. *Child Development, 60,* 1486–1496.

Dunn, J. (1988). *The beginnings of social understanding.* Cambridge, MA: Harvard University Press.

Dunn, J., Bretherton, I., & Munn, P. (1987). Conversations about feeling states between mothers and their young children. *Developmental Psychology, 23,* 132–139.

Dunphy-Lelii, S., & Wellman, H. M. (2004). Infants' understanding of occlusion of others' line-of-sight: Implications for an emerging theory of mind. *European Journal of Developmental Psychology, 1,* 49–66.

Eimas, P. D., Siqueland, E. R., Jusczyk, P. W., & Vigorito, J. (1971). Speech perception in infants. *Science, 171,* 303–306.

Ellsworth, C. P., Muir, D. W., & Hains, S. M. (1993). Social competence and person-object differentiation: An analysis of the still-face effect. *Developmental Psychology, 29,* 63–73.

Elsner, B., & Aschersleben, G. (2003). Do I get what you get? Learning about the effects of self-performed and observed actions in infancy. *Consciousness and Cognition, 12,* 732–751.

Fantz, R. L. (1961). The origin of form perception. *Scientific American, 204,* 66–72.

Fantz, R. L. (1964). Visual experience in infants: Decreased attention to familiar patterns relative to novel ones. *Science, 146,* 668–670.

Farrant, K., & Reese, E. (2000). Maternal style and children's participation in reminiscing: Stepping stones in children's autobiographical memory development. *Journal of Cognition and Development, 1,* 193–225.

Fenson, L., & Ramsay, D. S. (1980). Decentration and integration of the child's play in the second year. *Child Development, 51,* 171–178.

Fivush, R. (2001). Owning experience: Developing subjective perspective in autobiographical narratives. In C. Moore & K. Lemmon (Eds.), *The self in time: Developmental perspectives* (pp. 35–52). Mahwah, NJ: Lawrence Erlbaum Associates.

Fivush, R., & Fromhoff, F. (1988). Style and structure in mother-child conversations about the past. *Discourse Processes, 11,* 337–355.

Flavell, J., Everett, B., Croft, K., & Flavell, E. (1981). Young children's knowledge about visual perception: Further evidence for the Level 1–Level 2 distinction. *Developmental Psychology, 17,* 99–103.

Flavell, J., Flavell, E., & Green, F. (1983). Development of the appearance-reality distinction. *Cognitive Psychology, 15,* 95–120.

Fontaine, R., & Pieraut le Bonniec, G. (1988). Postural evolution and integration of the prehension gesture in children age four to ten months. *British Journal of Developmental Psychology, 6,* 223–233.

Fraley, R. C., & Spieker, S. J. (2003). Are infant attachment patterns continuously or categorically distributed? A taxometric analysis of strange situation behavior. *Developmental Psychology, 39,* 387–404.

Freud, S. (1964). An outline of psychoanalysis. In J. Strachey (Ed. And Trans.), *The standard edition of the complete psychological works of Sigmund Freud* (Vol. 23). London, England: Hogarth Press. (Original work published 1940).

Frye, D., & Moore, C. (1991). *Children's theories of minds: Mental states and social understanding.* Hillsdale, NJ: Lawrence Erlbaum Associates.

Frye, D., Zelazo, P. D., & Palfai, T. (1995). Theory of mind and rule-based reasoning. *Cognitive Development, 10,* 483–527.

Frye, D., & Ziv, M. (2005). Teaching and learning as intentional activities. In B. Homer & C. Tamis-LeMonda (Eds.), *The development of social cognition and communication* (pp. 231–258). Mahwah, NJ: Lawrence Erlbaum Associates.

Furrow, D., Moore, C., Davidge, J., & Chiasson, L. (1992). Mental terms in mothers' and children's speech: Similarities and relationships. *Journal of Child Language, 19,* 617–631.

Gallup, G. G. (1970). Chimpanzees: Self-recognition. *Science, 167,* 86–87.

Gentner, D., & Markman, A. B. (1997). Structure mapping in analogy and similarity. *American Psychologist, 52,* 45–56.

Gentner, D., & Medina, J. (1998). Similarity and the development of rules. *Cognition, 65,* 263–297.

Gentner, D., & Rattermann, M. J. (1991). Language and the career of similarity. In S. Gelman & J. Byrnes (Eds.), *Perspectives on language and thought: Interrelations in development* (pp. 225–277). New York: Cambridge University Press.

Geppert, U., & Küster, U. (1983). The emergence of "wanting to do it oneself": A precursor of achievement motivation. *International Journal of Behavioral Development, 6,* 355–369.

Gergely, G., & Watson, J. S. (1999). Early socio-emotional development: Contingency perception and the social-biofeedback model. In P. Rochat (Ed.), *Early social cognition: Understanding others in the first months of life* (pp. 101–136). Mahwah, NJ: Lawrence Erlbaum Associates.

Gerhardt, J. (1991). The meaning of the modals HAFTA, NEEDTA, and WANNA in children's speech. *Journal of Pragmatics, 16,* 531–590.

Goldberg, S. (2000). *Attachment and development.* London: Arnold.

Goldberg, S., Grusec, J., & Jenkins, J. (1999). Confidence in protection: Arguments for a narrow definition of attachment. *Journal of Family Psychology, 13,* 475–483.

Goodwyn, S., & Acredolo, L. (1993). Symbolic gesture versus word: Is there a modality advantage for onset of symbol use. *Child Development, 64,* 688–701.

Gopnik, A. (1993). How we know our minds: The illusion of first-person knowledge of intentionality. *Behavioral and Brain Sciences, 16,* 1–14.

Gopnik, A., & Astington, J. (1988). Children's understanding of representational change and its relation to the understanding of false belief and the appearance-reality distinction. *Child Development, 59*, 26–37.

Goren, C., Sarty, M., & Wu, P. (1975). Visual following and pattern discrimination of face-like stimuli by newborn infants. *Pediatrics, 56*, 544–549.

Gusella, J., Muir, D., & Tronick, E. (1988). The effect of manipulating maternal behavior during an interaction on three- and six-month-olds' affect and attention. *Child Development, 59*, 1111–1124.

Hains, S., & Muir, D. (1996a). Effects of stimulus contingency in infant-adult interactions. *Infant Behavior and Development, 19*, 49–61.

Hains, S., & Muir, D. (1996b). Infant sensitivity to adult eye direction. *Child Development, 67*, 1940–1951.

Haith, M. M. (1994). Visual expectations as the first step toward the development of future-oriented processes. In M. Haith, J. Benson, R. Roberts, & B. Pennington (Eds.), *The development of future-oriented processes* (pp. 11–38). Chicago: University of Chicago Press.

Haith, M. M., Hazan, C., & Goodman, G. S. (1988). Expectation and anticipation of dynamic visual events by 3.5-month-old babies. *Child Development, 59*, 467–479.

Harley, K., & Reese, E. (1999). Origins of autobiographical memory. *Developmental Psychology, 35*, 1338–1348.

Harner, L. (1975). Yesterday and tomorrow: Development of early understanding of the terms. *Developmental Psychology, 11*, 864–865.

Harris, P. L. (2000). *The work of the imagination.* Oxford, England: Blackwell.

Henderson, A., & Graham, S. A. (in press). Two-year-olds' appreciation of the shared nature of novel object labels. *Journal of Cognition and Development.*

Hertenstein, M., & Campos, J. (2004). The retention effects of an adult's emotional displays on infant behavior. *Child Development, 75*, 595–613.

Hilgard, E. R. (1980). The trilogy of mind: Cognition, affection, and conation. *Journal of the History of the Behavioral Sciences, 16*, 107–117.

Hirst, W., & Weil, J. (1982). Acquisition of epistemic and deontic meaning of modals. *Journal of Child Language, 9*, 659–666.

Hobson, R. P. (1993). *Autism and the development of mind.* Hillsdale, NJ: Lawrence Erlbaum Associates.

Hoffman, M. (1975). Developmental synthesis of affect and cognition and its implications for altruistic motivation. *Developmental Psychology, 11*, 607–622.

Huang, C. -T., Heyes, C., & Charman, T. (2002). Infants' behavioral reenactment of "failed attempts": Exploring the roles of emulation learning, stimulus enhancement, and understanding of intentions. *Developmental Psychology, 38*, 840–855.

Hudson, J. (2001). The anticipated self: Mother-child talk about future events. In C. Moore & K. Lemmon (Eds.), *The self in time: Developmental perspectives* (pp. 53–74). Mahwah, NJ: Lawrence Erlbaum Associates.

Hudson, J. (2002). "Do you know what we're going to do this summer?": Mothers talk to preschool children about future events. *Journal of Cognition and Development, 3*, 49–71.

Hume, D. (1911). *A treatise of human nature.* London: Dent. (Original work published 1739–40)

Identical twins closer than clones, experts say. Genetic blueprint can be trumped by environment. (2002, December 30). *Halifax Mail Star*, A4.

Isabella, R. (1995). The origins of infant-mother attachment: Maternal behavior and infant development. *Annals of Child Development, 10*, 57–81.

Isabella, R., & Belsky, J. (1991). Interactional synchrony and the origins of infant-mother attachment: A replication study. *Child Development, 62*, 373–384.

Jacobsen, T., Huss, M., Fendrich, M., Kruesi, M., & Zeigenhain, U. (1997). Children's ability to delay gratification: Longitudinal relations to mother-child attachment. *Journal of Genetic Psychology, 158*, 411–426.

Jacques, S., & Zelazo, P. D. (in press). On the possible roots of cognitive flexibility. In B. Homer & C. Tamis-LeMonda (Eds.), *The development of social understanding and communication* (pp. 53–81). Mahwah, NJ: Lawrence Erlbaum Associates.

James, W. (1950). *The principles of psychology.* Vol. 1. New York: Dover.

Jenkins, J. M., & Astington, J. W. (1996). Cognitive factors and family structure associated with theory of mind development in young children. *Developmental Psychology, 32,* 70–78.

Jenkins, J. M., & Astington, J. W. (2000). Theory of mind and social behavior: Causal models tested in a longitudinal study. *Merrill-Palmer Quarterly, 46,* 203–220.

Jenkins, J. M., Turrell, S., Kogushi, Y., Lollis, S., & Ross, H. (2003). Longitudinal investigation of the dynamics of mental state talk in families. *Child Development, 74,* 905–920.

Johnson, C. (1982). Acquisition of mental verbs and the concept of mind. In S. Kuczaj (Ed.), *Language development: Vol. 1. Syntax and semantics* (pp. 445–478). Hillsdale, NJ: Lawrence Erlbaum Associates.

Johnson, D. (1982). Altruistic behavior and the development of the self in infants. *Merrill-Palmer Quarterly, 28,* 379–388.

Johnson, M. H., Dziurawiec, S., Ellis, H., & Morton, J. (1991). Newborns' preferential tracking of face-like stimuli and its subsequent decline. *Cognition, 40,* 1–19.

Jones, S., & Hong, H. (2001). Onset of voluntary communication: Smiling looks to the mother. *Infancy, 2,* 353–370.

Jusczyk, P. W. (1997). *The discovery of spoken language.* Cambridge, MA: MIT Press.

Karmiloff-Smith, A. K. (1992). *Beyond modularity: A developmental perspective on cognitive science.* Cambridge, MA: MIT Press.

Kaye, K. (1979). Thickening thin data: The maternal role in developing communication and language. In M. Bullowa (Ed.), *Before speech: The beginning of interpersonal communication* (pp. 191–206). Cambridge, England: Cambridge University Press.

Kaye, K., & Fogel, A. (1980). The temporal structure of face-to-face communication between mothers and infants. *Developmental Psychology, 16,* 454–464.

Kestenbaum, R., & Nelson, C. A. (1990). The recognition and categorization of upright and inverted emotional expressions by 7-month-old infants. *Infant Behavior and Development, 13,* 497–511.

Király, I., Jovanovic, B., Prinz, W., Aschersleben, G., & Gergely, G. (2003). The early origins of goal attribution in infancy. *Consciousness and Cognition, 12,* 752–769.

Kirkham, N. Z., Slemmer, J. A., & Johnson, S. P. (2002). Visual statistical learning in infancy: Evidence for a domain general learning mechanism. *Cognition, 83,* B35–B42.

Kruger, A. C., & Tomasello, M. (1996). Cultural learning and learning culture. In D. R. Olson & N. Torrance (Eds.), *The handbook of education and human development: New models of learning, teaching, and schooling* (pp. 369–387). Cambridge, MA: Blackwell Publishers.

Kuhl, P. K., & Miller, J. D. (1975). Speech perception by the chinchilla: Voiced-voiceless distinction in alveolar plosive consonants. *Science, 190,* 69–72.

Kuhl, P. K., & Padden, D. M. (1982). Enhanced discriminability at the phonetic boundaries for the voicing feature in macaques. *Perception and Psychophysics, 32,* 542–550.

Lemmon, K., & Moore, C. (2001). Binding the self in time. In C. Moore & K. Lemmon (Eds.), *The self in time: Developmental perspectives* (pp. 163–179). Mahwah, NJ: Lawrence Erlbaum Associates.

Lemmon, K., & Moore, C. (2004). *The development of prudence in the face of varying future rewards.* Unpublished manuscript, Dalhousie University, Halifax, Nova Scotia, Canada.

Lempers, J. D. (1979). Young children's production and comprehension of nonverbal deictic behaviors. *Journal of Genetic Psychology, 135,* 93–102.

Lempers, J. D., Flavell, E. R., & Flavell, J. H. (1977). The development in very young children of tacit knowledge concerning visual perception. *Genetic Psychology Monographs, 95,* 3–53.

Leslie, A. M. (1987). Pretense and representation: The origins of "theory of mind." *Psychological Review, 94,* 412–426.

Leung, E., & Rheingold, H. (1981). The development of pointing as a social gesture. *Developmental Psychology, 17,* 215–220.

Lewis, M., & Brooks-Gunn, J. (1979). *Social cognition and the acquisition of self.* New York: Plenum Press.

Lewis, M., & Ramsay, D. (2004). Development of self-recognition, personal pronoun use, and pretend play during the 2nd year. *Child Development, 75,* 1821–1831.

Lewis, M., Stanger, C., & Sullivan, M. (1989). Deception in 3-year-olds. *Developmental Psychology, 25,* 439–443.

Lewis, M., Sullivan, M. W., Stanger, C., & Weiss, M. (1989). Self development and self-conscious emotions. *Child Development, 60,* 146–156.

Lillard, A. (1998). Ethnopsychologies: Cultural variations in theories of mind. *Psychological Bulletin, 123,* 3–32.

Liszkowski, U., Carpenter, M., Henning, A., Striano, T., & Tomasello, M. (2004). Twelve-month-olds point to share attention and interest. *Developmental Science, 7,* 297–307.

Lohmann, H., & Tomasello, M. (2003). The role of language in the development of false belief understanding: A training study. *Child Development, 74,* 1130–1144.

Loveland, K. A. (1986). Discovering the properties of a reflecting surface. *Developmental Review, 6,* 1–24.

Loveland, K. A. (1992). Self-perception and self-conception. *Psychological Inquiry, 3,* 125–127.

Lucariello, J. (1987). Concept formation and its relation to word learning and use in the second year. *Journal of Child Language, 14,* 309–332.

Lucariello, J., & Nelson, K. (1987). Remembering and planning talk between mothers and children. *Discourse Processes, 10,* 219–235.

Lyytinen, P., Poikkeus, A., & Laakso, M. (1997). Language and symbolic play in toddlers. *International Journal of Behavioral Development, 21,* 289–302.

MacDonald, K. (1992). Warmth as a developmental construct: An evolutionary analysis. *Child Development, 63,* 753–773.

MacPherson, A., & Moore, C. (2004, April). *New to me or new to you? Determining objects of attention and desire on the basis of novelty.* Paper presented at the International Conference on Infant Studies, Toronto, Canada.

MacWhinney, B., & Snow, C. (1990). The Child Language Data Exchange System: An update. *Journal of Child Language, 17,* 457–472.

Malatesta, C., & Haviland, J. (1982). Learning display rules: The socialization of emotion expression in infancy. *Child Development, 53,* 991–1003.

Mandel, D., Jusczyk, P., & Pisoni, D. (1995). Infants' recognition of the sound patterns of their own names. *Psychological Science, 6,* 315–318.

Masangkay, Z., McCluskey, K., McIntyre, C., Sims-Knight, J., Vaughn, B., & Flavell, J. (1974). The early development of inferences about the visual percepts of others. *Child Development, 45,* 357–366.

Maurer, D., & Barrera, M. (1981). Infants' perception of natural and distorted arrangements of a schematic face. *Child Development, 52,* 196–202.

McCabe, A., & Peterson, C. (1991). Getting the story: A longitudinal study of parental styles in eliciting narratives and developing narrative skill. In A. McCabe & C. Peterson (Eds.), *Developing narrative structure* (pp. 217–253). Hillsdale, NJ: Lawrence Erlbaum Associates.

McCune, L. (1995). A normative study of representational play and the transition to language. *Developmental Psychology, 31,* 198–206.

McCune-Nicholich, L. (1981). Towards symbolic functioning: Structure of early pretend games and potential parallels with language. *Child Development, 52,* 785–797.

Meins, E., Fernyhough, C., Wainwright, R., Das Gupta, M., Fradley, E., & Tuckey, M. (2002). Maternal mind-mindedness and attachment security as predictors of theory of mind understanding. *Child Development, 73,* 1715–1726.

Meltzoff, A. N. (1988). Infant imitation and memory: Nine-month-olds in immediate and deferred tests. *Child Development, 59,* 217–225.

Meltzoff, A. N. (1990). Foundations for developing a concept of self: The role of imitation in relating self to other and the value of social mirroring, social modeling, and self practice in infancy. In D. Cicchetti & M. Beeghly (Eds.), *The self in transition: Infancy to childhood* (pp. 139–164). Chicago: University of Chicago Press.

Meltzoff, A. N. (1995). Understanding the intentions of others: Re-enactment of intended acts by 18-month-old children. *Developmental Psychology, 31,* 838–850.

Meltzoff, A. N. (2002). Imitation as a mechanism of social cognition: Origins of empathy, theory of mind, and the representation of action. In U. Goswami (Ed.), *Blackwell handbook of child cognitive development* (pp. 6–25). Oxford, England: Blackwell.

Meltzoff, A. N., & Gopnik, A. (1993). The role of imitation in understanding persons and developing a theory of mind. In S. Baron-Cohen., H. Tager-Flusberg, & D. Cohen (Eds.), *Understanding other minds: Perspectives from autism* (pp. 335–366). New York: Oxford University Press.

Meltzoff, A. N., & Moore, M. K. (1977). Imitation of facial and manual gestures by human neonates. *Science, 198,* 75–78.

Meltzoff, A. N., & Moore, M. K. (1983). Newborn infants imitate adult facial gestures. *Child Development, 54,* 702–709.

Mischel, W. (1974). Processes in delay of gratification. In L. Berkowitz (Ed.), *Advances in experimental social psychology* (Vol, 7, pp. 249–292). New York: Academic Press.

Mischel, W., Shoda, Y., & Rodriguez, M. (1989). Delay of gratification in children. *Science, 244,* 933–938.

Mitchell, R. (1986). A framework for discussing deception. In R. Mitchell & N. Thompson (Eds.), *Deception: Perspectives on human and nonhuman deceit* (pp. 3–40). Albany: State University of New York Press.

Mitchell, R. (1997). Kinesthetic-visual matching and the self-concept as explanations of mirror self-recognition. *Journal for the Theory of Social Behavior, 27,* 17–39.

Mitchell, R., & Thompson, N. (1986). *Deception: Perspectives on human and nonhuman deceit.* Albany: State University of New York Press.

Moll, H., & Tomasello, M. (2004). 12- and 18-month-old infants follow gaze to spaces behind barriers. *Developmental Science, 7,* F1–F9.

Moore, C. (1999a). Gaze following and the control of attention. In P. Rochat (Ed.), *Early social cognition: Understanding others in the first months of life* (pp. 241–256). Mahwah, NJ: Lawrence Erlbaum Associates.

Moore, C. (1999b). Intentional relations and triadic interactions. In P. Zelazo, J. Astington, & D. Olson (Eds.), *Developing theories of intention: Social understanding and self-control* (pp. 43–61). Mahwah, NJ: Lawrence Erlbaum Associates.

Moore, C., Bryant, D., & Furrow, D. (1989). Mental terms and the development of certainty. *Child Development, 60,* 167–171.

Moore, C., & Corkum, V. (1994). Social understanding at the end of the first year of life. *Developmental Review, 14,* 349–372.

Moore, C., & Corkum, V. (1998). Infant gaze following based on eye direction. *British Journal of Developmental Psychology, 16,* 495–503.

Moore, C., & D'Entremont, B. (2001). Developmental changes in pointing as a function of attentional focus. *Journal of Cognition and Development, 2,* 109–129.

Moore, C., Furrow, D., Chiasson, L., & Patriquin, M. (1994). Developmental relationships between production and comprehension of mental terms. *First Language, 14,* 1–17.

Moore, C., Gilbert, C., & Sapp, F. (1995). Children's comprehension of the distinction between *want* and *need*. *Journal of Child Language, 22,* 687–701.

Moore, C., Jarrold, C., Russell, J., Lumb, A., Sapp, F., & McCallum, F. (1995). Conflicting desire and the child's theory of mind. *Cognitive Development, 10,* 467–482.

Moore, C., & Macgillivray, S. (2004). Social understanding and the development of prudence and prosocial behavior. In J. Baird & B. Sokol (Eds.), *Connections between theory of mind and sociomoral development: New directions for child and adolescent development* (pp. 51–62). San Francisco: Jossey-Bass.

Moore, C., Mealiea, J., Garon, N., & Povinelli, D. (2005). *The development of the bodily self.* Unpublished manuscript, University of Toronto, Canada.

Moore, C., & Symons, D. (2005). Attachment, theory of mind, and delay of gratification. In B. Homer & C. Tamis-LeMonda (Eds.), *The development of social cognition and communication* (181–199). Mahwah, NJ: Lawrence Erlbaum Associates.

Moore, D. S. (2002). *The dependent gene: The fallacy of nature vs. nurture.* New York: Times Books.

Moran, G., Krupka, A., Tutton, A., & Symons, D. (1987). Patterns of maternal and infant imitation during play. *Infant Behavior and Development, 10,* 477–491.

Morgan, C. L. (1894). *An introduction to comparative psychology.* London: Walter Scott.

Morton, J., & Johnson, M. H. (1991). CONSPEC and CONLERN: A two-process theory of infant face recognition. *Psychological Review, 98,* 164–181.

Moses, L., Baldwin, D., Rosicky, J., & Tidball, G. (2001). Evidence for referential understanding in the emotions domain at twelve and eighteen months. *Child Development, 72,* 718–735.

Muir, D., & Hains, S. (1999). Young infants' perception of adult intentionality: Adult contingency and eye direction. In P. Rochat (Ed.), *Early social cognition* (pp. 155–187). Mahwah, NJ: Lawrence Erlbaum Associates.

Mumme, D. L., & Fernald, A. (2003). The infant as onlooker: Learning from emotional reactions observed in a television scenario. *Child Development, 74,* 221–237.

Murray, L., & Trevarthen, C. (1985). Emotional regulation of interaction between two-month-olds and their mothers. In T. M. Field & N. A. Fox (Eds.), *Social perception in infants* (pp. 101–125). Norwood, NJ: Ablex.

Namy, L., & Waxman, S. (1998). Words and gestures: Infants' interpretations of different forms of symbolic reference. *Child Development, 69,* 295–308.

Neisser, U. (1988). Five kinds of self-knowledge. *Philosophical Psychology, 1,* 35–59.

Nelson, K. (1986). Event knowledge and cognitive development. In K. Nelson (Ed.), *Event knowledge: Structure and function in development* (pp. 1–19). Hillsdale, NJ: Lawrence Erlbaum Associates.

Nelson, K. (1993). The psychological and social origins of autobiographical memory. *Psychological Science, 4,* 7–14.

Nelson, K., & Fivush, R. (2004). The emergence of autobiographical memory: A social cultural developmental theory. *Psychological Review, 111,* 486–511.

Nelson, K., & Kessler Shaw, L. (2002). Developing a socially shared symbolic system. In E. Amsel & J. Byrnes (Eds.), *Language, literacy, and cognitive development: The development and consequences of symbolic communication* (pp. 27–57). Mahwah, NJ: Lawrence Erlbaum Associates.

Nichols, S. L. (2005). *Information processing abilities and parent-infant interaction: Prediction of imitative ability in the first year.* Unpublished doctoral dissertation, Dalhousie University, Halifax, Nova Scotia, Canada.

Nielsen, M., Dissanayake, C., & Kashima, Y. (2003). A longitudinal investigation of self-other discrimination and the emergence of minor self-recognition. *Infant Behavior and Development, 26,* 213–226.

Oakes, L. M., & Cohen, L. B. (1990). Infant perception of a causal event. *Cognitive Development, 5,* 193–207.

Olson, D. R. (1989). Making up your mind. *Canadian Psychology, 30,* 617–627.

Olson, D. R. (1993). The development of representations: The origins of mental life. *Canadian Psychology, 34,* 293–306.

Olson, D. R., & Bruner, J. S. (1996). Folk psychology and folk pedagogy. In D. R. Olson & N. Torrance (Eds.), *The handbook of education and human development: New models of learning, teaching and schooling* (pp. 9–27). Malden, MA: Blackwell.

O'Neill, D., & Gopnik, A. (1991). Young children's ability to identify the sources of their beliefs. *Developmental Psychology, 27,* 390–397.

Pascalis, O., De Schonen, S., Morton, J., Deruelle, C., & Fabre-Grenet, M. (1995). Mother's face recognition by neonates: A replication and an extension. *Infant Behavior and Development, 18,* 79–85.

Perner, J. (1991a). On representing that: The asymmetry between belief and desire in children's theory of mind. In C. Moore & D. Frye (Eds.), *Children's theories of mind* (pp. 139–155). Hillsdale, NJ: Lawrence Erlbaum Associates.

Perner, J. (1991b). *Understanding the representational mind.* Cambridge, MA: MIT Press.

Perner, J., Leekam, S., & Wimmer, H. (1987). Three-year-olds' difficulty with false belief. *British Journal of Developmental Psychology, 5,* 125–137.

Perner, J., Ruffman, T., & Leekam, S. (1994). Theory of mind is contagious: You catch it from your sibs. *Child Development, 65,* 1228–1238.

Peskin, J., & Ardino, V. (2003). Representing the mental world in children's social behavior: Playing hide-and-seek and keeping a secret. *Social Development, 12,* 496–512.

Peterson, C. (2000). Kindred spirits. Influences of siblings' perspectives on theory of mind. *Cognitive Development, 15,* 435–455.

Phillips, A. T., Wellman, H. M., & Spelke, E. S. (2002). Infants' ability to connect gaze and emotional expression to intentional action. *Cognition, 85,* 53–78.

Piaget, J. (1953). *The origin of intelligence in the child.* London: Routledge and Kegan Paul.

Piaget, J. (1962). *Play, dreams, and imitation.* London: Routledge and Kegan Paul.

Piaget, J., & Inhelder, B. (1956). *The child's conception of space.* London: Routledge and Kegan Paul.

Piaget, J., & Inhelder, B. (1969). *The psychology of the child.* London: Routledge and Kegan Paul.

Pillemer, D., & White, S. (1989). Childhood events recalled by children and adults. In H. Reese (Ed.), *Advances in child development and behavior* (pp. 297–340). New York: Academic Press.

Polak, A., & Harris, P. (1999). Deception in young children following noncompliance. *Developmental Psychology, 35*, 561–568.

Povinelli, D. P. (1995). The unduplicated self. In P. Rochat (Ed.), *The self in early infancy* (pp. 161–192). Amsterdam: North-Holland-Elsevier.

Povinelli, D. P. (2001). The self: Elevated in consciousness and extended on time. In C. Moore & K. Lemmon (Eds.), *The self in time: Developmental perspectives* (pp. 75–95). Mahwah, NJ: Lawrence Erlbaum Associates.

Povinelli, D. P., Bering, J. M., & Giambrone, S. (2000). Toward a science of other minds: Escaping the argument by analogy. *Cognitive Science, 24*, 509–541.

Povinelli, D. P., Landau, K., & Perilloux, H. (1996). Self-recognition in young children using delayed versus live feedback: Evidence of a developmental asynchrony. *Child Development, 67*, 1540–1554.

Povinelli, D. P., & Simon, B. (1998). Young children's understanding of briefly versus extremely delayed visual images of the self: Emergence of the autobiographical stance. *Developmental Psychology, 34*, 188–194.

Prencipe, A., & Zelazo, P. D. (2005). Development of affective decision-making for self and other: Evidence for the integration of first- and third-person perspectives. *Psychological Science, 16*, 501–505.

Reddy, V. (1991). Playing with others' expectations: Teasing and mucking about in the first year. In A. Whiten (Ed), *Natural theories of mind: Evolution, development and simulation of everyday mindreading* (pp. 143–158). Cambridge, MA: Basil Blackwell.

Reddy, V., Hay, D., Murray, L., & Trevarthen, C. (1997). Communication in infancy: Mutual regulation of affect and attention. In G. Bremner, A. Slater, & G. Butterworth (Eds.), *Infant development: Recent advances* (pp. 247–273). Hove: Psychology Press.

Reese, E. (2002). Social factors in the development of autobiographical memory: The state of the art. *Social Development, 11*, 124–142.

Reese, E., & Farrant, K. (2003). Social origins of reminiscing. In R. Fivush & C. Haden (Eds.), *Autobiographical memory and the construction of a narrative self: Developmental and cultural perspectives* (pp. 29–48). Mahwah, NJ: Lawrence Erlbaum Associates.

Reese, E., Haden, C., & Fivush, R. (1993). Mother-child conversations about the past: Relationships of style and memory over time. *Cognitive Development, 8*, 403–430.

Repacholi, B. M. (1998). Infants' use of attentional cues to identify the referent of another person's emotional expression. *Developmental Psychology, 34*, 1017–1025.

Repacholi, B. M., & Gopnik, A. (1997). Early reasoning about desires: Evidence from 14- and 18-month-olds. *Developmental Psychology, 33*, 12–21.

Richards, D., Frentzen, B., Gerhardt, K., McCann, M., & Abrams, R. (1992). Sound levels in the human uterus. *Obstetrics and Gynecology, 80*, 186–190.

Roberts, K. (1983). Comprehension and production of word order in stage 1. *Child Development, 54*, 443–449.

Rochat, P., & Hespos, S. J. (1997). Differential rooting response by neonates: Evidence for an early sense of self. *Early Development and Parenting, 6*, 105–112.

Rochat, P., & Morgan, R. (1995). Spatial determinants in the perception of self-produced leg movements in 3- to 5-month-old infants. *Developmental Psychology, 31*, 626–636.

Rochat, P., Neisser, U., & Marian, V. (1998). Are young infants sensitive to interpersonal contingency? *Infant Behavior and Development, 21*, 355–366.

Rochat, P., Querido, J., & Striano, T. (1999). Emerging sensitivity to the timing and structure of protoconversation in early infancy. *Developmental Psychology, 35*, 950–957.

Rochat, P., Striano, T., & Blatt, L. (2002). Differential effects of happy, neutral, and sad still-faces on 2-, 4-, and 6-month-old infants. *Infant and Child Development, 11*, 289–303.

Romanes, G. J. (1977). *Animal intelligence.* Washington, DC: University Publications of America. (Original work published 1883)

Ruffman, T., Perner, J., & Parkin, L. (1999). How parenting style affects false belief understanding. *Social Development, 8*, 395–411.

Russell, B. (1948). *Human knowledge: Its scope and limits.* London: Allen & Unwin.

Russell, J. (1995). At two with nature: Agency and the development of self-world dualism. In J. L. Bermudez, A. Marcel, & N. Eilan (Eds.), *The body and the self* (pp. 127–152). Cambridge, MA: MIT Press.

Russell, J. (1996). *Agency: Its role in mental development*. Hove, England: Psychology Press.

Russell, J., Mauthner, N., Sharpe, S., & Tidswell, T. (1991). The "windows task" as a measure of strategic deception in preschoolers and autistic subjects. *British Journal of Developmental Psychology, 9*, 331–349

Saffran, J. R., Aslin, R. N., & Newport, E. L. (1996). Statistical learning by 8-month-old infants. *Science, 274*, 1926–1928.

Scassellati, B. (2002). Theory of mind for a humanoid robot. *Autonomous Robots, 12*, 13–24.

Schaffer, H. R. (1984). *The child's entry into a social world*. London: Academic Press.

Searle, J. R. (1983). *Intentionality*. New York: Cambridge University Press.

Sethi, A., Mischel, W., Aber, J., Shoda, Y., & Rodriguez, M. (2000). The role of strategic attention deployment in development of self-regulation: Predicting preschoolers' delay of gratification from mother-toddler interactions. *Developmental Psychology, 36*, 767–777.

Shatz, M., Wellman, H., & Silber, S. (1983). The acquisition of mental verbs: A systematic investigation of first references to mental states. *Cognition, 14*, 301–321.

Shoda, Y., Mischel, W., & Peake, P. (1990). Predicting adolescent cognitive and self-regulatory competencies from preschool delay of gratification: Identifying diagnostic conditions. *Developmental Psychology, 26*, 978–986.

Slaughter, V., Dennis, M. J., & Pritchard, M. (2002). Theory of mind and peer acceptance in preschool children. *British Journal of Developmental Psychology, 20*, 545–564.

Slaughter, V., & Gopnik, A. (1996). Conceptual coherence in the child's theory of mind: Training children to understand belief. *Child Development, 67*, 2967–2988.

Slaughter, V., & McConnell, D. (2003). Emergence of joint attention: Relationships between gaze following, social referencing, imitation, and naming in infancy. *Journal of Genetic Psychology, 16*, 54–71.

Smith, P., & Pederson, D. (1988). Maternal sensitivity and patterns of infant-mother attachment. *Child Development, 59*, 1097–1101.

Sodian, B. (1991). The development of deception in young children. *British Journal of Developmental Psychology, 9*, 173–188.

Sodian, B., & Thoermer, C. (2004). Infants' understanding of looking, pointing, and reaching as cues to goal-directed action. *Journal of Cognition and Development, 5*, 289–316.

Spelke, E. S. (2000). Core knowledge. *American Psychologist, 55*, 1233–1243.

Sroufe, L. A. (1995). *Emotional development: The organization of emotional life in the early years.* New York: Cambridge University Press.

Sroufe, L. A., & Waters, E. (1976). The ontogenesis of smiling and laughter: A perspective on the organization of development in infancy. *Psychological Review, 83*, 173–189.

Stack, D., & Muir, D. W. (1992). Adult tactile stimulation during face-to-face interactions modulates 5-month-olds' affect and attention. *Child Development, 63*, 1509–1525.

Stern, D. (1977). *The first relationship: Infant and mother*. Glasgow, Scotland: Fontana.

Stern, D. (1985). *The interpersonal world of the infant: A view from psychoanalysis and developmental psychology*. New York: Basic Books.

Strauss, S., Ziv, M., & Stein, A. (2002). Teaching as a natural cognition and its relations to preschoolers' developing theory of mind. *Cognitive Development, 17*, 1473–1487.

Striano, T., & Rochat, P. (1999). Developmental link between dyadic and triadic social competence in infancy. *British Journal of Developmental Psychology, 17*, 551–562.

Suddendorf, T., & Whiten, A. (2001). Mental evolution and development: Evidence for secondary representation in children, great apes, and other animals. *Psychological Bulletin, 127*, 629–650.

Sullivan, M. W., & Lewis, M. (2003). Contextual determinants of anger and other negative expressions in young infants. *Developmental Psychology, 39*, 693–705.

Symons, L., Hains, S., & Muir, D. (1998). Look at me: Five-month-old infants' sensitivity to very small deviations in eye-gaze during social interactions. *Infant Behavior and Development, 21*, 531–537.

Tamis-LeMonda, C., Bornstein, M., & Baumwell, L. (2001). Maternal responsiveness and children's achievement of language milestones. *Child Development, 72*, 748–767.

Thelen, E., & Spencer, J. (1998). Postural control during reaching in young infants: A dynamic systems approach. *Neuroscience and Biobehavioral Reviews, 22,* 507–514

Thoermer, C., & Sodian, B. (2001). Preverbal infants' understanding of referential gestures. *First Language, 21,* 245–264.

Thompson, C., Barresi, J., & Moore, C. (1997). The development of future-oriented prudence and altruism in preschoolers. *Cognitive Development, 12,* 199–212.

Thompson, R. A. (1998). Empathy and its origins in early development. In S. Braten (Ed.), *Intersubjective communication and emotion in early ontogeny* (pp. 144–157). New York: Cambridge University Press.

Thorndike, E. (1965). *Animal intelligence: Experimental studies.* New York: Hafner. (Original work published 1898)

Tincoff, R., & Jusczyk, P. (1999). Some beginnings of word comprehension in 6-month-olds. *Psychological Science, 10,* 172–175.

Tomasello, M. (1992). *First verbs: A case study of early grammatical development.* New York: Cambridge University Press.

Tomasello, M. (1995). Joint attention as social cognition. In C. Moore & P. Dunham (Eds.), *Joint attention: Its origins and role in development* (pp. 103–130). Hillsdale, NJ: Lawrence Erlbaum Associates.

Tomasello, M. (1999a). *The cultural origins of human cognition.* Cambridge, MA: Harvard University Press.

Tomasello, M. (1999b). Social cognition before the revolution. In P. Rochat (Ed.), *Early social cognition: Understanding others in the first months of life* (pp. 301–314). Mahwah, NJ: Lawrence Erlbaum Associates.

Tomasello, M. (2003). *Constructing a language: A usage-based theory of language acquisition.* Cambridge, MA: Harvard University Press.

Tomasello, M., & Akhtar, N. (1995). Two-year-olds use pragmatic cues to differentiate reference to objects and actions. *Cognitive Development, 10,* 201–224.

Tomasello, M., & Farrar, M. J. (1986). Joint attention and early language. *Child Development, 57,* 1454–1463.

Tomasello, M., & Haberl, K. (2003). Understanding attention: 12- and 18-month-olds know what is new for other persons. *Developmental Psychology, 39,* 906–912.

Tomasello, M., Kruger, A. C., & Ratner, H. H. (1993). Cultural learning. *Behavioral and Brain Sciences, 16,* 495–511.

Tomasello, M., Strosberg, R., & Akhtar, N. (1996). Eighteen-month-old children learn words in non-ostensive contexts. *Journal of Child Language, 23,* 157–176.

Tomasello, M., & Todd, J. (1983). Joint attention and lexical acquisition style. *First Language, 4,* 197–212.

Trevarthen, C. (1979). Communication and cooperation in early infancy: A description of primary intersubjectivity. In M. Bullowa (Ed.), *Before speech: The beginning of interpersonal communication* (pp. 321–348). Cambridge, England: Cambridge University Press.

Tronick, E., Als, H., & Adamson, L. (1979). Structure of early face-to-face communicative interactions. In M. Bullowa (Ed.), *Before speech: The beginning of interpersonal communication* (pp. 349–370). Cambridge, England: Cambridge University Press.

Tronick, E., Als, H., Adamson, L., Wise, S., & Brazelton, T. B. (1978). The infant's response to entrapment between contradictory messages in face-to-face interaction. *Journal of the American Academy of Child Psychiatry, 17,* 1–13.

Tronick, E., Als, H., & Brazelton, T. B. (1980). Monadic phases: A structural descriptive analysis on infant-mother face-to-face interaction. *Merrill-Palmer Quarterly, 26,* 3–24.

Tulving, E. (1985). Memory and consciousness. *Canadian Psychology, 26,* 1–12.

Tulving, E. (2002). Episodic memory: From mind to brain. *Annual Review of Psychology, 53,* 1–25.

Turati, C., Simion, F., Milani, I., & Umiltà, C. (2002). Newborns' preference for faces: What is crucial? *Developmental Psychology, 38,* 875–882.

Van IJzendoorn, M., & Hubbard, F. (2000). Are infant crying and maternal responsiveness during the first year related to infant-mother attachment at 15 months. *Attachment and Human Development, 2,* 371–391.

Völker, S., Keller, H., Lohaus, A., Cappenberg, M., & Chasiotis, A. (1999). Maternal interactive behavior in early infancy and later attachment. *International Journal of Behavioral Development, 23*, 921–936.

Watson, A. C., Nixon, C. L., & Wilson, A. (1999). Social interaction skills and theory of mind in young children. *Developmental Psychology, 35*, 386–391.

Watson, J. S. (1972). Smiling, cooing, and "the game." *Merrill-Palmer Quarterly, 18*, 323–340.

Watson, J. S. (1985). Contingency perception in early social development. In T. Field & N. Fox (Eds.), *Social perception in infants* (pp. 157–176). Norwood, NJ: Ablex.

Watson, J. S. (1994). Detection of self: The perfect algorithm. In S. Parker & R. Mitchell (Eds.), *Self-awareness in animals and humans: Developmental perspectives* (pp. 131–148). New York: Cambridge University Press.

Waxman, S. R., & Markow, D. B. (1995). Words as invitations to form categories: Evidence from 12- to 13-month-old infants. *Cognitive Psychology, 29*, 257–302.

Weist, R. (1989). Time concepts in language and thought: Filling the Piagetian void from 2 to 5 years. In I. Levin & D. Zakay (Eds.), *Time and human cognition: A life-span perspective* (pp. 63–118). Amsterdam: North-Holland.

Welch-Ross, M. (1997). Mother-child participation in conversation about the past: Relationships to preschoolers' theory of mind. *Developmental Psychology, 33*, 618–629.

Wellman, H. (1990). *The child's theory of mind.* Cambridge, MA: MIT Press.

Wellman, H., Cross, D., & Watson, J. (2001). Meta-analysis of theory-of-mind development: The truth about false belief. *Child Development, 72*, 655–684.

Werker, J. F., & Tees, R. C. (1984). Cross-language speech perception: Evidence for perceptual reorganization during the first year of life. *Infant Behavior and Development, 7*, 49–63.

Werner, H., & Kaplan, B. (1963). *Symbolic formation.* New York: Wiley.

Whiten, A., & Byrne, R. (1988). Tactical deception in primates. *Behavioral and Brain Sciences, 11*, 233–244.

Wimmer, H., & Perner, J. (1983). Beliefs about beliefs: Representation and constraining function of wrong beliefs in young children's understanding of deception. *Cognition, 13*, 103–128.

Woodward, A. L. (1998). Infants selectively encode the goal of an actor's reach. *Cognition, 69*, 1–34.

Woodward, A. L. (1999). Infants' ability to distinguish between purposeful and non-purposeful behaviors. *Infant Behavior and Development, 22*, 145–160.

Woodward, A. L. (2003). Infants' developing understanding of the link between looker and object. *Developmental Science, 6*, 297–311.

Woodward, A. L., & Guajardo, J. J. (2002). Infants' understanding of the point gesture as an object-directed action. *Cognitive Development, 17*, 1061–1084.

Woodward, A. L., & Wilson-Brune, C. (2003, October). *Gaze-following and gaze comprehension in the first year of life.* Paper presented at the biennial meeting of the Cognitive Development Society, Park City, UT.

Yale, M., Messinger, D., Cobo-Lewis, A., & Delgado, C. (2003). The temporal coordination of early infant communication. *Developmental Psychology, 39*, 815–824.

Zahn-Waxler, C., & Radke-Yarrow, M. (1990). The origins of empathic concern. *Motivation and Emotion, 14*, 107–130.

Zahn-Waxler, C., Radke-Yarrow, M., Wagner, E., & Chapman, M. (1992). Development of concern for others. *Developmental Psychology, 28*, 126–136.

Zelazo, P. D. (1996). Towards a characterization of minimal consciousness. *New Ideas in Psychology, 14*, 63–80.

Zelazo, P. D., Carter, A., Reznick, J. S., & Frye, D. (1997). Early development of executive function: A problem-solving framework. *Review of General Psychology, 1*, 1–29.

Zinober, B., & Martlew, M. (1985). Developmental changes in four types of gesture in relation to acts and vocalizations from 10 to 21 months. *British Journal of Developmental Psychology, 3*, 293–306.

Author Index

A

Abbeduto, L., 168, 169
Aber, J., 200
Abrams, R., 59
Acredolo, L., 140, 142
Adamson, L. B., 76, 80, 93
Ainsworth, M., 84, 85, 86,
Akhtar, N., 148,149, 150, 152
Alexander, T., 78
Als, H., 72, 76, 80
Amsterdam, B., 122
Anderson, D., 84
Angelopoulos, M., 183
Anisfeld, M., 77, 140, 141
Appleton, M., 177
Ardino, V., 180, 181
Arterberry, M., 58
Aschersleben, G., 106, 107, 110
Asendorpf, J. B., 129,131, 132
Ashburn, L. A., 92
Ashley, J., 181
Aslin, R. N., 62
Astington, J. W., 157, 158, 167, 172, 174,
        178, 179, 182
Atance, C., 188

B

Bahrick, L., 64, 65, 66, 121
Baird, J. A., 112, 158
Bakeman, R., 93
Baldwin, D. A., 92, 94, 104, 112, 147, 158
Baldwin, J. M., 8

Barbu-Roth, M., 84
Baron-Cohen, S., 4
Barrera, M., 53, 57
Barresi, J., 8, 20, 24, 43, 121, 199, 201, 205
Bartsch, K., 161, 162, 163, 170
Bates, E., 97, 190
Bateson, M., 74
Baudonnière, P., 129, 131, 132
Baumwell, L., 146
Beeghly, M., 158, 159, 160, 162, 163
Beeghly-Smith, M., 158
Bell, S., 86
Bellagamba, F., 129
Belsky, J., 83, 86
Bering, J. M., 5
Berntson, G. G., 38, 41
Bertenthal, B., 122
Bigelow, A. E., 78, 82
Birch, S., 78
Bischof-Köhler, D., 131
Blatt, L., 81
Blehar, M., 84, 86
Block, N., 18
Borke, H., 171
Bornstein, M., 58, 146
Bowlby, J., 75, 84, 86
Boysen, S. T., 38, 41
Braine, M., 151
Brand, R. J., 92
Brazelton, T. B., 72, 76, 80
Bremner, J. G., 52
Bretherton, I., 98, 158, 159, 160, 162, 163,
        190
Bronson, G., 52

233

Subject Index

Date Du